Sustainable Environmental Management

Sustainable Environmental Management

Principles and Practice

Edited by
R. Kerry Turner

Published in association with

ECONOMIC AND SOCIAL
RESEARCH COUNCIL

BELHAVEN PRESS
a division of Pinter
Publishers, London

WESTVIEW PRESS
Boulder, Colorado

First published in Great Britain in 1988 by
Belhaven Press (a division of Pinter Publishers),
25 Floral Street, London WC2E 9DS

Published in 1988 in the United States by
WESTVIEW PRESS
Frederick A. Praeger, Publisher
5500 Central Avenue
Boulder, Colorado 80301

British Library Cataloguing in Publication Data
Sustainable environmental management:
  principles and practice.
  1. Environmental policy
  I. Turner, R. Kerry
  333.7   HC79.E5

  ISBN 1-85293-003-9

Library of Congress Cataloging in Publication Data

ISBN 0-8133-0744-9
CIP Data available from the Library of Congress

Typeset by Florencetype Ltd, Kewstoke, Avon
Printed by Biddles of Guildford Ltd

Contents

List of tables and figures   vii

List of contributors   x

Foreword *Timothy O'Riordan*   xi

1 Sustainability, Resource Conservation and Pollution
Control: An Overview
R. Kerry Turner   1

Part 1 Sustainable Growth and Development Principles

2 The Politics of Sustainability
Timothy O'Riordan   29
3 Economic Models and Environmental Values: A
Discourse on Theory
Michael Redclift   51
4 Resource Conservation, Sustainability and
Technical Change
D. Deadman and R. Kerry Turner   67
5 The Sustainable Use of Natural Resources in
Developing Countries
David Pearce   102
6 Alternative Approaches to the Valuation of
Environmental Resources
Chris Nash and John Bowers   118

Part 2 Sustainable Growth and Development Practice

7 Towards a Second Green Revolution in the Tropics:
From Chemicals to New Biological Techniques for
Sustained Economic Development
S. Ghatak   145
8 Pollution Control Objectives and the Regulatory
Framework
J. Rees   170
9 Market Mechanisms of Pollution Control: 'Polluter
Pays', Economic and Practical Aspects
John Pezzey   190

10   Valuation of Wildlife: A Case Study of the Upper Teesdale
     Site of Special Scientific Interest and Comparison
     of Methods in Environmental Economics
     K.G. Willis and J.F. Benson   243
11   Cost–Benefit Analysis in Theory and Practice: Agricultural
     Land Drainage Projects
     John Bowers   265

Index   290

List of tables and figures

Tables

4.1 World demand, production, reserves and resource depletion for selected strategic materials   70

4.2 Officially designated strategic (i.e. critical/vulnerable) materials   78

4.3 Levels of substitution and implementation lags   87

4.4 Survey of substitution and recycling potential for selected strategic materials   90

4.5 Short product lifetime case   94

4.6 Long product lifetime case   95

5.1 Carrying capacity in the Sahelian/Sudanian zones   104

5.2 Illustrative relative fuel prices, 1980   111

7.1 Relation of world expenditures on agricultural research to the value of agricultural product by income group   146

7.2 Estimated costs of azolla production in the Philippines   156

7.3 Expected nitrogen contribution and effective cost of nitrogen from azolla used as intercrop and green manure, by quality of irrigation   156

7.4 Economic return (cost-saving) of azolla use per hectare per season, South Cotabato, Philippines   157

7.5 Effect of herbicide treatment on coffee yield   159

7.6 Cost savings in weed control in rice and rubber crops   159

7.7 Research and development costs in the pharmaceutical and agro-chemical industries   163

9.1 Likely incidence of costs and benefits from reducing optimal effluent load   216

10.1 Financial and social costs of wildlife conservation at Upper Teesdale   248

10.2 Consumer surplus estimates from travel cost method   256

10.3 Summary and comparison of results from each valuation technique   261

Figures

1.1	Sustainable growth and development	7
1.2	Quantification of environmental values	9
1.3	Ecosystem change and environmental management in Broadland	11
2.1	Non-sustainable resource draw and international capitalism	40
2.2	Constraints on sustainable development	41
3.1	Typical components of growth/environment paradigms	58
4.1	Overview of the conventional approach to strategic materials policy	76
4.2	Resource contingency planning approach	84
4.3	Conventional economic view of substitution process	86
7.1	Sustainable growth	149
7.2	Impact of chemical fertilisers on rice production in India and Japan	151
7.3	Research and development cost constraint	163
7.4	Possible employment and income effects of new biotechnology	164
8.1	The 'rational' policy process	171
8.2	Management objectives	179
8.3	Pollution control tools	180
8.4	Variable consequences of management	181
9.1	Effluent control costs	199
9.2	Effluent damage costs	199
9.3	Socially optimal effluent load and definitions of pollution	202
9.4	Long-run and short-run optimal effluent	202
9.5	Pollution economics for an isolated firm	204
9.6	The pollution charge threshold	206
9.7	The Standard Polluter Pays Principle for a firm or industry	207
9.8	The Extended Polluter Pays Principle for a firm or industry	208

9.9   Changes in de facto pollution rights and control
       spending under the Standard PPP   211

9.10   Standard PPP: effect of increased demand for
       environmental services   211

9.11   Standard PPP: effect of more cost-effective effluent
       control   215

9.12   Control technology innovation incentive   219

9.13   Redistributive charging mechanism   220

9.14   Granted tradable discharge consents   223

9.15   Total market control and regulatory control costs   238

9.16   Marginal market control and regulatory control costs   239

9.17   Problems of economies of scale: original environmental
       demand   240

9.18   Problems of economies of scale: increased
       environmental demand   240

10.1   The social benefit/opportunity cost of agricultural
       output including costs and benefits to the public
       Exchequer for commodities where the United Kingdom
       is a net importer   249

10.2   The social benefit/opportunity cost of agricultural
       output including costs and benefits to the public
       Exchequer for commodities where the United Kingdom
       is a net exporter   250

List of contributors

J.F. Benson, Department of Biology, University of Newcastle Upon Tyne

John Bowers, School of Economic Studies, University of Leeds

D. Deadman, Department of Economics, University of Leicester

S. Ghatak, Department of Economics, University of Leicester

Chris Nash, Institute for Transport Studies, University of Leeds

Timothy O'Riordan, School of Environmental Sciences, University of East Anglia, Norwich

David Pearce, Department of Economics, University College, London

John Peezey, Department of the Environment, London

J. Rees, Department of Geography, London School of Economics

Michael Redclift, Department of Environmental Studies and Countryside Planning, Wye College (University of London)

R. Kerry Turner (editor), School of Environmental Sciences, University of East Anglia, Norwich

K.G. Willis, Department of Town and Country Planning, University of Newcastle

Foreword

In 1983 the Economic and Social Research Council (ESRC) in the United Kingdom funded a major programme of research under the banner of an environmental issues initiative. The Environment and Planning Committee of the Council was responsible for managing this programme and established a steering group to oversee the operation. I was invited to be Chairman of that Steering group. Within the intiative four Working Groups were formed to assess the state of the art in certain research areas, to develop innovative ideas and methodological approaches, and to give guidance on future research priorities.

One of these groups was the environmental economics group which convened its first meeting in October 1984 under the convenorship of my colleague Kerry Turner. This group met several times and focused its output on a workshop held at the University of East Anglia in July 1986. This volume of contributions, skilfully edited by Mr Turner, is the product of the group's work. I am very pleased to introduce this timely and valuable collection of essays on such a highly topical subject matter.

Timothy O'Riordan
University of East Anglia
April 1987

Chapter 1

Sustainability, Resource Conservation and Pollution Control: An Overview

R. Kerry Turner

Introduction

The decades of the 1960s and 1970s have been marked by the intensification and spread of pollution. There has also been a growing perception of 'environmental' problems based on a recognition of the importance and complexity of the interrelationships between mankind, the global resource base and the encompassing environment. The 1960s witnessed the rebirth of environmentalism, not as a unitary movement, but sectionalised into a diversity of groups and ideologies. According to O'Riordan (1981) this 'born again' environmentalism was essentially a dialectical phenomenon. He has classified environmentalists into opposing camps—technocentrists and ecocentrists—each with its own modes of thought and action (i.e. plural rationalities).

Four basic world-views can be distinguished (O'Riordan and Turner, 1983):

(a) 'cornucopian' technocentrism: an exploitative position supportive of a growth ethic expressed in material value terms (e.g. Gross National Product); it is taken as axiomatic that the market mechanism in conjunction with technological innovation will ensure infinite substitution possibilities to mitigate long-run real resource scarcity;

(b) 'accommodating' technocentrism: a conservationist position, which rejects the axiom of infinite substitution and instead supports a 'sustainable growth' policy guided by resource management rules;

(c) 'communalist' ecocentrism: a preservationist position, which emphasises the need for prior macroenvironmental constraints on economic growth and favours a decentralised socio-economic system;

(d) 'deep ecology' ecocentrism: an extreme preservationist position, dominated by the intuitive acceptance of the notions of intrinsic (as opposed to instrumental) value in nature and rights for non-human species.

A greater recognition and acceptance of these different environmental rationalities by participants in a given environmental resource conflict would aid the mitigation process. Effective environmental decision-making could then take into account both the irreconcilable differences and the potential areas of agreement in any given resource conflict situation.

It was into this ferment of opposing ideologies that the sub-discipline of environmental economics was born. Its development within the economics profession, during the 1960s, was in one sense a reaction to the prevailing conventional paradigm: a paradigm that stressed individualism, mechanicalism, self-interest, rationality and property rights. Revisionist analysts, therefore, perceived an opportunity to speed up the evolution of economics towards a paradigm that was 'relevant' to the coming transindustrial era. Other analysts, however, saw the sub-discipline as a means to better accommodate the environmental systems implications of the fast-growth society within a modified, but not radically different, set of economic models.

During its formative years the sub-discipline was a 'broad church', providing a home for adherents of the property rights approach to environmental management as well as for various revisionists. The profession has recently been reminded that because environmental economics addresses issues on the boundaries of economic and natural systems a pluralistic epistemology is appropriate and should not be jettisoned in favour of a narrow and over-specialised approach (Norgaard, 1985). Some revisionists claim an important role for economics in terms of a bridge between disciplines, including those concerned with societal ends and ethics and those facilitating and directing human activities. The contributions of this volume, in the editor's view, reflect an acceptance of the value of a pluralistic approach to environmental management.

Ecocentrists tried to bring to the forefront of public debate profound questions relating to the 'acceptability' of conventional growth objectives, strategies and policies. The social costs of living in a 'growth society' were highlighted and critically scrutinised. A central notion in the ecocentric world-view, as expressed in the 1960s and 1970s, was that environmental protection policies and the promotion of economic growth policies were incompatible. This led inevitably to calls for zero-growth strategies (Daly, 1977) and for the development of self-sustaining communities and, eventually, societies based on the principles of 'deep ecology', i.e. minimum resource-take communities relying on organic agriculture (Naess, 1973).

The re-birth of environmentalism in the 1960s was confined to the industrialised countries of the North. In the developing countries of the South, environmental policies, over and above a concern for basic necessities, were regarded as unaffordable luxuries. It was not until 1972, with the Stockholm Conference on the Human Environment, that a milestone was reached in the development of international environmental policy. It resulted in the establishment of the United Nations Environment Programme and the creation of national environmental protection agencies in the economies of the North. At the same time, the notion that the impending global environmental crisis was being hastened by the persistence of poverty in the South, as well as by ubiquitous industrial pollution, gained initial recognition. In the years that followed, developing countries while pressing for the establishment of a new 'International Economic Order' also came to realise that the health of the environment should concern them as much as it did the industrialised countries.

The same time period also saw the fabric of the international economic system (North and South) put under severe stress by, among other factors, the OPEC cartel action. As Gordon (1981) has put it: 'Around 1973/74 a quarter of a century of sustained economic growth at the highest rates in recorded history, interrupted by only mild and short-lived cyclical recessions, seemed to have given way to a new phase of uncertainty and perplexity.' At various times during the decade industrialised economies were faced with significant inflation and/or unemployment problems. Differential growth rates among the developing economies of the South widened and the poorest nations (the Group of Thirty-One) were afflicted with severe developmental constraints (including rapidly deteriorating local environments). One symptom of the underlying malaise in the international economy was the growing debt burden being carried by the developing economies and the start of the process of debt rescheduling.

In 1980, the US 'Global 2000 Report' (Barney, 1980) appeared to confirm environmentalist prophesies about the consequences of the neglect of the global 'common interest' and the overexploitation of open-access resources. But in a rerun of the original 'Limits to Growth' debate, 'Global 2000' stimulated a 'cornucopian technocentrist' backlash and the publication of *The Resourceful Earth* in 1984 (Simon and Kahn, 1984). The book sought to expose the data inadequacies present in the 'Global 2000' forecast. Optimism was the keynote of this 1984 report. Provided that market forces were not unduly interfered with, the development process would continue, and the expected stable population level forecasted for the globe in 2010 would be within the planet's carrying capacity.

The rejection of the physical limits to growth thesis, the appropriate role of market forces in the development process, the role of poverty in natural resource degradation and the need to recognise and build on common interests, are all themes that reappear in highlighted form in reports published recently (World Commission on Environment and Development, 1987; Repetto, 1985). In these documents it is accepted, in principle, that the world's resources are sufficient to meet long-term human needs. The critical issues under debate, therefore, concern the uneven spatial distribution of population relative to natural carrying capacities, together with the extent and degree of inefficient and irrational uses of natural resources.

These reports also contain an extended version of the interdependency thesis (i.e. a widening of the original Brandt Commission argument, which was largely confined to the question of the sustainability of the international trading system). The extended thesis has it that both North and South have common interests in alleviating the economic development pressures currently being exerted on the biosphere. Unfortunately, the mutual and common interests often identified by would-be reformers are of a very general nature. More often than not, it is national interests that dominate and determine government attitudes towards reform. While there may be a growing need for effective international cooperation to manage ecological and economic interdependency problems, the world has witnessed (since 1979) a significant retreat from multilateralism.

The first half of the 1980s has seen an improvement in developed economy growth rates, though whether the recovery will be maintained is far from clear. As far as the developing economies are concerned, their prospects are no brighter and recent forecasts predict a slowing-down in growth for even the relatively successful 'newly industrialised economies'. In 1980 the developing countries accounted for 28 per cent of the dollar value of world exports, but by 1986 their share had fallen to 19 per cent. The world debt crisis has also yet to be satisfactorily resolved. Western cultural (capitalist and socialist) influences on development planning and assistance for the South led to a stress on the twin goals of modernisation and industrialisation. But alternative paradigms of developmental strategy have increasingly been struggling for recognition since the early 1970s. Overall, it would seem that new forms of international cooperation and parallel institutions are required to foster 'growth' policies which enhance shared interests and minimise zero-sum national rivalries (World Commission On Environment and Development, 1987; G.O. Barney 1980).

Chapters 5 (David Pearce) and 7 (Subrata Ghatak) concentrate on environmental issues in developing countries. Pearce puts forward the argument that conventional economic analysis can provide valuable insights. He indicates that both price and fiscal reforms could do much in the short term to conserve scarce environmental resources. The market pricing of fuels and the imposition of resource exploitation taxes would both contribute to a more sustainable use of renewable resources in developing economies. The severity of the natural resource degradation (NRD) process can be assessed via measures of environmental carrying capacity and general economic indicators. In principle, the severity of NRD can be measured in terms of the marginal opportunity cost of non-sustainable resource use (MOC). MOC is made up of direct harvesting costs, user cost, externalities and some expected value of additional 'disaster' costs. The valuation of each of these costs is undoubtedly complex but significant progress has been made in the field of environmental resource valuation (see Chapters 6 and 10 in this volume).

Ghatak explores the issue of the transfer of biotechnological (BT) methods from developed to developing country agriculture. He emphasises that technology transfers have in the past been far from unqualified successes because of the neglect of local environmental and socio-economic conditions. In order to achieve a sustainable output from their agricultural sectors, developing countries need more than just inputs of agro-chemicals and BT. Sustainability requires an equitable distribution of the costs and benefits derived from any given 'green revolution'. Land reform is often a particularly important element in any sustainable agriculture strategy.

The 1980s have also seen a reorientation of some environmentalist thinking. The term *sustainability* has appeared in a range of contexts (environmental and developmental) and probably most prominently in publications like the *World Conservation Strategy* and the UK response to that document as set out by the Conservation and Development Programme for the UK, 1982. The precise meaning of terms such as 'sustainable resource usage', 'sustainable growth' and 'sustainable development' has so far proved elusive. Intuitively, sustainability arguments seem to be stressing the need to view environmental protection and continuing economic growth (in terms of growth of per capita real incomes over time) as mutually compatible and not necessarily conflicting objectives. Sustainability could therefore imply compatibility with natural resource base limitations and biospherical waste assimilation carrying capacities, and require a search for what Clark (1976) has termed bioeconomic equilibria.

In terms of the technocentric/ecocentric taxonomy and given the acceptance of plural rationalities, the argument appears to be that there exists some common ground where a fruitful and politically practicable partnership of ideas, values and policies—from across the spectrum of environmentalist groups—might develop. In particular, a coalition of 'accommodating' technocentrism and 'communalist' ecocentrism seems possible. Although it has to be said that 'cornucopian' technocentrism, as expressed by writers such as Simon and Kahn (1984), with its complete reliance on market forces, the power of technological progress and substitution processes, is unlikely ever to be acceptable to ecocentrics and vice versa.

In development planning and economics circles, sustainability is a key concept in some of the alternative eco-development paradigms that have been advocated (Norgaard, 1984). Debate about the sustainability of the international economic system inevitably involves notions of justice and equity, both on an intragenerational and intergenerational basis. A recent international report concluded that several transitions were essential to a world at once sustainable and renewed:

(a) a demographic transition to a stable world population;
(b) an energy transition to an era in which production efficiency is achieved with minimum environmental damage costs;
(c) a resource transition from non-renewables to renewables;
(d) an economic transition to sustainable growth encompassing a resource redistribution process;
(e) a political transition to a global bargain based on complementary objectives between North and South (Repetto, 1985).

Definitions of sustainability

From the conventional economic viewpoint 'sustainable growth', in the context of short-run growth policy, would be interpreted as a situation in which macroeconomic management policies had succeeded in minimising business-cycle fluctuations. Through such demand management policy, national growth rates (conventionally measured in terms of GNP) would be kept close to the feasible maximum growth path. The latter would be conditioned by labour-force growth, capital investment and technological and institutional constraints. But clearly, sustainability notions in the 1980s refer almost exclusively to the longer-term growth context and, as was hinted at in the introduction, have much broader connotations. In this context it seems reasonable to talk about sustainability in two modes:

1. *the sustainable growth mode*;
2. *the sustainable development mode*.

Figure 1.1 illustrates these two notions (roughly similar to Ophuls's 'maximum feasible sustainable state' society and his 'frugal sustainable state' society (Ophuls, 1977). The distinction between these two modes is not of course absolutely clear-cut and various intermediate positions are possible.

In the sustainable growth mode, conservation would be one of several goals within an overall materials policy which would include waste-recycling options and waste-reduction strategies. Policy analysis could then be undertaken using as determinate a monetary cost benefit analysis (CBA) as is practicable, or via a fixed standards approach. In the latter

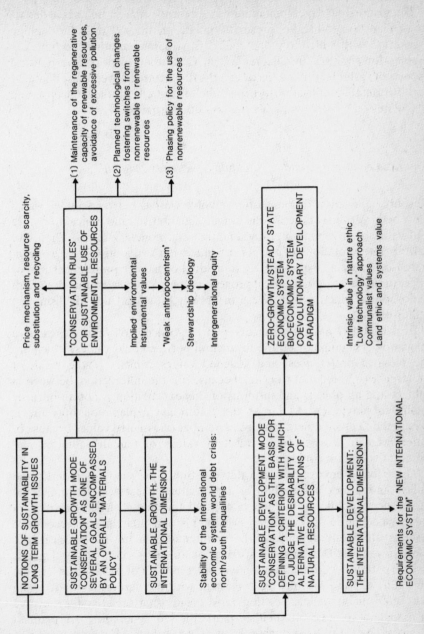

Figure 1.1   Sustainable growth and development

approach CBA would be limited by pre-emptive conservation limits.

The sustainable development mode represents some more radical departures. Conservation and/or preservation become the sole basis for defining a criterion with which to judge policy. Environmental ethics become key themes for analysis. In Chapter 2 Tim O'Riordan explores the political aspects of sustainability (in his terms, the distinction between sustainability and sustainable utilisation), traces the evolution of the concept, and speculates on possible impediments to future progress.

Environmental values and sustainability: wetlands example

Resource allocation disputes often involve clashes between values which have been variously described as fragile, qualitative, and ethical in nature and values that are more easily quantified in monetary terms. There are various interpretations of the term 'value', but economists have concentrated on value as expressed via individual consumer preferences and/or opportunity costs. Such an approach is compatible with the dominant philosophical doctrines in Western society, such as individualism and utilitarianism.

Brown (1984) has recently surveyed the concept of value in resource allocation. He emphasised the distinction between held values, which are the basis of preferences, and assigned values, which are the result of preferences. Value only occurs because of the interaction between a subject and an object, and in terms of this explanation is not an intrinsic quality of anything. As far as the traditional explanation of value is concerned, a given object can have a number of assigned values because of differences in the perception of held values of human valuators and different valuation contexts.

Three basic environmental value relationships seem to underlie the policy and ethics adopted in society: values expressed via individual preferences; public preference value; and functional physical ecosystem value (see Figure 1.2). Human ecosystems and their internal economic systems ultimately depend on the maintenance of the biospherical life-support system. The long-run survival of human social systems depends also on certain functional requirements met by a set of social norms. In the long run, such norms must be consistent with the natural laws governing ecosystem maintenance, i.e. they must ensure that social systems evolve in a sustainable fashion (neither market-based economies nor planned economies seem to be systems with in-built features that would guarantee sutainability). Within the context of physical requirements and social norms, individuals operate according to their own preferences. Environ-

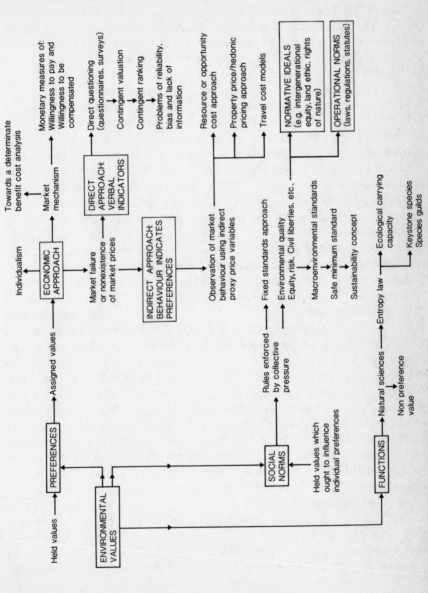

Figure 1.2 Quantification of environmental values

mental conflict situations most often involve clashes between social norms, or between those norms and individual preferences.

For instance, Figure 1.3 summarises the conflict pressures (development versus conservation) that have impinged on a complex wetland ecosystem, Norfolk Broadland. Wetlands provide a range of functional and structural values. Increasing demands on the productive use of the wetlands' resources in terms of more agricultural output, more use of the rivers for recreation (boating and fishing), and more use of water for domestic and industrial consumption and effluent assimilation, have generated negative externalities. There has been an accelerated enrichment of the watercourses by nutrients (eutrophication), which in turn leads to algal growth and decay, and the associated loss of vegetation and organic decay. Changes in the characteristic landscape of the region have also been stimulated, e.g. loss of reedbanks, channelisation and quay-heading of river banks, loss of grazing marsh and of related dyke habitats, natural ornithological and invertebrate interest. The formulation of an 'acceptable' management plan and operational guidelines sufficient to moderate and direct the process of change in this wetland has turned out to be a formidable task.

The comparatively greater depletion of British wetlands suggests that the 'balance' struck between conservation and agricultural interests in the United Kingdom should serve as a signal to other countries whose stock of wetlands is still relatively large. In Chapter 11, John Bowers takes a detailed look at land drainage investment policy up to 1985 in the United Kingdom. He concludes that because of the institutional setting, official CBAs undertaken on behalf of Water Authorities and Land Drainage Authorities were technically deficient and biased in favour of agricultural development. Past experience in the United Kingdom may, in some respects, serve as a prologue to the future of, for example, US interior wetlands, unless a balance is struck in the immediate future which is more favourable to conservation (Nelson, 1986). Despite the prevailing political climate on both sides of the Atlantic which is favourable to public expenditure constraints and deregulation, government intervention, via a package of incentive instruments centred around a core of regulatory change, is likely to be the most cost-effective and sustainable wetlands management strategy.

The purpose of Figures 1.2 and 1.3 is to emphasise, among other things, that economic value measures are context-specific, assigned values and may therefore be inappropriate as the *sole* value measures for public resource allocation. The appropriateness of held values and the assumption that all individuals operate on the basis of a flat plane of substitutable wants are also contentious issues.

Willingness to pay (WTP) and willingness to be compensated (WTBC)

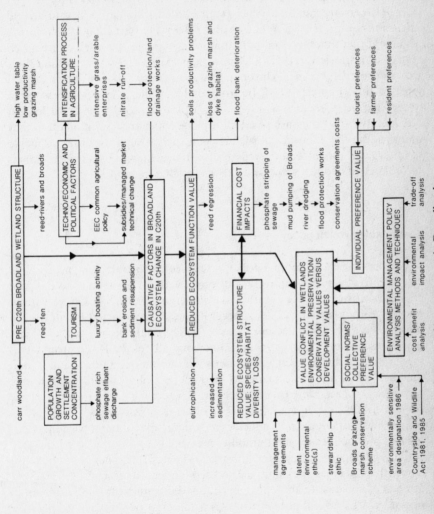

Figure 1.3   Ecosystem change and environmental management in Broadland

measures operate best in a private rather than a social group context. Sagoff (1981) contends that private and public preferences belong to different logical categories, with the latter involving opinion or beliefs and not wants or desires. Ecocentric ideologies seek to base environmentally sustainable policy on social norms that individuals accept as members of a community. Deep ecology positions place primary emphasis on a distinction between instrumental value (expressed via human held values) and intrinsic, non-preference-related value. They lay particular stress on the argument that functions and potentials of ecosystems themselves are a rich source of intrinsic value. This value would exist even if humans and their experiences were extinct. The environmental ethics debate will be analysed later in this chapter. It will be argued that while it is not necessary to accept the deep ecology world-view in order to protect the environment adequately, it is necessary to adopt a more collectivist approach to policy and to admit the relevance of social norms such as support for the principle of intergenerational equity and the existence of what some economists have labelled bequest value and existence value in nature.

Sustainable growth policy

In principle, such an optimal policy would seek to maintain an 'acceptable' rate of growth in per-capita real incomes without depleting the national capital asset stock or the natural environmental asset stock. Conservation, then, is to be viewed as one of several goals encompassed by an overall *materials policy*. Such a comprehensive policy would be one that explicitly considered in one management framework all residuals, environmental media and feedback mechanisms between and among both residuals and media. The three basic elements of such a policy would be *resource recovery programmes* (materials/energy recycling in various forms); *residuals management* (pollution control targets, instruments and institutions); and *waste reduction policies* (including 'low and non-waste technologies', product design and durability measures).

Only elements (often not fully coordinated) of such a policy are currently in place in the industrialised economies. In the United Kingdom, interest in and debate about the concept of 'best practicable environmental option' marks an initial step towards a material policy and the possible future implementation of a management framework such as that explored, mostly in theory, in 'regional environmental quality modelling' studies (Basta *et al.*, 1978).

It is possible to identify three 'conservation rules' for realising an efficient use of natural environmental assets, i.e. for the sustainable use of environmental resources:

Conservation Rule One: maintenance of the regenerative capacity of renewable resources, and avoidance of excessive pollution which could threaten biospherical waste assimilation capacities and life support systems.

Conservation Rule Two: guidance of technological changes in an indicative planning process such that, wherever physically possible, switches from non-renewable to renewable resources (stock and flow variants) are fostered.

Conservation Rule Three: utilisation of the growing body of scientific data on geological and geochemical processes in order to formulate a 'phasing' policy for the use of non-renewable resources. In principle, the aim should be to move gradually over time from relatively scarce to more scarce resources. It makes no sense to talk about the sustainable use of a non-renewable resource (even with substantial recycling effort and use rates). Any positive rate of exploitation will eventually lead to exhaustion of the finite stock (Cornucopian technocentric analysts would argue that 'in practice' resources are virtually 'infinite in supply, provided that a 'back-stop' energy resource is available and technological progress is not artificially hindered.)

Conservation Rule One: bioeconomic equilibria

If extinctions of non-renewable resources are to be avoided, harvesting rates should not be allowed to exceed the rate of natural growth of the resource over prolonged periods of time. There is a maximum stock level, constrained by the 'carrying capacity' of the host ecosystem, beyond which no renewable resource can grow. At the other end of the scale, there may be a critical minimum stock for some resources, below which resource population survival is not possible. Natural resource economics has fostered the development of a number of theorems concerned with the optimal use of a renewable resource (strictly stock renewable resources). The analysis is complex and serves to warn against an over-reliance on the simple 'maximum sustainable yield' criterion. Socially optimal resource management rules vary as different resource stock growth curves, harvest/effort rates and costs/revenues are assumed. Further, once the analysis is made dynamic, variations in the discount rates assumed greatly complicate the search for stable bioeconomic equilibria. Nevertheless, the intuitive notion of sustainability as 'sustained yield' management has been found to be generally a prudent basis for long-term management.

However, the theory developed so far does not provide concrete management policies for multipopulation ecosystems subject to non-selective harvesting (Clark, 1976).

Policy analysis: fixed standard versus cost–benefit frameworks

In the face of the complexity of ecological interdependence and uncertainties surrounding resource development policies, two alternative general policy approaches have been suggested in the environmental economics literature. Some analysts have argued for the adoption of a *cost–benefit framework*, utilising monetary valuations but also incorporating explicit recognition of uncertainty and irreversibilities. Others urge the adoption of a fixed standard approach, either in selected cases or as a way of implementing a general 'macroenvironmental policy'. Macroenvironmental standards could encompass land-use zoning policy, ambient environmental quality standards for air and water and land, population targets, etc. In this form such standards would operate as binding constraints, and, although perhaps flexible over time (as knowledge increases), would limit the scope of cost-benefit analysis to cost effectiveness analysis.

Taking the latter approach first, according to Bishop (1978), SMSs, 'safe minimum standards' (related to biophysical and other quantifiable criteria), are required in order to safeguard against, in particular, irreversibilities in the loss of critical zone resources. Public decision-making should be guided by a modified form of the minimax principle derived from game theory. Thus a safe minimum population of, for example, an endangered species should be maintained unless the social costs of doing so are unacceptably high. Conservation, then, is to be evaluated in terms of its social opportunity costs. The decision process concerned with the level at which costs actually do become excessive will have to incorporate considerations of intergenerational equity and other ethical concerns.

While it is necessary to bear in mind that no simple generalised model of ecological impacts can be formulated to allow for the numerous potential interactions between environmental parameters and ecosystems, certain criteria (species diversity, carrying capacity, species and habitat rarity, etc.) appear to be pertinent to evaluating biological impacts.

The goal of preserving the structural integrity of ecosystems should not be confused with preserving species or habitat diversity. The self-regulating (homeostatic) interactions among a coevolved grouping of species in an ecosystem is what is sought to be preserved, if balance is to be maintained. But species and habitat rarity is also important because of the growing recognition of the extent of *instrumental value* possessed by the natural biota. Advances in medicine, agriculture and industry have often occurred only because a wide variety of genetic information was available. Brown and Goldstein (1984) have investigated this particular economic argument for preserving some endangered species. The basic assumption of the analysis is that the distribution of species which are expected to be the repository of future products is, other things being equal, more valuable than species which are not, in some way, potentially fruitful sources for experimentation. They concluded that the minimum information required for a rational preservation policy would be knowledge of the probabilities of discovering improved products and how these probabilities are changed by the loss of particular species. Interdependencies between phenotypes and species greatly complicate matters. Further, market structures will also have an effect on the pace of new discoveries, and genetic engineering holds out the promise of synthetic substitutes for some 'natural' genetic configurations.

The data do appear to be available at least to formulate a set of 'rough' working guidelines, necessary to identify the most 'valuable' landscapes and ecologically important or fragile habitats and areas. However, this is not to suggest that the knowledge concerning the physical production and transformation linkages between public policies and environmental values is by any means totally adequate. Environmental Impact Assessment methods and techniques clearly have a continuing and important role to play in this context. The overall policy strategy would, then, be to try and conserve the 'priority areas' (in combination they would represent the overall SMS) in any trade-off situation.

This type of evaluation approach and these criteria do not, however, offer a panacea to the complex problem of conservation and land-use conflict. In particular the criteria suggested only rank order (in ordinal terms) sites/areas within a given general land use (e.g. recreation, landscape quality, agriculture, etc.). They do not provide a cardinal measurement scale which allows different land uses to be accurately evaluated on a comparative basis. A great deal of research effort has gone into the development of formal multi-criteria evaluation methods, such as 'concordance analysis', but it remains to be seen how operational such devices prove to be (Nijkamp, 1980). The potential facility to provide a common monetary measurement scale for diverse costs and benefits is of course the great attraction of the *economic cost–benefit approach*.

Research into the monetary valuation of environmental commodities is also still in a state of flux and it is probably too early to tell how ultimately useful some of the experimental approaches being tested will be. In the absence of a demand curve and market price (the area under the demand curve being an approximate welfare measure of benefits) for many environmental commodities (non-exclusive and non-rival or congestible goods (Randall, 1983)), a number of non-market methods for estimating value have been devised.

Four value data collection techniques, in particular, have received much attention: activity substitution models, such as the Clawson–Knetsch travel cost method, for estimating recreational values; participation models, incorporating the unit day value method for recreation values; hedonic price approaches; and contingent valuation methods, using questionnaires to simulate actual markets or creating hypothetical market situations. In Chapter 6 John Bowers and Chris Nash survey the environmental resource valuation literature. While noting the progress that has been made by analysts attempting to produce monetary estimates of environmental quality changes and of the value of various environmental resources themselves, Bowers and Nash conclude that a fixed standards approach still has much merit. Given the environmental uncertainties that remain, the 'shadow project' idea is advocated for a number of resource conflict situations. Where locally irreversible environmental losses are likely, the costs of the development scheme responsible for these losses (such as the destruction of a particularly valuable wetland) should be increased by an amount sufficient to fund a 'shadow' project designed to substitute for the lost environmental asset. It may be possible for example, to restore a partly degraded wetland somewhere else in the region.

A growing literature has suggested that non-use values should also be counted as part of the total value of a natural resource. Option value can be interpreted as the effect of uncertainty on value, i.e. an adjustment to convert the expected value of consumer surplus to an *ex ante* value to allow for uncertainty. Option value becomes significant to resource allocation problems when conditions of uncertainty as to future demand and/or supply exist.

It is therefore possible to conceive of aggregate environmental preservation value as an amalgam of use value, option value and two further elements, bequest value and existence value. Economists have sought to identify an individual's option price for conservation. This is defined as that payment which an individual is prepared to make in order to keep his/her expected utility (satisfaction) constant for differing levels of nature conservation. The difference between option price and actual current use value is the option value. Use value can be expressed in terms of expected consumer surplus from the actual recreational use of a wetland, for example. The desire to keep one's options open on the possible future use of the environment will be partly individual but may also involve bequest motivations towards one's children or even future generations. Individuals may also place existence value on environmental resources, i.e. the knowledge that such assets will continue to be conserved, even though no individual current or future use is anticipated, may itself generate utility

(Smith and Desvousges, 1986). A number of interpretations of existence value are possible and it could be argued that existence value encompasses altruism towards non-human nature and a wider conservation ethic. Deep ecologists would then want to go on to argue the case for intrinsic value in nature. But while this notion might partially overlap with the existence value concept, it also differs from it in the sense that the eco-imperative world-view would still acknowledge the existence of value in a world totally devoid of all humans.

A number of studies, based on the contingent valuation approach, have been undertaken to estimate option value empirically (Cummings, Brookshire and Schulz, 1986). Critics of contingent valuation have been concentrating their attention on the existence of biases claimed to be inherent to the technique (Rowe and Chestnut, 1983; Boyle et al., 1985). Some, but not yet enough, empirical work has been directed at the question of the practical extent of the biases. There seems little doubt that biases have affected many of the studies undertaken so far. Further, too little attention has been paid to the question of the comparative validity of economic monetary value estimates derived from the alternative methods (Seller et al., 1985). Despite these shortcomings it seems reasonable to conclude that option value is a real phenomenon. In Chapter 10 Ken Willis and John Benson provide some empirical results from a study attempting to place monetary values on wildlife benefits in selected sites in the United Kingdom. Both travel cost and contingent valuation estimates of the willingness to pay for wildlife benefits are presented. Initial results indicate that willingness to pay measures are positive and significant.

Open-access environmental resources: waste assimilation and life support services

The second part of Conservation Rule One serves to remind us that the residuals disposal and life support services of the environment must not be neglected in a sustainable growth strategy. Pearce (1976) has demonstrated that conventional neoclassical economic analysis is not appropriate when so-called persistent stock pollutants (i.e. those which have no counterpart degrader populations in the biosphere) are present. There is the possibility, especially because of the open-access nature of the assimilative capacity resource, of a basic incompatibility between the conventional economic optimum level of pollution and an ecologically 'sound' optimum level. Stock pollutants also typically present latency and damage perception problems.

It became clear during the 1970s that societies would have to face this

new type of environmental problem which has been labelled 'environmental risk' (Page, 1978). The growing degree of this type of risk
exemplified, for example, by the storage, transport and disposal of
radioactive and chemical wastes, seems to be causing much anxiety
amongst increasing numbers of individuals. Both local communities (in a
severe form) and larger populations are now subject to a relatively new
group of facilities that pose hazards to human health and safety and that
can be classified as low-probability/high-risk facilities. Between four and
five million tonnes of hazardous and potentially hazardous waste, for
example, are generated annually in England and Wales. The bulk of this
waste is disposed of via less than a hundred large sites in thirteen local
authority areas. Over 90 per cent of the waste is untreated when it is
landfilled or disposed of at sea. The uneven regional distribution of
treatment and disposal facilities clearly has distributional implications as
far as the social costs and benefits of hazardous waste disposal policy are
concerned. The benefits of the disposal policy are spread widely through
society but the potential negative externalities are concentrated on relatively small 'target' populations living in close proximity to, say, a landfill
'co-disposal' site.

Discussion of technological risk inevitably boils down to a debate about
'acceptable' levels of risk and the weighting of this risk against actual
or anticipated benefits to be derived from technological innovations.
O'Riordan et al. (1985) have recently argued that there is no agreed level
of safety that is 'acceptable'. Those responsible for managing and regulating safety believe that they can establish adequate parameters, but they
recognize that these standards must meet with 'public approval'. Social and
political conflict (threatening sustainable growth) induced by environmental risk problems can occur at various levels—local, national and
international. At the local level, a neighbourhood or community may have
to bear a disproportionate share of the negative externalities associated
with a given technological advance and related waste disposal requirement.
These so-called LULUs (locally unwanted land uses) often force the
affected minority into a conflict situation. Increasingly it would seem to be
the case that the degree of public risk aversion will have a considerable
influence on the cost and/or uptake of certain disposal options. Economic
risk–benefit analysis will need to take on board these distributional issues,
as well as the difficult question of compensation for 'target' populations.

Randall (1983) has suggested that, in the spirit of what he terms the
Coase–Buchanan approach to the law and economic efficiency issues,
LULU problems could be ameliorated by way of a compensation auction.
The low bidding community would become fully compensated and there-
fore prepared to accept a facility such as a hazardous waste disposal site.
If no community submitted a 'low enough' bid, the 'need' for the facility or

the possibility of a technological fix via a low and non-waste technology innovation would be re-evaluated. Thus a market would be established which would tend to achieve efficiency in determining the total number of such facilities and their locations. But as Randall admits, two crucial details remain to be worked out—'(1) the collective decision process leading to submission of the community bid, and (2) the mechanism for determination of intra-community compensation in cases where various sections of the community were differently impacted'. Conflict resolution methods and laws have been tested in some US states, usually involving mandatory mediation or negotiation processes. In the United Kingdom, the planning inquiry system is still relied on despite its increasing cost and protracted time-scale.

The irreversible nature of stock pollution also inevitably raises the question of intergenerational equity and the thorny problem of trying to value the preferences of future generations.

In the light of uncertainties concerning pollution transfer and damage cost functions (and in particular the lack of knowledge about synergistic damage costs in certain media), pollution control policy should be seen in terms of an iterative search process. Data deficiencies are such that neither optimal standards nor Pigovian taxes for pollution abatement are feasible. Roberts (1976) sees the process of pollution abatement decision-making proceeding sequentially, with policy continually being adjusted as information accumulates. Pollution control is therefore undertaken via a satisficing rather than an optimising approach. For flow pollutants the aim would be to maintain an average level of ambient quality most of the time. 'Acceptable' ambient environmental quality standards need to be set and then the range of potential policy instruments scrutinised in order to determine the most 'cost-effective' package of instruments required to achieve the chosen ambient quality states. So far most governments have favoured the direct regulatory approach, in a majority of pollution contexts, in preference to the market-based economic incentive instruments (taxes, tradable emission rights and deposit–refund systems).

In Chapter 8 Judith Rees argues the case for a multi-criteria approach to the evaluation of pollution control policy. According to Rees, the economic efficiency aspects of any instrument package must be balanced by considerations of distributional equity and political feasibility. Not enough research has been conducted on the way various interested parties actually react to policy instruments. In Chapter 9 John Pezzey takes an in-depth look at the efficiency of economic incentive mechanisms (taxes and rights) for pollution control. He brings together an economic analysis of the instruments most often mentioned in the literature and an appreciation of the institutional framework within which the instruments must operate. The concepts of the 'acceptable level of pollution' and the 'economically optimum' level of pollution are analysed in the context of UK and EEC pollution control policy.

Conservation Rules Two and Three

In principle, what is being argued under these rules is that sustainable use of renewable resources must be supplemented by a strategy that seeks to substitute renewable for non-renewable resources at some rate consistent with an 'optimal' use of non-renewables. The optimum path for non-renewables is predetermined by substitution possibilities. Data are lacking on the full extent of substitution constraints and on the practical magnitude of the global non-renewable resource stock. The technocentrist world-view rejects, in any case, the notion that material shortages are likely to occur in the foreseeable future (within a hundred years or so). According to neoclassical economic theory, the depletion of high-quality mineral deposits and the consequent rise in real prices will stimulate conservation and substitution processes as real resources scarcity begins to pinch. All that is needed is a lead time and gradually rising prices, which serve as market signals restricting demand.

This optimistic outlook should, however, be tempered. The required energy 'backstop' is not yet available and the rate of increase in techno-logical innovation is not guaranteed to continue in the future as it has in the past. In any case, increasing degrees of environmental risk would also have to be accepted by society if exploitation of the resource base is to continue at the same rate. Costs of safeguarding exposed populations from potential environmental damage will also rise in the future as perceived 'accepta-bility' levels change. The cornucopian technocentrist view has until recently been buttressed by the classical study of Barnett and Morse (1963), which indicated that real resource scarcity was not increasing over time. This general conclusion has now come under challenge. There is now some evidence to suggest that the end of the 1960s might have been a resource scarcity turning-point (Hall and Hall, 1984). Further, industrial economies would still have to face the risk (perhaps increasing) of transitional Malthusian scarcity in the short run. Resource exploitation and the diffusion of technological innovation are subject to time lags of six to ten years. Material shortages can occur suddenly because of a variety of factors—war, embargoes, cyclical surges in demand, strikes, accidents, natural disasters and inadequate investment in mining and processing. The globally inequitable distribution of resources is also a potential security threat to industrialised economies because of their need to import a range of 'important' (critical) materials.

In Chapter 4 Derek Deadman and I examine a sustainable growth strategy for industrialised economies in the context of strategic materials supply sources and future demand requirements. The traditional approach to strategic resource contingency planning has focused on the concepts of supply vulnerability and demand criticality. This approach is rejected in favour of a strategy that concentrates more attention on processing technologies and substitution opportunities.

Technological alternatives exist which are capable of mitigating resource scarcity and supply vulnerability problems. A broad-based mitigation strategy (a materials policy) based on the so-called 'Materials Technology Triad' (US OTA, 1983) is recommended. The basic objective of this strategy would be to diversify, where possible, potential supply sources and more generally to reduce demand via conservation. The latter process would include a programme for effective materials utilisation which encompassed: product design and developments tailored to reduced materials intensity and increased recyclability; industrial process changes aimed at the minimisation of the waste to output ratio and the input–output ration, i.e. low and non-waste technologies (Pearce and Turner, 1984); and efforts to increase material and functional substitution.

Sustainable development policy

Sustainability notions in this mode all represent, to varying degrees, more radical departures from the conventional growth-orientated society. Conservation becomes the sole basis for defining a criterion with which to judge the desirability of alternative allocations of natural resources. It is further argued that a paradigm shift is required in economics in order to take into account more efficiently environmental constraints on the economic growth process.

In Chapter 3 Michael Redclift argues that conventional economics is not well suited to an adequate analysis of complex environmental interrelationships. Redclift looks at both the Marxist and Deep Ecology positions for a more satisfactory analysis but finds that limitations (especially in the latter position) are present there, too. He finds much to support in the coevolutionary economics paradigm being developed by Norgaard (1984). This embryonic paradigm has been designed to address directly the question of whether economic progress (in material value terms) is sustainable over the long run. Coevolution refers to any ongoing feedback process between two evolving systems. During coevolution, energy surpluses are generated within systems and these are then available for stimulating new interactions between systems. If the interactions prove favourable to society the development process continues. Thus the overly deterministic view of entropy characteristic of the earlier steady state models is rejected in favour of a negentropic interpretation of evolution. Because of evolution, it is argued, the biosphere has acquired a better order as far as human needs are concerned. The 'selfish gene' interpretation of past evolution (i.e. as merely a chance process) has masked the importance of learned preferences. Learning, knowledge and evolution are interrelated and additional coevolutionary development potential remains untapped. Uncertainty surrounds the magnitude and extent of this development potential which will determine how tolerable survival will be. Over the long run, perhaps only basic human needs can be catered for on a sustainable basis.

The need for and possibilities of an environmental ethic

Analysts supportive of the sustainable development world-view claim to have detected a growing sense of unease in industrialised societies about the current man–nature relationship and the lack of normative insight into this relationship. These analysts seem to be appealing to some kind of intuitive ethic, for example, that humans ought not to overexploit other less advantaged humans and nature in general. Efforts should be made to protect nature's ongoing holistic integrity.

There is little consensus among philosophers, however, as to whether this intuitive ethic can be given rational and theoretical support, or what the content of the ethic should be. A number of writers have suggested that traditional forms of ethical reasoning must be broadened or even abandoned. There must be an extension of the moral reference class beyond current individuals to cover the rights and interests of non-human nature and/or future generations of humans. Regan (1981) distinguishes between an ethic 'of the environment' and an ethic 'for the use of the environment'. The former environmental ethic requires that non-human nature (both conscious and non-conscious) be capable of being inherently valuable (i.e. both possess intrinsic value). It would seem, however, that trying to justify judgements of inherent value is an almost impossible task. In any case, I would argue that an ethic 'for the use of the environment', which restricts rights to humans and recognises only instrumental value in nature, can offer sufficient environmental safeguards.

Conclusions

I have surveyed elsewhere (Turner, 1987) the various positions for and against an extended ethic. In this chapter I will merely highlight my own conclusions both on the debate over the need (in terms of adequately safeguarding the biosphere) for an extended ethic and the sustainability debate:

1. An 'ethic for the use of the environment' does, suitably interpreted, offer adequate environmental safeguards.
2. There is no requirement to accept any of the more radical 'deep ecology' positions and ethics.
3. Instead, it is the individualistic basis of utilitarianism and conventional economic thinking that needs modification.
4. Acceptance of the 'justice as opportunity' position in the intergenerational equity context (Page, 1983) offers a way forward towards a sustainable growth policy. What is proposed is that future generations are owed compensation for any reduction (due to the activities of the current generation) in their access to easily extracted and conveniently located natural resources. So the future's loss of productive potential must be compensated for if justice is to prevail. The current generation pays the compensation via improved technology and increased capital investment designed to offset the impacts of depletion. Adopting a more collectivist approach allows us to recognise 'generalised obligations' (Norton, 1984)—obligations of the current generation to maintain a stable flow of resources into the indefinite future, in order to ensure ongoing human life, rather than just meeting individual requirements.
5. The passing-on of the resource base 'intact' over the generations can be achieved via the three 'conservation rules' for sustainable growth and their related policy strategies. Further optimal management of renewables and 'constrained' development of non-renewables (so as to limit environmental damage costs) will necessarily ensure the survival of the majority of non-human nature and its natural habitats.
6. The sustainable growth mode does not have to be abandoned in favour of any of the variants of sustainable development policy.

References

Barnett, H. and Morse, C., 1963, *Scarcity and Growth: The Economics of Natural Resource Availability*, Johns Hopkins University Press, Baltimore.

Barney, G.O., 1980, *The Global 2000 Report to the President of the US*, 2 vols., Pergamon Press, Oxford.

Basta, D. *et al.*, 1978, *Analysis for Residuals: Environmental Quality Management*, RFF, Washington, D.C.

Bishop, R., 1978, 'Endangered Species and Uncertainty: The Economics of a Safe Minimum Standard', *American Journal of Agricultural Economics*, 61 (5).

Boyle, K. *et al.*, 1985, 'Starting Point Bias in Contingent Valuation Bidding Games', *Land Economics*, 61 (2).

Brown, G. and Goldstein, J., 1984, 'A Model for Valuing Endangered Species', *Journal of Environmental Economics and Management*, 11 (3).

Brown, T., 1984, 'The Concept of Value in Resource Allocation', *Land Economics*, 60 (3).

Clark, C., 1976, *Mathematical Bioeconomics*, John Wiley, New York.

The Conservation and Development Programme for the UK, 1982, *A Response to the World Conservation Strategy*, Kogan Page, London.

Cummings, R.G., Brookshire, D.S. and Shultz, W.D. (eds), 1986, *Valuing Environmental Goods*, Rowan and Allanheld, Totowa, N.J.

Daly, H., 1977, *Steady-State Economics*, Freeman, San Fransisco.

Gordon, L., 1981, 'Changing Growth Patterns and World Order', in Cleveland, H. (ed), *The Management of Sustainable Growth*, Pergamon Press, New York.

Hall, D.C. and Hall, J.V., 1984, 'Concepts and Measures of Natural Resource Scarcity, with a Summary of Recent Trends', *Journal of Environmental Economics and Management*, 11 (3).

IUCN (International Union for the Conservation of Nature), 1980, *World Conservation Strategy: Living Resource Conservation for Sustainable Development*, IUCN–UNEP–WWF, Gland, Switzerland.

Naess, A., 1973, 'The Shallow and the Deep, Long-Range Ecology Movement: A Summary', *Inquiry*, 16 (1).

Nelson, R.W., 1986, 'Wetlands Policy Crisis: United States and United Kingdom', *Agriculture Ecosystems and Environment*, 18 (3).

Nijkamp, P., 1980, *Environmental Policy Analysis*, Wiley, Chichester.

Norgaard, R., 1984, 'Coevolutionary Development Potential', *Land Economics*, 60 (2).

—— 1985, 'Environmental Economics: An Evolutionary Critique and a Plea for Pluralism', *Journal of Environmental Economics and Management*, 12 (4).

Norton, B., 1984, 'Environmental Economics and Weak Anthropocentrism', *Environmental Ethics*, 6 (2).

Ophuls, W., 1977, *Ecology and the Politics of Scarcity*, Freeman, San Francisco.

O'Riordan, T., 1981, *Environmentalism*, Pion Press, London.

O'Riordan, T. and Turner, R.K., 1983, *An Annotated Reader in Environmental Planning and Management*, Pergamon Press, Oxford.

O'Riordan, T. *et al.*, 1985, 'On Weighing Gains and Investments at the Margin of Risk Regulation', Working Paper, School of Environmental Sciences, UEA, Norwich.

Page, T., 1978, 'A Generic View of Toxic Chemicals and Similar Risks', *Ecology Law Quarterly*, 7 (2).

Page, T., 1983, 'Intergenerational Justice as Opportunity', in Brown, P. and Maclean, D. (eds), *Energy and the Future*, Rowman and Littlefield, Totowa, N.J.

Pearce, D.W., 1976, 'The Limits of Cost Benefit Analysis as a Guide to Environmental Policy', *Kyklos*, 29, Fass 1.

Pearce, D.W. and Turner, R.K., 1984, 'The Economic Evaluation of Low and Non-Waste Technologies', *Resources and Conservation*, 11 (1).

Randall, A., 1983, 'The Problem of Market Failure', *Natural Resources Journal*, 23 (1).

Regan, T., 1981, 'On the Nature and Possibility of an Environmental Ethic', *Environmental Ethics*, 3 (1).

Repetto, R. (ed), 1985, *The Global Possible*, Yale University Press, New Haven.

Roberts, M., 1976, 'Environmental Protection: The Complexity of Real Policy Choice', in Swainson, N. (ed), *Managing the Water Environment*, University of British Columbia Press, Vancouver.

Rowe, R.D. and Chestnut, L.G., 1983, 'Valuing Environmental Commodities: Revisited', *Land Economics*, 59 (4).

Sagoff, M., 1981, 'Economic Theory and Environmental Law', *Michigan Law Review*, 79 (7).

Seller, C. *et al.*, 1985, 'Validation of Empirical Measures of Welfare Change: A Comparison of Non Market Techniques', *Land Economics*, 61 (2).

Simon, J. and Kahn, H. (eds), 1984, *The Resourceful Earth: A Response to Global 2000*, Basil Blackwell, Oxford.

Smith, V.K. and Desvousges, W.H., 1986, *Measuring Water Quality Benefits*, Kluwer Nijhoff, Boston.

Turner, R.K., 1987, 'Wetlands Conservation: Economics and Ethics', in Collard, D. *et al.* (eds), *Economics, Growth and Sustainable Environments*, Macmillan, London.

US Office of Technology Assessment, 1983, *Strategic Materials: Technologies to Reduce US Import Vulnerability*, Gov. Printing Office, Washington, D.C.

World Commission on Environment and Development, 1987, *Our Common Future*, Oxford University Press, Oxford.

World Resources Institute, 1985, *The Global Possible*, Washington, D.C.

Part I

Sustainable Growth and Development Principles

Chapter 2
The Politics of Sustainability
Timothy O'Riordan

Introduction and summary

Sustainability appears to be accepted as the mediating term designed to bridge the gulf between 'developers' and 'environmentalists'. Its beguiling simplicity and apparently self-evident meaning have obscured its inherent ambiguity. Its survival attests to the fact that developmental interests now recognise that much more serious attention must be paid to incorporating a thorough understanding of environmental processes into project investment calculus, if for no other reason that failure to do so may result in environmental side-effects that carry economic losses. But the perseverance of the concept goes far beyond that. Developers now realise that under the guise of sustainability almost any environmentally sensitive programme can be justified. They thereby seek to exploit the very ambiguities that give sustainability its staying power. Similarly, environmentalists abuse sustainability by demanding safeguards and compensatory investments that are not always economically efficient or socially just. It may only be a matter of time before the metaphor of sustainability becomes so abused as to be meaningless, certainly as a device to straddle the ideological conflicts that pervade contemporary environmentalism. Once the notions that underlie sustainability are politicised, the concept is effectively devalued.

Placing sustainability in perspective

The notion of sustainability applies most conveniently to the replenishable use of renewable resources. The aim is to benefit from the advantages provided by such resources to the point where the rate of 'take' equals the rate of renewal, restoration or replenishment. So in agriculture the farmer derives fertility from soil equal to the ability of the soil to supply nutrition. Similarly, the woodsman removes trees or tree products at a rate equal to tree regeneration. The fisherman catches marine resources in amounts that are equivalent to their refurbishment. This begs the question of whether inherent rates of renewability can be enhanced through scientific management. Even under those conditions, however, the basic principles of sustainability apply.

Implicit in this narrow definition are four seemingly justifiable precepts:

(i)   *knowability*: the amount, rate and other characteristics of renewability are knowable and calculable.

(ii) *homeostasis*: renewable resource systems operate broadly around equilibria or can be manipulated to approximate steady states following human intervention—homeostasis is a preferential state of nature.

(iii) *internal bioethics*: the act of drawing upon a renewable resource even below some threshold of take has implications only for the tightly confined ecosystem that is that resource.

(iv) *external bioethics*: utilising a renewable resource up to the point of sustainable yield is morally justifiable even though that resource, below the threshold of optimal 'take', may have other ecological values and functions.

We shall see below that none of these principles or conditions is realistic, practicable or justifiable. Yet, if sustainability in this narrow sense is to be operational, then these principles must at least set boundaries for acceptable action.

The argument that follows draws upon a distinction between sustainable utilisation and sustainability. This is similar to the theme introduced by Kerry Turner in the opening chapter, between sustainable growth and sustainable development. Turner visualises sustainable growth primarily as a technical concept, bound by formalistic rules of efficiency and administration. This is akin to the treatment of sustainable utilisation in this chapter. Sustainability is a much broader phenomenon, embracing ethical norms pertaining to the survival of living matter, to the rights of future generations and to institutions responsible for ensuring that such rights are fully taken into account in policies and actions. The first two of the four premises of sustainability outlined above, those pertaining to knowability and homeostasis, apply to the concept of sustainable utilisation. The latter two, which embrace a more bioethical perspective with implications for a great variety of rights and obligations, impinge more directly on the notion of sustainability. Sustainable utilisation is a prior condition for sustainability, but not a sufficient one. The analysis which follows asserts that sustainable utilisation is manageable and politically acceptable because it is safely ambiguous. Sustainability, on the other hand, is politically treacherous since it challenges the status quo. Paradoxically, the objectives of sustainibile utilisation cannot be met without incorporating the principles of sustainability—hence the confusion of misunderstanding that has grown up around the sustainability debate.

Interpretations of sustainability

Sustainability within Gaian laws

The concept of sustainability has a long historical lineage. The very brief historical account that follows is written to illustrate that sustainability has been a desirable objective throughout human history. Interpretations, however, have differed noticeably, depending upon the character of the man–land relationship.

As a specific notion, sustainability probably appeared first in the Greek vision of 'Ge' or 'Gaia' as the Goddess of the Earth, the mother figure of natural replenishment. The historian, Donald Hughes (1983, 55) summarises the Gaian perspective: '[Gaia] nourishes and cares for all creatures as her own children. From her all things spring; to her return all things that die. Her creative womb bore all that is, including the first of all the sky and all that it contains . . .' So important was the practice of sustainability to the Greeks that provincial governors were rewarded or punished according to the look of the land. Signs of erosion or other features of environmental damage led to admonishment or even exile, whereas a healthy-looking land, regardless of the real well-being of its people, would be accorded approval.

Hughes takes the Gaian interpretation of sustainability one stage further by showing that linked to Gaia was her daughter, Themis, the goddess of law or justice. As Hughes (1983, 56) comments:

It is because the Earth has her own law, a natural law in the original sense of these words, deeper than human enactments and beyond repeal . . . Who treats her well receives blessings; who treats her ill suffers privation, for she gives with evenhanded measure. Earth forgives, *but only to a certain point, only until the balance tips and then it is too late* . . . [emphasis added]

There is far more to the Greek concept of Gaia, and its more scientific contemporary interpretation attributed to Lovelock (1979), than this rather confined version of sustainability. Nevertheless, the principles of *adherence to natural laws*, or what scientists prosaically term fundamental environmental processes and the *evenhandedness of retribution* (at least in terms of consequence, if not in terms of final impact which relates to poverty and technological adaptability), are pertinent in the original, simple formulation.

Sustainable utilisation as democratic resource management

We can move almost two thousand years to see the notion of sustainability taken into the modern era. The principal advocates were the new elite of scientific environmentalists operating under the Progressive political ideologies found in the United States at the turn of the century. Their champion was President Theodore Roosevelt, but their intellectual leader was Gifford Pinchot, Roosevelt's chief forester and mentor.

Pinchot regarded sustainable utilisation as the application of 'common sense'. To Pinchot, conservation and sustainability were as one:

Conservation advocates the use of foresight, prudence, thrift, and intelligence in dealing with public matters. It proclaims the right and duty of the people to act for the benefit of the people. Conservation demands the application of common sense to the common problems for the common good. [written in 1910, quoted in Nash, 1968, 61].

Conservation is the foresighted utilisation, preservation and/or renewal of forests, waters, lands and minerals for the greatest good of the greatest number for the longest time. [ibid., 61]

Pinchot was a forester. During the latter part of the nineteenth century, foresters had developed a series of management principles around the application of sustained yield silviculture. Sustained yield management was very tightly defined, referring to the replanting of commerical species over logged areas so that productive biomass was sustained. Nothing was said about concomitant ecological losses. However, foresters had also linked their profession into soil conservation. Indeed, the early British forest reserves in India were known as 'conservancies' as their prime role was to protect the soil and control runoff, rather than to provide timber. It is from this derivation that Pinchot extended the meaning of conservation, and ecologists later coined the phrase 'sustainable utilisation'. Pinchot and his associates were primarily interested in efficiency of economic transactions over natural resource utilisation. This meant blocking the monopoly power of the major resource-owning monoliths, and extending access to the benefits of natural resources to as many people as possible. Enlightened regulation was supposed to apply the brakes on selfishness or the inherent tendency towards corporatist aggrandisement. Grafted on to the fundamentals of replenishment were the more contemporary themes of *efficiency*, i.e. minimisation of wastage, achieved by appropriate pricing and/or regulation. Sustainability therefore cannot be divorced from the *mechanisms for determining resource allocation*, and hence is of central concern to contemporary environmental politics. The contributions by Rees (Chapter 8) and Pessey (Chapter 9) reflect this continuing interest, as does that by Deadman and Turner (Chapter 4).

Samuel Hays (1959, 266), the eminent student of the history of American conservation, was probably the first to reveal how the principles of sustainability, if vaguely defined and drawn from insecure scientific principles, could be exploited for political ends:

The conservation movement did not involve a reaction against large scale corporate business, but, in fact, shared its views in a mutual revulsion against unrestrained competition and undirected economic development. Both [developers and conservationists] placed a premium on large scale capital organisation, technology and industry—wide cooperation and planning to abolish the uncertainties and waste of competitive resource use.

Hays's analysis goes further. Roosevelt used the Progressive conservation rhetoric to bypass Congress and to outflank established economic institiutions and major interest lobbies in his quest to democratise resource use decision-making and management. He exploited the 'common sense' intepretation of Pinchot and his scientific colleagues in his belief that a decentralised society would be more enlightened and frugal in resource utilisation, and that democratic accountability could be extended into the nascent realms of environmental regulation.

Here we begin to see the stretching of the concept of sustainability to embrace institutions and devices capable of reducing waste and ensuring adequate surveillance. Sustainability is only promoted if it is seen to be achievable.

Sustainability and protective buffers

The first economist to appreciate that the 'knowability' and 'equilibrium' precepts that were built into the early interpretations of sustainability were not practicable was Ciriacy-Wantrup (1963). Wantrup was alive to the economic dangers of the irreversibility—or what he termed 'the critical zone'—and argued for a buffer to protect managers from folly, annoyance or ignorance. He termed this buffer, or sub-threshold optimum for resource draw, the 'safe minimum standard'. But even Wantrup erred on the side of a technical analysis of the economic–ecological relationship. He gave no indication of an interest in or the relevance of any eco-morality issues associated with the 'sub-threshold' take, nor in the possible ecological side-effects as renewable resources are drawn. This is how he interprets the safe minimum standard:

In *many* practical situations, maintenance of a safe minimum standard does not involve any use foregone; rather it involves a change in the technical ways (*not the quantities*) of utilisation . . . with proper timing and choice of tools . . . costs of maintaining the safe minimum standard are not only small in absolute amount, but very small relative to the loss which is being guarded against, a decrease of flexibility in the continuing development of a society. [quoted in Burton and Kates, 1965, 577] [second emphasis added]

For Ciriacy-Wantrup sustainability was regarded primarily as a technical matter, involving appropriate economic incentives for correcting resource mismanagement. The buffer against misuse was determined through what he termed 'economic rationale', not ecological morality.

One should compare this with the powerful analysis offered by Charles Frankel (1976, 111–12). Frankel was considering what are the 'messages' or 'rights' of nature which should provide maxims for sustainability. He concluded that nature ought to provide a moral brake on arrogant prescriptions about knowledge of environmental processes:

Indeed the appeal to 'Nature' may well be a useful reminder that human purposes fade, and that the sacred truths of an era are usually only collective follies. It also reminds us that, although there are laws, presumably, that explain what happens in human life, we do not know these laws and, from our partial point of view, we must accept Nature as in part random, unpredictable, mysterious. *So it is that the experts must be wrong, are destined to be wrong, unless they make explicit provision for reversing their plans and hedging their bets* . . . Perhaps when people say 'Nature has rights' they mean only to say that we ought to have institutional protection against being carried away by temporary enthusiasms. [emphasis added]

This is a far cry from Ciriacy-Wantrup, but a useful bridge into the contemporary politics of sustainability. Frankel was seeking to establish a set of rules for sustainability that transcended short-term practicalities. He provided no coherent set of new guides to assist those responsible for allocating environmental resources. This question is addressed by Nash and Bowers (Chapter 6), by Pearce (Chapter 5) and by Turner (Chapter 1). Each of these authors recognises that economic transactions now have to contain and/or be constrained by an ecological element if full valuation of resource use is to be undertaken. Each also admits that it is extra-ordinarily difficult to do this under present practices. The time has come to go beyond rhetoric. The contemporary politics of sustainability attempt to deal with this problem.

The new imperative of sustainability

The modern view of sustainability adds three crucial dimensions:

(a) the possibility of global ecological disturbance leading to serious national and international economic collapse along with perturbations in availability of key resources, notably food, timber and wholesome water;

(b) an explicit linkage between the rights of nature and the rights of minority cultures, adding a new ethical dimension to the social and ecological justice aspects of sustainability;

(c) the recognition that sustainability extends to institutions, and especially to mechanisms of accounting and allocation based on collective and long-term analytical approaches, not just to rather narrow technical issues of renewability and appropriate pricing.

These dimensions were given an impetus in the publication of the *World Conservation Strategy*, published by the International Union for the Conservation of Nature (IUCN) (1980).

That document placed the concept of sustainable utilisation on the international political agenda. The idea was not new to IUCN circles, but the *Strategy* was instrumental in causing the international community to focus upon it from the viewpoint of what Kerry Turner terms sustainable growth. Because the thesis here is that sustainability is deliberately treated in an ambiguous and inconsistent fashion, it is worth looking at the history of the phrase 'sustainable utilisation' in the lexicon of international nature conservation.

It all began with a series of African-based conferences in the mid-1960s. In December 1962 the United Nations passed a resolution that natural resources were of central importance to economic development, and that economic development in the developing countries would be jeopardised if the conservation and restoration of natural resources were not given due attention (*IUCN Bulletin*, 6, 1963). The following year, a conference of international conservation concluded that 'only through the planned utilisation of wildlife as a renewable natural resource can its conservation and development be economically justified in competition with agriculture, stock raising and other forms of land use'. This established the trend toward equating sustainable utilisation with nature conservation and wildlife management. Ten years later, in 1973, the Assembly of the IUCN moved nearer to the concept by defining conservation as 'the management (which includes survey, research, preservation, utilisation) of air, water, soil, minerals and living systems including man so as to achieve the highest sustainable quality of life'.

By this time, a number of ecologists at IUCN were attempting to link renewability to wildlife protection and improvement of the human condition. Notable amongst these was Raymond Dasmann, Duncan Poore and Max Nicholson. These men realised the importance of incorporating conservation principles within development, and sought to encourage the new interest within IUCN in favour of strategic planning and tactical initiatives based on a clearly defined set of objectives.

The result was a set of guidelines, based on ecological principles, for the management of tropical forests and mountains respectively. Initially these were orientated towards wildlife protection, but Poore also spoke of a need to establish 'a framework of wise use which ensures that the potential of renewable natural resources is maintained' (*IUCN Yearbook 1975–76*). About this time appeared the word 'eco-development', also an IUCN notion. This was applied to the development of a locality taking fullest sustainable advantage of its physical, biological and cultural resources. The objective was to connect this location-specific approach to a general global strategy within which conservation and development were fused, with due attention given to cultural, administrative and aspirational differences amongst communities.

The result was a series of drafts which wound their tortuous way through various IUCN General Assemblies between 1976 and 1980. By 1978 the Assembly resolved that its philosophy

while continuing to concentrate on conservation issues, shall place conservation firmly in its socio-economic context, with due reference to population and such other major influences as poverty, economic growth, the conservation of energy and raw material, inappropriate technologies and the satisfaction of basic human needs. [*IUCN Yearbook 1978*]

This important sentiment was never properly incorporated in the final *Strategy*. Instead that document remained fairly superficial and bland, dodging the fundamental institutional and political impediments to genuine global eco-development. The sustainable utilisation theme remained firmly rooted in technological principles allied to renewable resource management:

[sustainable utilisation means] ensuring utilisation [does] not exceed the productive capacity of exploited species, reducing sustainable yields to sustainable levels, reducing incidental take, maintaining the habitats of exploited species, carefully allocating timber concessions and limiting firewood consumption, and regulating the stocking of grazing lands. [IUCN, 1982]

The *Strategy* marked a turning-point in the international confidence of the environmental movement which had compromised on some of its more unrealistic positions to recognise that, by infusing ecological principles into development, the gulf between the anti-growth groups and the development-at-all-costs advocates could be bridged. Sustainable utilisation became the language of mediation, an attempt to implant scientific rigour into land-use planning and project management.

The *World Conservation Strategy* was a transitional statement, seeking to be a mediating bridge between the conservationists of the developed world and the suspicious leaderships of the developing world. They were angry that what they regarded as wealth creation might be denied in the interests of sustainability. Starving people, they claimed, do not think about the day after tomorrow. What was missing from the *Strategy* was any apparent understanding of why sustainable utilisation was not being followed. It also failed to address how this concept could be connected to the global eco-moralities that were emerging around the usurped rights of threatened species and cultures, as championed by a new breed of aggressive environmental activists such as Greenpeace and the Chipko tree preservation movement of the Himalayas. The drafters of the *Strategy* were also anxious not to lay blame on the causes of underdevelopment and social and environmental exploitation. The implications that aid schemes, the activities of international corporations, and the selfish expropriation of profits by many Third-World leaders, cosseted by corruption, might be the culprits were all carefully avoided. Sustainability was to be a virtuous concept operating from the middle ground of Pinchotian common sense.

Also absent from the compromise version of sustainability was the integration of the emerging theory of 'basic needs'. This had also arisen from the UN Conference on the Environment in the mid-1970s, and had blossomed into powerful rhetoric through the sponsorship of the UN Environment Programme. Ghabbour (1982, 19, 21) provided one of the best analyses of this concept:

All needs which go to make up the human character as we know it are basic. The search for dignity is inherent in man and is itself an ultimate basic human need. . . . Generally basic needs satisfaction is defined in terms of development strategies that aim at minimally satisfying primary needs for those segments of the population unable to satisfy them by their own efforts.

The basic needs approach is much more people-directed than land-directed, with emphasis on removing the causes of poverty and enabling self-help through cooperative endeavour to flourish in a myriad of co-ordinated ways.

What we see is a triple-level approach to sustainability. *Basic needs* provides the fundamental objective, *eco-development* emphasises the location/culture-specific application of the concept, and *sustainable utilisation* becomes the 'common sense' mechanism for application. The *Strategy* did not initially visualise its task in these terms, but, in response to criticism, has subsequently moved this way.

This triangular approach is akin to that recently developed by Chambers (1986). Chambers distinguishes between three approaches to development, namely *environment-orientated* (similar to the early IUCN view of sustainable utilisation), *development-orientated* (approximating to traditional developmental viewpoints as expressed by many Third-World leaders at the UN Environment Conference), and *livelihood-orientated* (close to the 'basic needs' approach). He suggests a fusion of the three into sustainable livelihood development which is close to the recent thinking on eco-development.

It sees sustainable development as achievable by securing more and more sustainable livelihoods for the critical group of the poor, thus stabilising use of the environment, enhancing productivity and establishing a dynamic equilibrium, above the sustainable livelihood line, of population and resources. It seeks to create and maintain conditions in which poor people are less poor and see and work for themselves in sustainable development. [Chambers, 1986, 13]

Chambers thus approaches the core area of sustainability, which is an enabling condition, freeing people to uplift their impoverished condition through means appropriate to their cultures and aspirations.

Despite these important conceptual developments, the immediate aftermath of the *Strategy* has been an excessive reliance on sustainable utilisation. The outcome, even to this restricted initiative is a modest response. To date, only forty countries of the 123 nations that contribute to the IUCN have prepared conservation development strategies. Excessive attention has been paid to environmental appraisal (i.e. estimates of resource availability according to various technical options of extraction and management in the spirit of Ciriacy-Wantrup's safe minimum standard) and to environmental assessment of major development projects.

These national strategies vary very much in terms of quality and comprehensiveness. Yet they all address the fundamental issue that development can only be successful if it is firmly rooted in scientific understanding of environmental processes and that cultural aspirations for human needs are adjusted to these realities. At a recent conference in Ottawa, where the *Strategy* was reassessed, linkage to basic human needs became more firmly established within sustainable utilisation. That conference followed the Chambers thesis by accepting that a primary objective was to maintain sustainable living conditions for the poorest of the poor as part of a general momentum to insert sustainable utilisation into the very heart of the developmental process. The crucial triad of

basic needs

eco-development   sustainable utilisation

is now becoming part of the currency of international development. This may not appear to be much of a breakthrough, but in global terms it is of

nmense importance in establishing sustainability as a viable political
bjective.

Impediments to the application of the sustainability principle

Both the interpretation and enactment of sustainability embrace political
values and the exercise of power. For sustainability to become implanted in
the political culture, the character of developmental and resource management institutions will require reform and remodelling. Opposition to such
eforms is ideological and structural. Sustainability is not regarded seri-
usly by those who really count, namely those at the top of political
uctures and those who control the flows of national and international
tal. The promotion of sustainability implies a reorganisation of agency
ments and priorities which cuts across the prejudices of those at the
he full application of sustainability also demands new arrangements
lget-sharing and cross-organisational responsibilities that are
nacceptable or unworkable by those who benefit and operate
isting arrangements. By contrast, sustainable development,
where it can be shown that thoughtless mismanagement of
systems can result in economic disaster and unprofitable capital
t, is now visualised as an appropriate way forward. But the
f sustainable development is simply not enough.
y of illustration, let us look at three levels at which sustainability
es might operate:

vironmental–economic development in poor Third-World coun-
es;
utting into effect the concept of best practicable environmental
ption;
rading environmental losses for environmental gains in project evaluation.

se three themes are chosen to reflect important arenas where the ideas
ained in other chapters of this volume apply most directly.

e Third-World dilemma

he Third World is a diverse collection of countries facing a myriad of
vironmental, social and economic problems with an equally varied mix
developmental histories and political–military governments. What
lows is a generic analysis of the difficulties of putting sustainability into

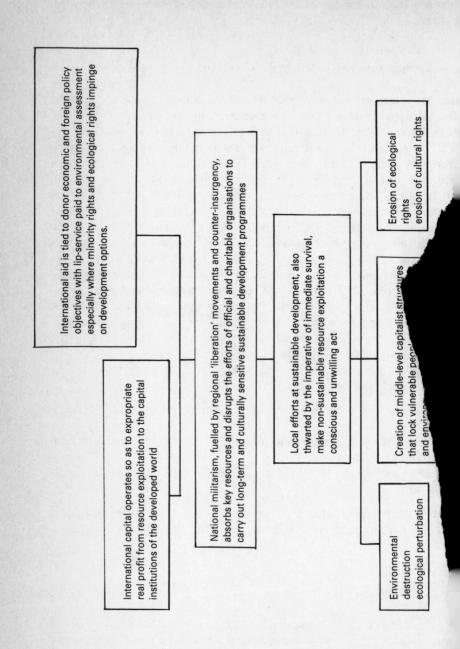

International aid is tied to donor economic and foreign policy objectives with lip-service paid to environmental assessment especially where minority rights and ecological rights impinge on development options.

International capital operates so as to expropriate real profit from resource exploitation to the capital institutions of the developed world

National militarism, fuelled by regional 'liberation' movements and counter-insurgency, absorbs key resources and disrupts the efforts of official and charitable organisations to carry out long-term and culturally sensitive sustainable development programmes

Local efforts at sustainable development, also thwarted by the imperative of immediate survival, make non-sustainable resource exploitation a conscious and unwilling act

Creation of middle-level capitalist structures that lock vulnerable peo[...] and envir[...]

Environmental destruction ecological perturbation

Erosion of ecological rights erosion of cultural rights

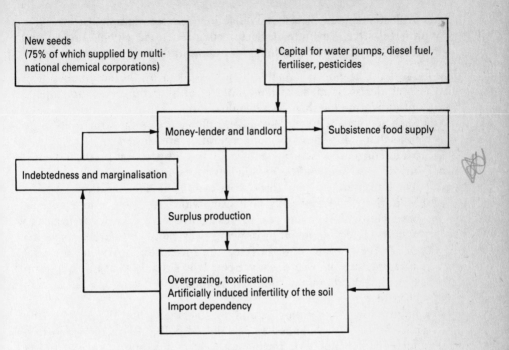

Figure 2.2   Constraints on sustainable development

practice. The arguments cannot be applied neatly to any particular Third-World country.

We start with Figure 2.1. This illustrates the relationship between the pressures for non-sustainable resource draw and the imperatives of international capitalism, international aid, national militarism and counter-insurgency, and cultural conflict which render sustainable development impossible.

Making this more specific, Figure 2.2 illustrates the links between capital movement, the seed–fertilizer–pesticide axis of major multinational chemical corporations, desertification and indebtedness, all leading to marginalisation of the vulnerable who intensify the degradation of the soil in their desperate efforts to survive. The solution requires coordination between agriculture, soil management, forestry, aid schemes and industrial regeneration departments, integrating their efforts at a regional and local level through extensive use of *animateurs*, locally-based extension agents acting as catalysts for local self-help schemes.

The following conclusions emerge from current studies of the three great environmental dilemmas facing the Third World, namely soil erosion, desertification and tropical forest depletion (see, for example, Brown 1986; World Resources Institute, 1986 for comprehensive global studies; and Pearce (Chapter 5) in this volume for a more concise statement):

(i) Most of the non-sustainable action is taken by the accumulation of small decisions made at household level by people who are trapped into undermining their own livelihood.

(ii) Such actions are essentially uncontrollable unless the structural conditions that induce poverty and desperation are altered.

(iii) Middlemen who take advantage of the desperation of the poverty-stricken and the landless exploit any propensity to accumulate surplus by expropriating capital through extortion and debt-creation.

(iv) Militarism, and especially civil war, which is now commonplace in poor Third-World countries, strikes against any successful approach to sustainable development by drawing away capital into arms, removing able-bodied labour into warfare, and physically destroying the vital infrastructure of rural development. It is unlikely that any long-term agricultural programme built on sustainability principles can remain unscathed.

(v) International aid is not geared to sustainable development at the micro-scale. Aid is linked to established political structures and to a degree is dependent on recipient government support. Recent studies of World Bank aid, even those programmes which allegedly have a specific environmental component, indicate outcomes which are socially divisive and environmentally destructive.

Criticism of the World Bank has been most furiously developed by the *Ecologist Magazine* coordinated by its editor, Edward Goldsmith. Five issues of the magazine have been devoted to this cause (Vol. 14, Nos. 5 and 6, 1984; Vol. 15, Nos. 1 and 2, 198.; Vol. 16, Nos. 2 and 3, 1986). Goldsmith (1985, 7) sums up his views:

Environmental degradation in the Third World is the . . . inevitable consequence of present development policies, and Third World people are poor, because they have been impoverished by previous development, because they have been robbed by developers of their means of sustenance, and are now condemned to scratching an ever more marginal existence from land that ever more closely resembles the surface of the moon.

This reads like unsubstantiated rhetoric. But World Bank ecologist Robert Goodland (quoted in World Resources Institute 1986, 199) admits that World Bank-financed major water projects have caused 'massive damage' and that there is an acute shortage of environmental specialists on the Bank staff. The US Treasury, also quoted in the World Resource Institute study suspects that the problems encountered in the environmental aspects of projects may be an instance of the over emphasis of quantity rather than quality. If environmental considerations threaten expeditious project processing, the environment is assigned low priority and is left to be dealt with later.

The World Resources Institute report indicates that progress is being made, but at an agonisingly slow pace.

Despite numerous studies of the need for global sustainability, and even more reports on global ecological disturbance, no serious attempts at institutional reform are being made by those who are capable of mobilising and implementing these reforms.

David Pearce offers a more optimistic appraisal. He recognises the impediments but argues that corrective taxes and various distributional aids would stem the destruction of renewable resources and generate sufficient indigenous capital to allow some beginnings to locally based sustainable development projects. The key to his analysis is the effective implementation of corrective taxes to account for the uncompensated natural resource rents. For the tropical forests this will require coordinated intervention by a number of national governments, or quasi-dictatorial action by an international agency such as IUCN or UNEP. The tax take will affect the rich more than the poor in Third-World countries, the very people who prop up the governments that currently act in such a thoughtless, non-sustainable manner. Part of the secure middle classes are the security force personnel who may not take kindly to the reduction in their living standards in the name of the poor and the restless, many of whom grant them a role to play in a militaristic state. Solutions for sustainability can be devised, but the achievement involves such dramatic political dangers, that it is much easier to shelter under the less threatening umbrella of sustainable development. As has been discussed, however, such a concept is not essentially effective. Analysis and action is left to non-governmental bodies who, almost by definition, are ineffective at the structural level. One can see no realistic way out of this dilemma. At one level, namely the tremendous response of millions of individuals to the tragedy of Africa, there is much scope for hope. But these efforts raise miniscule amounts in relation to existing aid programmes and the required injection of money necessary to implement genuine and sustainable programmes. In any case, the political response to this national and cross-party expression of solidarity is depressingly feeble. Perhaps worse has to befall the Third World before we really take note and comprehend that whatever happens there affects us all. But by then it may be too late: the blocks to the realistic application of sustainability practices may by then prove impregnable.

Best practicable environmental option

At quite another level of environmental activity is another group of
conceptual and pragmatic impediments to the effective implementation
of sustainability. This is the superficially imaginative idea first proposed by
the Royal Commission on Environmental Pollution for applying the
concept of best practicable environmental option to pollution control,
waste management, and, by recent extension, to risk assessment.

The idea originated in the Commission's Fifth Report (1976, 76). The
Commission was looking at the management of air pollution control, and
came to the conclusion that while the principles underlying best practicable
means were sound, the idea should be extended to a more 'whole
environment' concept:

We therefore propose a new unified inspectorate with widened responsibilities. The
essential aim of creating this body (HMPI) would be to ensure an integrated
approach to difficult industrial pollution problems at source, whether these affect
air, water, or land. HMPI would seek the optimal environmental improvement
within the concept of 'best practicable means', employing the knowledge of
industrial processes and many of the present techniques of the Alkali Inspectorate
to reduce or modify the wastes produced. In effect we have in mind an expansion of
the concept of 'best practicable means' into an overall 'best practicable environmental option'.

In its initial formulation of BPEO, the Commission considered only a very
modest extension of bpm practice, though it emphasised the multi-media
option for the most appropriate waste discharge sink. The key was the
establishment of a unified pollution control agency, embracing land, water
and air pollution and extending from a central, specialised body into the
less technically experienced domains of local authority environmental
health departments.

In its response, delayed for over six years, the British Government all
but killed the HMPI and BPEO ideas. Officially the line taken was that
circumstances where truly integrated approaches to pollution control were
rare, and that there was 'little evidence that the present system is seriously
failing in terms of achieving a sensible balance in the control of pollution in
different forms' (Department of the Environment, 1982, 2). Behind the
scenes, however, the major inspectorate responsible for air, land and water
pollution were frankly unwilling, indeed unable, to coordinate their
approaches to pollution control, approaches noted for their economic or
environmental rationality. In addition, the myriad of local environmental
health departments did not like the idea of being bound to more cumber-
some and intricate analytical approaches to their craft. They most certainly
did not wish to be dominated by central agency guidelines. So the idea was
suffocated by institutional inertia and prejudice.

Here is a classic example of the difference between sustainable utilisation and sustainability. The best practicable means approach, if operated to its full intent, could verge on the application of sustainable utilisation. Bpm is supposed to take into account the assimilative capacities of the receiving medium, the effects of other effluent discharges, and public sensitivities to emissions in their midst. This desideratum is not achieved in practice. In concluding their study of water pollution control enforcement, Richardson and her colleagues (1983, 195–6) observed that definitions of unlawfulness were influenced by context, costs and benefits were never properly considered, and officials manœuvred within the system to codify their own rules of what was right and wrong. In effect the bpm principle is flouted in favour of expediency, personal predicament and prejudice.

The Commission returned to this theme with much more vigour in the Tenth Report (1984, 34–56, 176–7) suggesting that the idea was not only likely to lead to more optimal allocation of pollution abatement resources, but should guide a timetable for determining the priorities for pollution abatement. Nevertheless, in the Commission's mind there still seems to lurk a technically orientated approach to BPEO. The concept, as currently being debated, is aimed at administrative efficiency and improved value for pollution abatement money. As yet there is no evidence of an effective commitment to the non-monetary aspects involved in the calculus of BPEO. Many of the suggestions made in this volume would not be welcome in official pollution abatement circles.

In its response to the Commission, the Department of the Environment (1985, 3) reaffirmed its commitment in principle to BPEO:

It is clearly right that wastes should be disposed of in the way which causes least harm to the environment as a whole, taking account of possible interactions as well as economic, geographic, technical and other relevant factors. Such decisions require very complex analysis but it is important that over waste disposal policies should stand the test of the BPEO principle.

Yet in the only report so far that has attempted to promote this principle, namely the DoE study of radioactive waste disposal options (Department of Environment, 1986) it looks as though the wider advantages of the BPEO approach have yet to be grasped. That report narrows the appraisal of radioactive waste streams into neatly compartmentalised pathways, it provides only 'guestimates' of weightings that might be accorded non-monetary values (most notably the political weight of public opinion), and it draws upon the rather dubious technique of decision analysis to compare environmental options. Decision analysis is appropriate as a management tool, most especially for industry and commerce, but its failure to capture the dynamic subtleties of political realities, notably the changing public evaluations of risk, health and amenity, render it vulnerable as a decision-aiding advice.

This discussion assumes a link between sustainability and BPEO. One should be cautious that such a link can be made, certainly as BPEO is currently envisaged. The problem lies in the structure of institutional responsibilities from the management of waste, including appraisals of the processes that lead to the creation of waste. There is also a difficulty in that mechanisms for determining how effluent discharges should be handled are also in a state of flux. There is a continuous battle between the advocates of media-wide quality standards and 'discharge point' effluent quality determination, and between those who pursue 'market-orientated' approaches as opposed to those who prefer the regulatory licence-driven style of effluent limitation. These points are admirably covered by Rees and Pezzey in accompanying chapters (Chapters 8 and 9).

Because the exciting potential of the sustainability theme has most penetrated the intellectual analysis of BPEO, that concept is in danger of being confined to a retrospective tool to encourage institutional efficiency rather than environmentally harmonious pollution management strategies. Ideally BPEO should be extended into the realms of anticipatory environmental policy analysis, as well as the rounded environmental appraisal of new technologies, or programmes of investment. For example, should the Central Electricity Generating Board agree to, or be forced into, the removal of sulphurous and nitrogenous emissions from coal-fired power stations, the BPEO idea should be applied to the comprehensive environmental appraisal of the technology involved, the materials used, the extraction and transportation of limestone (for the flue gas desulphurisation medium) and the disposal of the lime-rich sludge. This would call for some very revealing environmental trade-off analyses, since the additional limestone quarrying and transport would almost certainly stir up other environmental objections.

Here is where a comprehensive foresight capability, coupled with imaginative use of decision weightings, could be incorporated into BPEO, making it a useful tool for sustainable analyses of a major pollution control strategy.

As matters currently stand, in this whirlpool of confused claim and counter-claim, sustainability has little to offer in the way of practical assistance. The notorious vagueness of the term, and its scope for varied and seemingly legitimate interpretation by different parties, make it all but useless as an operational guide. But conceptually, the idea drives at the heart of the dilemma, namely the need to devise agencies and budgets that coordinate approaches to the multi-media management of the discharge of waste, that have an adequate capacity for foresight, can stimulate appropriate R & D into the necessary future abatement technologies, and can analyse and justify measures for giving weight to non-monetary aspects of environmental production and risk. At present, this is an impossibly demanding agenda, but it is the agenda that sustainability sets out. It will be interesting to see how far the Royal Commission takes these points in its forthcoming reappraisal of BPEO.

Trading one set of environmental values for another

A third area where sustainability is relevant and challenging is the now fashionable approach in project appraisal where one set of environmental values is created to compensate for the loss of another set. This idea is not new; indeed, it is enshrined in the public trust doctrine that derives from Roman law. This provides that certain natural amenities, associated with environmental benefits, are in effect unalienable to the common good, and so cannot totally be usurped by a private landowner (Sax, 1970, 167–9).

There is no such legal convention in Britain, but there are parallels in the practice of *planning gain*, through which a developer bargains with a local planning authority in order to obtain consent, or appropriate conditions to a planning application, in order to proceed. Planning gain is becoming an increasingly attractive arena for developer–planner negotiations, notably where development proposals impinge on scenic areas or on sites of importance for natural conservation.

The principle of planning gain is relatively easy to state: to provide some kind of equivalent compensation for the amenities that are lost. Applying the precepts of sustainability, one should be looking for equivalent compensation in a kind of environmental Pareto optimum. Transactions should take place whereby nobody is worse off in total amenity terms, and at least somebody is better off.

This is an impossible objective. Amenities are not tradable in any conventional sense, and losses of habitat or psychological feelings of anxiety because of the proximity of a potentially dangerous installation (a chemical plant or nuclear waste dump) have implications for future generations that cannot readily be bargained away. Attempts to arrive at surrogate prices for such values will run into trouble. This will be not just because money may not be regarded as an appropriate currency. There will also be certain losses which people will regard as non-negotiable, i.e. which have no effective price. Already this is evident in attempts to devise compensation packages for communities living adjacent to proposed radioactive waste disposal sites. This may also be a factor in decisions to introduce the genetically manipulated products of biotechnology into a suspicious world.

Nevertheless, for many developments equivalent compensation via an extension of the planning gain approach has much potential. For example, the Central Electricity Generating Board and British Petroleum have drawn up guidelines through which areas of nature conservation will be replaced by equivalent new conservation assets, subject to the agreement of the Nature Conservancy Council and the local planning authority. The Euro-tunnel Group have begun similar negotiations with local conservation interests over the detailed planning for conservation and amenity protection. To date, however, progress is slow and results are far from satisfactory.

Here is where many of the suggestions made by those advocating a more ethically and ecologically based accounting framework from cost benefit analysis and resource valuation have much to offer. The ideas promoted by Nash and Bowers (Chapter 6), by Willis and Benson (Chapter 10), and by Turner in his introductory chapter outline fruitful possibilities for application. Environmental trade-off analysis provides an excellent vehicle for experimentation. It would also encourage the use of sensitivity testing of variables to examine the significance of ranges of valuations and should at least approach the goal of an environmental optimum.

This approach can be placed on a surer footing. A limited interpretation of sustainability is relevant here. The aim would be to establish negotiating principles and bargaining procedures based on experience elsewhere and informed consultation with local interests. Guidelines, of the kind being agreed with respect to onshore oil and gas development and electricity generation, are an important first step. But guidelines are no substitute for balanced bargaining. The value of the sustainability theme is that it should emphasise the need to reach a genuine consensus, based on a firmer negotiating hand from local parties than has heretofore been the case. The Americans set aside up to 2 per cent of development costs for local environmental mediation and compensation. An equivalent arrangement should become the practice in the United Kingdom. There is still much to be gained.

Future prospects for sustainability

One can only be cautious about an effective future role for the concept of sustainability. It is probably going to languish as a 'good idea' which cannot sensibly be put into practice—like 'democracy' and 'accountability'. Its advantage is that it establishes a useful moral position which can be exploited by reformists. Its disadvantage is that it can be manipulated into tinkering adjustments to the status quo by established interests which, in order to retain respectability, have to make certain relatively minor concessions. The real threat is that the concept becomes widely misunderstood, it is confined to the flow rates of depletion and replenishment, it remains regarded essentially as a scientific and managerial device, and it has no role either in institutional reform, mobilisation of new power relationships, or in the extension of a more pragmatic eco-morality.

References

Brown, L.C., 1986, *State of the World 1986*, Norton, New York and London.

Burton, I. and Kates, R., 1965, *Readings in Resource Management and Conservation*, University of Chicago Press, Chicago.

Chambers, R., 1986, 'Sustainable Livelihoods: An Opportunity for the World Commission on Environment and Development', Institute of Development Studies, University of Sussex, Brighton, England.

Ciriacy-Wantrup, S.V., 1963, *Resource Conservation*, University of California Press, Berkeley.

Department of the Environment, 1982, *Air Pollution Centre: The Government Response to the Fifth Report of the Royal Commission on Environmental Pollution*, Pollution Paper 18, HMSO, London.

_____ , 1985, *Controlling Pollution: Principles and Prospects: The Government's Response to the Tenth Report of the Royal Commission on Environmental Pollution*, Pollution Paper 22, HMSO, London.

_____ , 1986, *Assessment of Best Practicable Environmental Options (BPEOs) for the Management of Low and Intermediate Level Solid Radioactive Wastes*, HMSO, London.

Frankel, C., 1976, 'The Rights of Nature', in Tribe, L.H., Shelling, C.S. and Voss, J. (eds), *When Values Conflict*, Wiley, New York, 93–114.

Goldsmith, E., 1985, 'Open letter to Mr. Clausen, President of the World Bank', *The Ecologist*, **15** (21–2).

Ghabbour, S.I., 1982, 'Definitions, Issues and Perspectives', in UN Environmental Programme, *Basic Needs in the Arab Region: Environmental Aspects, Technologies and Policies*, UNEP, Nairobi, 19–46.

Hays, S.P., 1959, *Conservation and the Gospel of Efficiency*, Harvard University Press, Cambridge, Mass.

Hughes, D., 1983, Gaia: an ancient view of our planet, *The Ecologist*, **13** (2, 3).

International Union for the Conservation of Nature, 1980, *World Conservation Strategy*, IUCN, Geneva.

Lovelock, J., 1979, *Gaia: A New Look at Life on Earth*, Oxford University Press, Oxford.

Nash, R., 1968, *The American Environment: Readings in the History of Conservation*, Addison Wesley, Reading, Mass.

Pinchot, G., 1910, *The Fight for Conservation*, Garden City, New York.

Richardson, G., Ogns, A. and Burrows, P., 1983, *Policing Pollution: A Study of Regulation and Enforcement*, Clarendon Press, Oxford.

Royal Commission on Environmental Pollution, 1976, *Fifth Report: Air Pollution Control: An Integrated Approach*, Cmnd. 6971, HMSO, London.

Royal Commission on Environmental Pollution, 1984, *Tenth Report: Tackling Pollution: Experience and Prospects*, Cmnd. 9149. HMSO, London.

Sax, J., 1970, *Defending the Environment*, Knopf, New York.

World Resources Institute, 1986, *World Resources 1986*, Harper and Row, New York and London.

Chapter 3

Economic Models and Environmental Values: A Discourse on Theory

Michael Redclift

Introduction and summary

This chapter begins by comparing the claims that economics can success-fully incorporate environmental values with the alternative view that, since this is impossible, it is economics itself which needs to change. To resolve this debate we need to be clear about what is meant by environmental goods and environmental values. In contrast with mainstream environ-mental thinking, some perspectives, such as 'Deep Ecology', emphasise that nature has value other than to human beings or as 'natural' resources. Most thinking about conservation fails to make this distinction explicit, and assumes a less than holistic view of the environment.

Moving from the theoretical to the policy debate, the chapter then examines the alternative environmental agenda first contained in *The Limits to Growth* (Meadows *et al.*, 1972) in the light of subsequent events. Fifteen years later, the effects of economic development on the environ-ment and the rural poor in the South seem to confirm the earlier negative prognosis. However, these effects have accompanied a contraction in global demand, unlike that predicted in the 1960s. Today economic growth is still recommended in the South, as well as the North, as a way of addressing problems associated with environmental degradation—them-selves partly a consequence of the single-minded pursuit of economic growth. International restructuring and the debt crisis in Africa and Latin America have often served to undermine policies aimed at achieving sustainable development, rather than assisting in the search for a solution.

Finally, the chapter considers the contribution of Marxist analysis to environmental problems. This perspective has some of the same limitations as the orthodox economic paradigm, in that traditionally Marxism has failed to regard the environment as a system in which human productive activities are constrained as well as realised. However, the implication of considering environmental values are even more profound for Marxists than for orthodox economists, since for Marxists the very existence of commodity production under capitalism makes environmental problems inevitable. In Marxist terms the environmental crisis is a contradiction of capitalism which can only be resolved by history. In the intervening period Marxist analysis is just as incapable of resolving the contradiction between economic growth and ecological vulnerability as any other perspective. The point at which the costs in destroying the environment, and non-market social relationships, exceed the benefit of further commodity production has already arrived. This, rather than capitalism *per se*, explains the urgency of environmental problems.

In the final section of the chapter it is argued that elements from within Marxism and other perspectives deserve to be given greater attention in seeking answers to the complex relationship between economic growth and the environment. One of these is the 'mediation' of nature: a position which takes issue with the idea that the 'natural' world and the 'human' world are separate and distinct domains, and seeks to identify the processes through which nature is 'humanised' (conservation, amenity, recreation) while human beings are 'naturalised' (in most productive activity using 'natural' resources). An integrated theoretical approach to economics and the environment is not an exclusive concern of economists or environmentalists: it is a concern of those who wish to see the environment transformed in ways that enlarge human experiences, without doing irreparable damage to nature.

Inclusive and exclusive economics

There are several schools of thought on the relationship between the environment and economic growth. They range from what O'Riordan (1986) has termed the 'environmental moralists' who deny that the environment is a commodity at all, to those who argue that environmental goods should be treated exactly like any other commodity for which there is a market. In the view of some writers, neo-classical economics has 'largely been devoted to the refinement, expansion and implications of thinking of the environment as a commodity' (Pearce, 1985, 9–10). Other economists, such as Norgaard, point to the difference between examining how scarce resources can best be allocated (the definition of most economists today) and turning this framework on its tail 'to determine from how resources are allocated *whether* they are scarce' (Norgaard, 1985b, 3). Economists, in other words, are interested in scarcity as the underlying reality behind human choice. Environmentalists are concerned that economic growth is the reality which makes human choice less and less possible under conditions of scarcity.

Economists like Pearce argue that it is possible to consider the environment within the governing economic paradigm, and that the field of 'bioeconomics' has already made substantial progress. They argue that extended cost–benefit analysis is already of considerable use as a decision-making tool. Being able to quantify and measure human concern for the environment is then of major assistance to the environmental lobby, and a step forward in building bridges with non-economists interested in the environment. Pearce is concerned that the environmental movement is either oblivious to this fact or actually opposed to it, believing (wrongly in his view) that the esteem in which economics is held by planners and policy-makers partly accounts for the problems encountered in the environment. The alternative view is that a concern with the environment entails the abandonment of a unitary economic paradigm. This is essentially the position of economists like Norgaard (1985a and b).

Pearce's position, like that of most of the economists he cites, is that economic modelling is increasingly sophisticated and able to attach quantitative weight to human desires and preferences. Experimental economics has led to 'the extension and measurement of our value concepts beyond those of direct use value' including, critically, those pertaining to environmental uses (Pearce, 1985, 12). By being able to incorporate measurable data into policy work on the environment the interests of sustainability are served, though this is not a guarantee that they will be adhered to by policy-makers. Economics is traditionally interested in value that can be expressed through consumer preferences, for example, in the notion of 'opportunity cost'. These methods can be extended to cover environmental goods in a number of ways.

There is, then, a recognition in this approach that any costs of development which lie outside ecological constraints, that pose difficulties for sustainability, are both injurious to life-support systems and serve to reduce the future resource base. At one level this is little more than the admission that market mechanisms and public choices do not necessarily bring about sustainable development. It is also an affirmation of the strength of economics in being able to measure the effect of these allocative mechanisms in areas, such as environmental preference, which have only received attention recently. Pearce reiterates that the pursuit of better living standards is captured in the concept of economic growth, and that it would be unwise to fail to acknowledge this fact (1985, 16).

The ability to model human preferences for environmental goods, through the 'willingness to pay' principle, rests on ways of discounting present and future preferences. The rules for assessing anticipated future losses 'can be modelled and analysed in a framework which incorporates both economic and ecological considerations' (Pearce, 1985, 20). The claim is that 'economic science has been ahead of the game, developing the foundations of bioeconomics, the integrative analysis of biological and economic systems of man [sic] and the natural environment' (1985, 25).

Pearce's position can be criticised from within economics, as well as from without. A recent paper concerned with developing methods of environmental evaluation on the basis of people's choices concluded that there were important divisions within economics '. . . not only as to the appropriate rate of discount but even as to whether long term environmental changes should be the subject of discounting at all' (Hodge, 1986, 9). Many economists remain unconvinced that environmental resources represent a challenge which neo-classical economics can and should address. Some, following a utilitarian position, would argue that there is no moral justification for extending individual rights to future generations, for example. Some economists clearly do not see the environment as a problem for economics, even if economics is a problem for the environment.

Another position, and one which takes issue with much that Pearce is saying, argues that economists are still giving the environment much less attention than it deserves. In a series of trenchant, closely argued papers, Norgaard (1984, 1985a, 1985b) has suggested that neo-classical economics is incapable of fully incorporating environmental considerations into its methodology without what amounts to a 'paradigm shift' (Kuhn, 1970). Norgaard insists that economic models do need to meet the challenge of future discounting. For one thing, future generations need to inherit an improved capital stock and better technology that will equip them to substitute resources and overcome scarcity. The need to treat future generations as if they are living now, he argues, is not just a requirement of equity but of the competitive conditions assumed by the economist's model, which assumes exchange between generations. He notes that the world which has been formally modelled by economists is an '. . .imaginary world without surprise or resources'. It is also a world which assumes general public policies and allocations by public agencies, a position which few of the economists concerned would be prepared to defend for political reasons (Norgaard, 1985a, 4).

The problem with environmental resources is partly that of determining optimal behaviour. Allocations which account for environmental preferences, in the way referred to by Pearce, frequently assume that behaviour is optimal when it is not. For example, people have inadequate knowledge of the decision-makers whose behaviour is altering their environment, and little knowledge of whether their behaviour is appropriate. Since many natural resources are located on public lands, the assumptions of the economic model also frequently concern the public's knowledge of how public agencies work. This leads us into particularly dangerous waters. If, on the other hand, economic indicators give the correct signals without considering new areas of behaviour and new preferences, '. . . then resource owners are already fully informed about scarcity' and are practising 'optimisers' (Norgaard, 1985a, 6). Norgaard argues, convincingly,

I believe, for a much more ecumenical view of the environment and development in which long-run resource scarcity is considered together with the technological drive to offset it. In his view, developing and adapting to technology 'have restructured what is a benefit and what a cost' in the environment (1985, 14).

The problem of marrying economics to the environment is not confined to methodological postures, however important these may be. It begins with the assumptions of the disciplines concerned. Neo-classical economics assumes that resources are divisible and can be owned. It does not acknowledge that resources bear a relationship to each other in the natural environment, as part of environmental systems. Market mechanisms fail to allocate environmental goods and services efficiently precisely because environmental systems are not divisible, frequently do not reach equilibrium positions, and incur changes which are not reversible. In other words, the properties of ecological systems run counter to those of what Norgaard terms 'the atomistic–mechanical world view' of neo-classical economics (1985b). Economics is not adapted to consider total changes. Resting as it does on the concept of the margin, it is epistemologically predisposed towards a reductionist view of resources and their utility.

Similarly, economic theory has difficulty in recognising that both ecological and social systems evolve over time, in ways which change both of them. This evolution brings uncertainty and the uncertainty of evolving systems is not adequately accounted for by economists interested in risk within a neo-classical model. The implication is that economics can only handle environmental factors successfully if it breaks free from its mainstream epistemology.

This is not to argue that human environmental preferences cannot be modelled, by economists, or anyone else. Such modelling, however, is only useful when 'environmental' goods can be clearly distinguished from other goods. This is frequently not the case. Moreover, human preferences for environmental goods need to take account not only of the value of the environment to human beings, but also the value of the environment itself. Ecosystems are themselves a source of value. The 'deep ecology' position addresses just this concern, as we shall see below. Finally, the real world of resources and the environment only weakly resembles that of the economists' models, since the environment is constantly evolving together with the social system in ways which alter its nature, whether human actors are aware of it or not. Genetic engineering, for example, is an area in which environmental changes are occurring without the knowledge of anybody but a specialised, scientific elite. For the moment, however, we need to examine the question of environmental values in more detail.

Environmental goods and values

The discussion of growth takes on a completely different character if we do not regard the market as the ultimate barometer of peoples' needs. Writers like Maslow (1954) have argued that 'needs' can be ranked in different societies. The priority of peoples' needs changes in the course of development, from the satisfaction of basic needs such as food and shelter to the satisfaction of aesthetic and existential 'needs' (or wants) which play such a large part in developed countries. In poor countries environmental goods are 'survival goods': fuelwood, clean water, staple food supplies. In developed countries what Hirsch (1976) calls 'positional goods' play an increasingly important part in personal well-being. The countryside is a good example of a 'positional good' in that its value declines as access to it increases. In a sense, then, it is subject to market mechanisms, but differs from most commodities (although not all) in that it cannot be produced in larger quantities to satisfy demand. The challenge of environmental social science is to link the priority of needs to their conditions of scarcity (Inglehart, 1981). We need to know to what extent economic growth makes an increasingly marginal contribution to peoples' needs, but at the same time creates scarcity where it did not exist before. The observation that an inverse relationship exists between human preferences for goods and the likelihood that they will become more scarce is not confined to environmental goods, but the environment is an area in which these considerations loom large. This is also an area in which social scientists, including economists, have a large role to play (Lowe and Rudig, 1986). One of the things which distinguishes the late 1980s from the 1960s is that today, in most parts of the developed world, the pursuit of economic growth, and the production of more goods, is being effected through cuts in the contribution of the public sector, in relative if not in absolute terms. Public sector cuts have reduced social service provision, in many cases bringing a decline in the slow process of inner city rehabilitation, industrial decline in the regions and, most dramatically, employment. Less developed countries have been affected by the same processes, often in an exaggerated form, as passed on to them by international financial institutions and the increasing protectionism of the industrialised countries. The technologies which are credited with the potential for reversing the depressed pattern of economic growth—microelectronics and biotechnology, for example—are unlikely to reverse the environmental effects which have accompanied a restructuring of the economies of the developed countries. Indeed, the expansion of new industries in most industrialised countries is being achieved by depressing public expenditure still further in areas of environmental concern. The position taken by liberal environmentalists is thus beset with a paradox: as long as environmental provisions are counted as part of Gross National Product (GNP), a reduction in economic growth and expenditure—sought by many of the champions of 'zero growth'—is harmful to the environment.

Deep Ecology

Other ecological positions take issue with the centrality of economic growth in determining environmental values. An example of an environmental philosophy with an epistemology radically different from that of the 'bioeconomics' referred to by Pearce is that of 'Deep Ecology'. Deep Ecology is the name given to the philosophical position of a series of writers whose roots lie in Scandinavia, California and Australia (Naess, 1973, 1983; Tobias, 1984; Sylvan, 1985). According to its adherents, Deep Ecology is metaphysical at base; it represents a search for a sustaining metaphysics of the environment. The underlying conviction that informs this view is that human beings should seek to emphasise their underlying unity with other living beings and processes. Deep Ecology is biocentric, not anthropocentric (Sylvan, 1985, 2). Unlike reformist environmentalism, Deep Ecology is 'not a pragmatic, short-term social movement with a goal like stopping nuclear power or cleaning up the waterways' (Devall, 1979). The defining characteristic of 'deep', as opposed to 'shallow', environmental positions is that they do not take an 'unrestricted' view of the purposes to which the natural environment can be put. This is in contrast with dominant Western culture which emphasises that people can do more or less what they like with nature, which exists for humans to exploit or manage. According to deeper positions, humans are not the sole items of value which bestow value in the world, 'and not all things of value are valuable because they answer back in some way to human concerns' (Sylvan, 1985, 5). A deep ecological position would part company with both Pearce's 'bioeconomics' and Norgaard's plea for a transdisciplinary approach to environmental economics. A deep ecology position sees primary value in nature, rather than in its transformation.

Deep Ecology has a small following, partly because some of its tenets, such as biospheric egalitarianism, can easily be dismissed as eccentric or untenable. It is not obvious, as Sylvan points out, that something has value because it has life. Nevertheless, elements of a deep ecological concern can be identified in a much wider range of writing and thinking about the environment (Cotgrove, 1982; Russell, 1982; Rifkin, 1985). The existence of philosophical positions like that of Deep Ecology, and social movements committed to 'deep' ecological objectives like the animal rights movement, should serve to remind us of the impossibility of incorporating environmental values fully within a unitary economic paradigm.

Figure 3.1 sets out some of the contrasts between the 'deeper' ecological paradigm and what we might term the 'dominant social paradigm' which places considerable emphasis on economic growth. The dominant social paradigm expresses the value placed on utilising rather than conserving resources in industrialised society. It is not synonymous with neo-classical economics which, according to economists such as Pearce, is capable of accommodating to environmental 'values'. Most conservation positions occupy the 'shallow' ground between this dominant social paradigm and Deep Ecology. Setting out the variables in this way enables us to bring together the different components of these paradigms, and serves to illustrate the multifaceted character of environmental value systems.

Dominant social paradigm	Deep Ecology paradigm
Dominance over nature	Harmony with nature
Natural environment as a resource	Values in nature/biosphere impartiality
Material goals/economic growth	Non-material goals/ecological sustainability
Ample reserves/perfect substitutes	Finite natural reserves
High-technology/science solutions	Appropriate-technology solutions
Consumerism	Basic needs/recycling
Centralised/large scale	Decentralised/small scale
Authoritarian/coercive structures	Participatory/democratic structures
SHALLOW	DEEP

Figure 3.1 Typical components of growth/environment paradigms (adapted from Sylvan (1985))

Marxist perspectives

Just as an interest in attaching value to the environment is not the preserve of deep ecological positions alone, so economic development is not the province of neo-classical economics alone. Contending theories of economic development must necessarily include Marxist perspectives. Marxist analysis has traditionally looked upon environmental problems as a necessary, but unfortunate, consequence of the development of capitalism. This position has proved unsatisfactory for a number of reasons. First, it is clear that such problems are not confined to capitalist societies, despite the elaborate and disingenuous claim that Soviet society takes ecological issues seriously (Khozin, 1979). Second, it has become increasingly clear that '. . . the goal of expanding the productive forces is in conflict with the original revolutionary goals of eliminating exploitation and alienation' which are central to Marxism (Lashof, 1986, 13). Since Enzensberger's seminal essay on the subject, a new generation of the European Left has claimed to be both socialist and pro-ecology (Enzensberger, 1974). Third, it has become increasingly clear that the ecological breakdown forecast in the 1960s and 1970s has already occurred in parts of the South, providing a curious footnote to Marx's stark choice between socialism and barbarism. The imminence of this choice has led some recent writers to talk of 'abandoning affluence' in the North as a first step towards achieving development in the South, contrary to what most development theory contends (Trainer, 1985). Finally, and most importantly, Marxist theory and method, divorced from orthodox dogma, still represents one of the most fertile intellectual traditions in which to locate ecological ideas, based as it is upon both the social construction of nature and the 'naturalisation' of human consciousness (Schmidt, 1971; Smith, 1984).

A Marxist view of the environment needs to encompass a number of closely related, but separable, issues. In the first place it needs to address the issue of the way nature is transformed under capitalism, and the implication of this process for developing countries today. In this context the question of commodity production is of paramount importance, and distinguishes Marxism from both neo-classical and Radical Ecology perspectives, as we shall see. Second, Marxist approaches to the environment are necessarily concerned with the distribution of environmental costs and benefits, not simply from a 'welfare' standpoint, but because the distributive effects of environmental change have important implications for the kinds of social movements which are likely to emerge from ecological degradation. Third, Marxists are concerned about the ideological content of environmental ideas, and their relationship both to bourgeois processes of legitmation, and to central Marxist concepts such as alienation and the class struggle.

The concept of 'the environment' appears in Marxist writing in a number of guises. The most common is that of 'natural resources'. As Schmidt (1971) has argued, 'natural resources' are the product of a conversion process through which labour (and capital) is applied to nature. There is nothing 'natural' about 'natural resources' to begin with—this property is socially determined in any given environment. Natural resources are those which are of potential use to human beings. They are socially determined in the sense that their value is related to the technologies used to exploit them, and the existence of people to consume them. Without a social formation comprising, among other things, an internal market of consumers and a technology capable of linking them to the production process, natural resources remain 'unresourced'.

This leads to the question of underdevelopment. As Ojeda and Sanchez have put it:

. . . private capitalist accumulation, within the ambit of the international division of labour and the growing specialisation that this implies, makes the consideration of what is a natural resource depend upon the manner in which each society is inserted within the world market [Ojeda and Sanchez, 1985, 36]

Capitalist development transforms nature and the environment within a logic which needs to be understood in global terms, as both Lenin (1972) and Luxemburg (1951) argued, and which has characteristics today which it did not possess fifty or a hundred years ago. This internationalisation of the environment within the global capitalist system has clear implications for the way resources are used. The implication of viewing resource uses as the conservation of *stocks* rather than the utilisation of *flows* has informed some important work currently being undertaken in Latin America by the United Nations Economic Commission for Latin America (ECLA) and the United Nations Environment Programme (UNEP) (Sunkel and Gligo, 1980).

To some extent Marxists encounter the same problem in approaching the environment as neo-classical economists. This is that the environment exists as a system. It follows that '. . . a basic difficulty in the construction —or refutation—of ecological hypotheses is that the processes involved do not take place serially, but in close interdependence' (Enzensberger, 1974, 6). As we saw, the systems in which resources are located provide difficulties for neo-classical economists, whose paradigm is atomistic, if not reductionist. For Marxists the problem is one of the underlying logic of the environmental system rather than the system itself. Neo-classical economists have attempted to get around the problem of environmental values by attaching a price to 'externalities', enabling them to be treated as if they were part of an optimising resource model. This does not necessarily enable economists to incorporate the environment successfully within their analysis, as we have seen, but it does enable them to model human preferences in the environment, at least at a theoretical level.

The problem for Marxists is more complex, however. As Harris has written, Marxist methodology

. . . points in an opposite direction. It suggests that it is not possible to flout the market system. If a system of commodity production prevails, merely raising the price of some commodities will not eliminate them from use . . . It will not change people's relation to nature, their attitudes or their desire for material possession. [Harris, 1983, 49]

In Marxist terms scarcity will only disappear when the necessity to make commodities in order to realise a profit disappears. While some neo-classical economists assert that environmental goods should be approached for their use values as well as their exchange values, Marxists are concerned, primarily, with the process through which use values are converted to exchange values. The point of Marxist analysis is not to espouse economic growth as an end in itself, but to argue that the increased production of commodities under capitalism necessarily implies economic growth. Together with radical ecologists, Marxists agree that the market allocates natural resources in an inefficient way through time, ultimately destroying the basis of survival for future generations. Nevertheless, Marxists see the commitment to commodity production under capitalism as making ecological externalities inevitable. Indeed, it is part of the contra-dictory nature of capitalism that 'the environmental crisis presents a massive threat' to the earning powers of entrepreneurs, as underwritten by the capitalist state (Enzensberger, 1974, 11).

The inevitability of ecological collapse was not a concern of early Marxist writing, although Marx referred to the problem of maintaining soil fertility in a celebrated passage from *Capital* (1974). Similarly, Engels (1970a, b), although aware of the fact that nature could not be plundered without cost, still emphasised the potential that nature afforded economic growth. What distinguishes the position adopted by radical ecologists, and some Marxists, from that of orthodox Marxism, is the conviction that '. . . long before it becomes physically impossible to grow, it becomes socially undesirable to do so' (Lashof, 1986, 10). The costs of environ-mental degradation, especially in the South, are such that the final scenario of capitalism destroying itself through ecological attrition is unacceptable on this analysis. The point at which the costs in destroying the environ-ment, and non-market social relationships, exceed the benefits of further commodity production has already arrived. The Promethean quality of early Marxism is therefore placed in doubt. As Enzensberger wrote during the 1970s, when radical ecology was primarily a critique of 'successful' economic growth:

. . . [the ecologists] have one advantage over the Utopian thinking of the Left in the West, namely the realization that any possible future belongs to the realm of necessity not that of freedom, and that every political theory and practice—includ-ing that of socialists—is confronted not with the problem of abundance, but with that of survival. [Enzensberger, 1974, 3]

These sentiments showed some prescience in 1974 when they were written. After the recurring crises of African famine, Bhopal, and the recent nuclear catastrophe at Chernobyl, they look increasingly realistic. Clearly, environmental disasters can anticipate the point at which the limits to economic growth are finally reached.

In this context it is worth reflecting that the production of commodities under capitalism can be taken to include 'free goods' in nature, which originally had no market value. The transformation of nature under capitalism has largely been conceptualised in terms of the specialisation of labour and technology. Human dependence on technology has already reached the point, however, where nature itself can only be maintained through recourse to technology. For example, chemical fertilisers and pesticides are necessary to agricultural production under some conditions, whatever their long-term effect. Similarly, even air and water cease to be 'free goods' in a pure form, and become highly valued commodities when the environment is sufficiently degraded. This is the case, for example, in a sprawling urban environment like Mexico City, where house prices are heavily influenced by the smog which covers much of the city. Those who are able to pay the market price can live surrounded by 'natural' advantages, relatively clean air and water, through reduced exposure to the worst effects of pollution.

This brings us to the issue of distribution, which is central to a Marxist approach to the environment. During the nineteenth century most ecological degradation was more class-specific in the industrialised countries than it is today. The housing and working conditions of the poor were extremely bad, and lay outside the experience of the middle and upper classes. The circumstances in much of the South today bear comparison, in that environmental problems are differentially distributed in ways that can hardly be overlooked. One view is that as environmental degradation in the North has become 'universalised', ecological issues have caught the attention of the middle classes. The 'cost of a private environment' (like that of the middle classes in Mexico City) is '. . . already astronomical' in the industrialised countries (Enzensberger, 1974, 10). The environmental movement, it is argued, has great appeal to those who can do little to remove themselves from environmental hazards such as acid rain, nuclear fall-out, industrial pollution. The Club of Rome, it should be remembered, was composed of top industrialists and urban bureaucrats who were also concerned at the cost to the quality of *their* life posed by pollution, industrial waste and urban decay. Today this list of the undesirable consequences of economic growth would have to be lengthened to include some less proximate factors: the survival of natural species, the difficulty in gaining access to the countryside, the erosion of farmlands in parts of North America and Western Europe.

The importance of distributive factors in the way environmental effects are manifested has been the focus of considerable attention (Sandbach, 1980; Sandbrook, 1982), but it requires a much more systematic analysis than Marxists have hitherto provided. Enzensberger, for example, argues *both* that the environmental crisis is a threat to the earning power of the bourgeoise (1974, 11) *and* that 'the eco-industrial complex' is able to profit from pollution at the expense of the community as a whole (ibid., 12). These observations, which are contradictory, require careful dissembling. In the late 1980s the political assumption is that the earning power of the capital-owning classes is being put at risk by 'expensive' controls to protect the environment, rather than by degraded environments. Similarly, Enzensberger's observation that bourgeois social movements only became interested in the environment when the middle classes were adversely affected conceals as much as it reveals. One might equally argue that Marxists were not interested in the environment until it became an issue in 'bourgeois' political debate. The environmental problems which were the product of class oppression only assumed political importance for many Marxists because the movements which sought to improve environmental conditions since 1945 evolved largely independently of the labour movement. At the same time, radical environmental groups, such as the Green parties in West Germany and The Netherlands, have made the distributive consequences of economic growth for the environment a central part of their analysis and their political manifesto.

The full impact of Marxist thinking on the relationship between society and nature will inevitably depend on the degree to which Marxism fully incorporates the implications of unsustainable development. This implies a rethinking of political economy, which takes seriously both feminist and Green positions (Barrat-Brown, 1985). The concept of 'mediation', which has been employed within Marxist theory to examine the role of culture and political process, is one way in which the political economy tradition could be extended to include nature and the environment. In attempting to unmask the ideology of the environmental movement, Left critics have signally failed to elaborate on their own ideological position. Marxist theory has tended to lay claim to an explanation of both 'base' and 'superstructure' in the environmental debate, but without integrating them sufficiently.

Capitalism necessarily concerns the transformation of nature and the development of value around market conditions of production and exchange, but this has become divorced from what Burgess (1978) identifies as the neo-idealist concern with human consciousness. The Marxist concept of nature should aspire to make the connections 'between attitudes towards nature and the day-to-day practice of man's [*sic*] economic activity', as Pepper (1984, 159) argues, but this aspiration needs to be grounded in a theoretical project. This theoretical project, in turn, can only succeed if Marxism is prepared to question some of the assumptions of nineteenth-century theory, while making full use of its method. Enzensberger

(1974) has criticised the ecological movement for its lack of ideological sophistication, declaring that it is ill equipped to make the transfer from the natural world to its social mediation. Radical ecology, he argued, has no theory of society and no sense of the historical process.

However, the central contradiction of advanced capitalism, and its relations with the developing world, still eludes Marxism. This is that the labour process, the means by which the social mediation of nature is achieved, succeeds in transforming the environment in ways that ultimately make it less productive. At the same time, the 'externality' effects that have attracted the attention of economists in Western societies are central to the 'survival algorithm' of many households in the South. Technology is not simply a means to harness nature in industrial society. It is also frequently the instrument through which alienation is effected in rural areas of the South: people are separated from their land; women from their control over household resources; cultural practices that evolved to sustain both production and the environment are lost. The assertion that human interests in the environment need not be ultimately prejudicial to it cannot wait on the removal of all class oppression, any more than women's rights can wait on the overthrow of all forms of patriarchy. Whatever the eventual outcome, the problem is that as we develop new ways of exploiting nature, we lose our capacity to maintain limits on our own Promethean urges. We have substituted 'societies of appropriation', which are unsustainable, for 'societies of production', which depended for their very existence on an accommodation to environmental values (Sohn-Rethel, 1986). We should not seek to achieve understanding of the environment in one paradigm or even one epistemology.

References

Barrat-Brown, M., 1985, *Models in Political Economy*, Penguin, London.

Brandt Commission, 1980, *North–South: A Programme for Survival*, Pan, London.

Brown, L., 1984, *State of the World: 1984*, W.W. Norton and Co., New York.

Burgess, R., 1978, 'The Concept of Nature in Geography and Marxism', *Antipode*, 10 (2).

Cotgrove, S., 1982, *Catastrophe or Cornucopia: The Environment, Politics and the Future*, Wiley, Chichester.

Devall, B.B., 1979, 'The Deep Ecology Movement', *Natural Resources Journal*, **20**, University of New Mexico.

Engels, F., 1970a, 'Introduction to the Dialectics of Nature', in Marx, K. and Engels, F., *Selected Works* (one vol.) Lawrence and Wishart, London.

Engels, F., 1970b, 'The Part Played by Labour in the Transition from Ape to Man', in Marx and Engels, *Selected Works*.

Enzensberger, H., 1974, 'A Critique of Political Ecology', *New Left Review*, **84**.

Global 2000, 1982, *A Report to the President*, Penguin, London.

Harris, A., 1983, 'Radical Economics and Natural Resources', *International Journal of Environmental Studies*, **21**.

Hirsch, F., 1976, *The Social Limits to Growth*, Routledge and Kegan Paul, London.

Hodge, I., 1986, 'Approaches to the Value of the Rural Environment', paper given to the Annual Conference of the Rural Economy and Society Group of the British Sociological Association, University of Loughborough, 16–18 December.

Inglehart, R., 1981, 'Post-materialism in an Environment of Insecurity', *American Political Science Review*, **75**.

IUCN, 1980, *World Conservation Strategy*, IUCN, Gland, Switzerland.

Khozin, G., 1979, *The Biosphere and Politics*, Progress Publishers, Moscow.

Kuhn, T.S., 1970, *The Structure of Scientific Revolutions*, University of Chicago Press, Chicago.

Lashof, D., 1986, 'The Ecology of Socialism', Energy and Resources Group, University of California, Berkeley (ms).

Lenin, V., 1972, *Imperialism, the Highest Stage of Capitalism*, Progress Publishers, Moscow.

Lowe, P. and Rudig, W., 1986, 'Political Ecology and the Social Sciences: the State of the Art', *Political Studies* (in press).

Luxemburg, R., 1951, *The Accumulation of Capital*, RKP, London.

Marx, K., 1974, *Capital*, vol. III, Progress Publishers, Moscow.

Maslow, A.H., 1954, *Motivation and Personality*, Harper and Row, New York.

Meadows, D. *et al.*, 1972, *The Limits to Growth*, Pan Books, London.

Naess, A., 1973, 'The Shallow and the Deep, Long-Range Ecology Movement', *Inquiry*, **16**.

Naess, A., 1983, 'Philosophical Aspects of the Deep Ecological Movement', Oslo (ms).

Norgaard, R., 1984, 'Coevolutionary Development Potatentional', *Land Economics*, **60**.

Norgaard, R., 1985a, 'Environmental Economics: An Evolutionary Critique and a Plea for Pluralism', *Journal of Environmental Economics and Management*, **12**, No. 4.

Norgaard, R., 1985b, 'The Scarcity of Resource Economics', paper presented at the Annual Meeting of the American Economics Association, New York.

Ojeda, O. and Sanchez, V., 1985, 'La Cuestión Ambiental y la Articulación Sociedad Naturaleza', in *Estudios Sociologica*, **III**, No. 7, El Colegio de Mexico, Mexico.

O'Riordan, T., 1985, 'Future Directions in Environmental Policy', *Environment and Planning*, 9 (3).

Pearce, D., 1985, Inaugural Lecture, University College, London.

Pepper, D., 1984, *The Roots of Modern Environmentalism*, Croom Helm, London.

Rifkin, J., 1985, *Declaration of a Heretic*, RKP, London.

Russell, P., 1982, *The Awakening Earth: Our Next Evolutionary Leap*, RKP, London.

Sandbach, F., 1980, *Environment, Ideology and Policy*, Basil Blackwell, Oxford.

Sandbrook, R., 1982, Chapter 5 in *The Conservation and Development Programme for the UK: A Response to the World Conservation Strategy*, Kogan Page, London.

Schmidt, A., 1971, *The Concept of Nature in Marx*, New Left Books, London.

Smith, N., 1984, *Uneven Development*, Basil Blackwell, Oxford.

Sohn-Rethel, A., 1986, 'Science as Alienated Consciousness', in Levidow, L. (ed.), *Radical Science Essays*, Free Association Books, London.

Sunkel, O. and Gligo, N., 1980, *Estilos de Desarrollo, Energia y Medio Ambiente*, Estudios e Informes de CEPAL, United Nations, Santiago, Chile.

Sylvan, R., 1985, 'Deep Ecology', *Radical Philosophy*, Summer/Autumn, **40** and **41**.

Tobias, M. (ed.), 1984, *Deep Ecology*, Avant Books, San Diego, Calif.

Trainer, F., 1985, *Abandon Affluence*, Zed Books, London.

Chapter 4

Resource Conservation, Sustainability and Technical Change

D. Deadman and R. Kerry Turner*

In this chapter sustainable growth on a national scale is interpreted exclusively in terms of the need for, and content of, a broad-based policy initiative which has resource conservation as one of several goals. The ultimate aim of the policy would be the formulation and operation of a 'materials policy'. Such a policy would explicitly consider in one management framework all residuals, environmental media and feedback mechanisms between and among both residuals and media. The three basic elements of such a policy would be resource conservation and recovery programmes (materials substitution, recycling and/or energy recovery); residuals management (pollution control targets, instruments and institutions); and waste reduction policies (including process changes, design and product durability measures). Only elements (often not fully coordinated) of such a materials policy are currently in place in the industrialised economics.

The sustainability concept has both national and international dimensions. International economic interdependence is increasingly the norm, with the majority of industrialised economies dependent to a significant degree on continued supplies of industrial minerals and metals originating from developing economies. Concurrent with this trend has been a rise in political and economic instability in many of the important resource supplier developing countries. The international economic system has been rocked by a series of destabilising events since 1973—in particular, the OPEC actions and consequent debt burdens for Latin American and African countries. Some analysts also claim that the potential for instability has increased as the Soviet Union has become more involved in overseas minerals supplies and markets for politicostrategic reasons. Moreover, despite the apparent lack of any concerted and successful attempt to imitate the OPEC action, potential future cartelisation is still, it is argued, a possible future threat.

* We are indebted to David Jacobson and Tony Challis for their comments and criticisms of earlier drafts. All remaining errors are our responsibility.

From the industrial economy viewpoint, an important element in any sustainable growth policy would be the strategic requirement for continued access to 'critical' raw material supplies. Raw materials management must be linked to balance of payments management and to policies designed to minimise economic and strategic security risks. Resource contingency planning, then, is a required element in any sustainable growth strategy.

In succeeding sections the conventional policy framework for the management of 'important' (strategic) materials will be critically examined, and a more systematic approach to resource contingency planning suggested. It will be argued that the conventional strategic materials stockpile is an inadequate means of attempting to secure the supply of critical materials for manufacturing industry. A much broader based strategy is required for effective contingency planning, encompassing:

(a) the setting-up of a highly selective physical materials stockpile, which would have to be actively managed and continually updated;
(b) the development and maintenance of an adequate range of processing facilities;
(c) the development and updating of an information stockpile;
(d) the promotion of an ongoing scientific and technological programme aimed at increasing substitution possibilities, recycling and other materials conserving actions.

The required institutional framework for resource contingency planning, one that is broadly based and at the same time fully integrated, is lacking in Europe. The European Economic Community does not have any collective policy on contingency planning of raw materials, but this must be remedied in the near future. Elements of the French, Swiss, Swedish and Japanese strategies for strategic materials could be encompassed within the model framework provided by the National Critical Materials Council in the United States and operated on an EEC-wide basis.

A policy framework for strategic materials

The conventional approach to strategic sensitivity

At various times of stress and heightened international tension during this century, the governments of the industrialised economies have become concerned about potential shortages of 'important' materials. Since the rise of modern environmentalism in the 1960s, official fears about short-run (largely institutionally induced) scarcity have been supplemented by concern over possible long-run physical depletion and environmental damage constraints on future materials exploitation. In the light of these considerations, both governments and minerals markets have over time come to recognise the existence of a category of 'important' materials and have labelled them strategic. What the inventory of strategic materials ought to contain and over what time period are, however, controversial questions. A debate has continued intermittently since the 1920s over what exactly is meant by the term 'strategic material'. Both the concept and the issue are characterised by ambiguity (Hagland, 1984).

Two basic positions emerged from the conventional debate over the strategic sensitivity of materials:

1. a broad-based view, which held that the defining characteristics of a strategic material were essential to national defence and imported to some significant degree;
2. a restrictionist view, critical of the wide coverage of the former position and its consequent high costs (e.g. thus the US Strategic Stockpile's ninety-eight items were valued in 1981 at $US12.6 billion).

According to the restrictionists a strategic material is defined as: '. . . one for which the quantity required for essential civilian and military uses exceeds the reasonably secure domestic and foreign supplies, and for which acceptable substitutes are not available within a reasonable period of time' (OTA, 1983). This definition encompasses two central strategic sensitivity criteria for any given material, namely supply vulnerability and the critical/essential nature of its use.

The vulnerability criterion: Supply vulnerability supplants import dependence and, in principle, can be analysed in both a short-run and long-run context. In the former context, it is argued that excessive import dependency could increase an economy's susceptibility to institutionally induced shortages (transitional Malthusian scarcity). Cartel action, war, cyclical surges in demand, strikes, accidents and natural disasters can all produce shortages or sharp price escalations which, although transitional (rarely lasting more than one to five years), may still impose significant economic dislocation costs.

The potential problems of Soviet and African mineral supplies are those most often cited in this context. The consensus seems to be that while the Soviet Union probably has no 'grand design' in terms of a systematic strategy to deny the West access to strategic minerals, or to gain assured access itself, it may still collaborate with mineral exporters on an opportunistic and *ad-hoc* basis. More problematic is the vulnerability of mineral supplies from Southern African countries. On a positive note, all of these states are crucially dependent on mineral export revenue and so sustained embargoes are unlikely. Nevertheless, a prolonged period of turmoil (a

Table 4.1 World demand, production, reserves and resource depletion for selected strategic materials

Material	(1) World mine production (tonnes) metal content average 1979–81	(2) World demand 1978 (tonnes)	(3) Demand growth per annum 1978–2000 (%)	(4) World demand in year 2100 (tonnes)	(5) Four major non-OECD producer approx. share of world production (%)	(6) Change in resources 1950–81 (%)	(7) Estimated current resources (tonnes)	(8) Static reserve life based on average mined production 1979–81 and proven reserves	(9) Depletion of resources by year 2100 (%) based on (2), (3), (4) and (7)	(10) Depletion of current plus 'extended' resources by 2100 (%)
Chromium	3.1m	3.2×10^6	3.3	1.5×10^7	South Africa USSR 79 Albania Zimbabwe	> 300	1.0×10^{10}	346 years	12	*
Cobalt	31,000	2.3×10^4	2.8	9.7×10^4	Zaire Zambia USSR 68 New Caledonia	> 300	5.4×10^6	105 years	150	36
Manganese	26.4m	8.7×10^6	2.7 to 3.3	4.0×10^7	USSR South Africa 76 Brazil Gabon	> 200	2.8×10^9	131 years	120	18
Molybdenum	107.667	1.0×10^5	4.5	6.3×10^5	Chile USSR 26 China Peru	> 200	2.1×10^7	93	249	5
Nickel	719,000	7.1×10^5	4.0	3.8×10^6	USSR New Caledonia 42 Indonesia Cuba	> 200	2.1×10^8	76	152	35
Niobium	15,000	1.1×10^4	5.9	8.6×10^4	Brazil USSR Nigeria 88	–	1.7×10^7	329	41	–
Titanium	81,000	1.7×10^6	3.8	8.6×10^6	USSR 49 (but remainder in OECD countries)	–	7.1×10^8	88	102	38
Tungsten	50,000	4.0×10^4	3.4	1.9×10^5	China USSR 56 S. Korea Bolivia	10–39	6.8×10^6	42	236	11
Vanadium	34,367	3.2×10^4	3.6	1.6×10^5	S. Africa USSR 78 China Chile	–	5.6×10^7	444	23	–

Table 4.1—cont.

	(1)	(2)	(3)	(4)	(5)	(6)	(7)	(8)	(9)	(10)
Antimony	60.867	6.7×10^4	2.2	2.5×10^5	S & SW Africa Bolivia USSR China	10-39 70	5.2×10^6	68	402	—
Bismuth	4.272	4.4×10^3	1.7	1.4×10^4	China Peru Mexico Brazil	— 48	1.9×10^5	30	656	—
Mercury	6,400	5.5×10^3	2.4	2.1×10^4	Algeria USSR China Czechoslovakia	10-39 53	5.8×10^5	24	305	—
Selenium	1,900 to 2,000	1.6×10^3	3.5	7.9×10^3	Zambia Mexico Peru Chile	— 9	4.1×10^5	30-40	161	6
Zinc[†]	6.1m	6.4×10^6	2.0	2.2×10^7	USSR Peru Mexico China	>200 30	3.3×10^8	26	581	37
Platinum group	211	1.9×10^2	2.1	6.9×10^2	USSR S. Africa Colombia China	>1000 94	1.0×10^5	180	58	—
Germanium	125 (refinery production)	69	4-6	3.7×10^2	USSR	20	$5.0\text{-}8.6 \times 10^3$	39	366	‡ small if coal and its combustion products are included

Notes: * Assumes no insurmountable energy, technological or environmental constraints; estimates taken from Goeller and Zucker (1984). † By-product elements cadmium, germanium, indium and thallium are found mainly exclusively to zinc ores. ‡ Germanium has been extracted commercially (1950–70) in the UK from flue dust produced in coal gas plants.

Sources: Ray (1984); Goeller and Zucker (1984); Metallgesellschaft (1982, 1983, 1984); Institute of Geological Sciences (1985).

tribal/regional conflict) in one or several countries could still badly disrupt international trade.

The degree of vulnerability will depend on factors such as:

(a) the degree of production concentration;
(b) the 'reliability' of the supplying country;
(c) the prospects for raising domestic production at reasonable economic (including environmental damage and energy) costs;
(d) the existence of alternative non-domestic supply sources;
(e) the 'thinness' of material markets;
(f) status of the material as a by-product or not;
(g) politico-economic conditions in the international economy.

This type of scarcity problem can be compounded by potential time lags which afflict resource exploitation cycles and lengthen the time interval between research and development innovation and the widespread diffusion of resource conserving technology.

The conventional view of short-run vulnerability and the need for some sort of an 'insurance policy' would be supported by those analysts that view the current, globally inequitable distribution of resources as a potential security threat. The Brandt Reports, for example, have warned that economic inequalities within national economies and on a global North–South basis have the potential to spread social and political unrest.

On a long-run basis, a majority of analysts support the hypothesis that physical resource scarcity is unlikely to become a problem within the next hundred years or so, for most of the materials currently in use (Goeller and Zucker, 1984). Table 4.1 summarises depletion prospects for a selected range of important materials. It is assumed that the market mechanism will be able to cope with the slow onset of scarcity as certain high-quality mineral deposits are depleted and lower-quality deposits are exploited with increasing cost penalties. The gradual rise in prices will stimulate new technologies, substitution processes, materials recycling activities and generally encourage materials conservation.

The more alarmist Malthusian 'limits to growth' forecasts are based on 'static reserve index' calculations which in fact only provide a lower limit to resource stocks. A dynamic relationship exists between the known resource base of a given material and the reserves of the material. An increasing price profile for a given material results, over time, in more exploration effort, increased exploitation/processing technology innovation and cost reductions, and consequent increases in reserves. For example, direct leaching techniques such as *in-situ* solution mining and biotechnology, which bypass costly mineral benefication processes, are enabling the recovery of precious metals and copper from relatively low-grade ores (Harris, 1986).

On the other hand, the more optimistic 'cornucopian technocentrist' resource availability forecasts are underpinned by a set of assumptions which do require some qualification. It is assumed that an energy 'backstop' technology will be found and that technical progress over a broad front will continue indefinitely. Infinite substitution possibilities over time are taken as axiomatic in many studies, so a number of caveats are in order. Some geochemists have argued that for certain minerals the general assumption that grade decline is partly compensated for by deposit size increases is not correct. For some minerals it is argued that, at least down to fairly low-grade levels, grade and quantity decline simultaneously (Harris and Skinner, 1982). It is also the case that the continued exploitation of lower-grade resources will impose an increasing degree of environmental risk on society. Energy requirements will escalate sharply if possible mineralogical thresholds are breached and thermal pollution risks will consequently rise. Other forms of pollution, caused by increased waste disposal loading in the biosphere, will also increase. The costs of safeguarding exposed populations from potential environmental damage are likely to rise significantly in the future, as perceived 'acceptability' levels are pushed up because of political pressures. Health, safety and environmental protection regulations have all become increasingly stringent over time. Moreover, conventional research and development advances are also not best fitted to alleviating the impacts of scarcity on the production of environmental amenities.

The resource scarcity measurement debate—Barnett and Morse revisted: The cornucopian viewpoint has until recently been buttressed by the classical study of Barnett and Morse (1963) which indicated that, with the exception of forest products, the real unit costs of extractive output (agricultural and minerals) fell in the United States over the period 1870–1957. The general conclusion that real economic scarcity was not increasing over time was confirmed in analyses which included resource data to the end of the 1970s (Barnett, 1979, 1982). The escalation in some real resource prices during the 1970s was attributed to a combination of government intervention on environmental and safety grounds and changing market structures (notably the OPEC oil cartel) and not to real scarcity. Hall and Hall (1984) have emphasised that it is difficult to reach a consensus on what natural resource scarcity really is. The available resource price data are biased because of government intervention in markets and the failure of the market mechanism to internalise adequately pollution damage costs imposed on common property resources (e.g. clean air and water). They concluded that the Barnett (1979) argument, that rising prices in the 1970s did not represent indicators of real economic scarcity but were merely indicators of institutional pressures, is open to reinterpretation. The regulatory and governmental intervention pressures on prices can be seen as the mechanism by which real resource constraints (previously hidden scarcity, in terms of the assimilative capacities of the environmental media being put at risk) were being properly internalised. The authors also pointed out that materials recycling activities play an ill-defined role in the aggregate supply process.

Hall and Hall (1984) proposed a typology of physical scarcity based on four categories: Malthusian stock and flow scarcity (MSS and MFS), and Ricardian stock and flow scarcity (RSS and RFS). RFS applies to resources whose average costs depend upon the rate of extraction and which represent an infinitely available stock. RFS is a special case of RSS which applies to resources whose average costs depend upon the total extracted to date in addition to the rate of extraction. RSS is in turn a special case of MFS which involves a binding constraint on the total available stock of a resource (which if it is of uniform quality is encompassed by MSS) and has average resource extraction costs dependent upon the rate of extraction. The important point about this typology is that it serves to emphasise the fact that the appropriate measure (index of unit costs, *in-situ* resource prices or relative prices of output) of resource scarcity depends upon the nature of scarcity. The unit cost index favoured by Barnett and Morse is an insufficient scarcity measure for non-renewable resources characterised by RSS, MFS or MSS. Nevertheless, it also has to be recognised that all the available indexes suffer from deficiencies of one type or another. Hall and Hall (1984) test the hypothesis of increasing general scarcity in the 1970s by reference to two indexes, relative prices and unit costs. Their results confirm the hypothesis that scarcity increased in the extractive sector in the 1970s for non-renewable energy resources and for some renewable resources. Their work, although not conclusive, should at least lead to a serious reconsideration of the conventional wisdom that real resource scarcity is static or diminishing.

The criticality criterion: The critical nature of a material is interpreted in terms of its essentiality to the military and industrial well-being of a country. The degree of criticality will depend on factors such as:

(a) the opportunities for substitution, effective materials utilisation and/or recycling;
(b) the degree of domestic economic damage likely from supply failure/ price escalation.

For any given raw material input criticality will depend directly on the ability to substitute for that input in production, and to substitute in consumption from products in which the input is used intensively.

It has been argued that it seems reasonable to label a material 'possibly critical' as long as one 'important user' of the material input would face a significant increase in costs if the input price rose rapidly. Constraints on substitution also increase the degree of criticality. But defining just what is and what is not in the 'national interest', and which are the 'important' users of any given material input is inherently subjective. Forecasting substitution possibilities is also a complex task.

Criticality and economic efficiency: In principle, the degree of criticality can be assessed in terms of the changes in economic welfare (efficiency) that would be induced by a supply disruption. An input–output model can be used to estimate the change in Gross National Product that is stimulated when imports of a given material are disrupted over a short time period. Over a longer period, changes in inventories and supply and demand responses need in principle to be taken into account via a market model approach. Quantification of welfare changes (producers and consumer surplus) initially requires the determination of the supply effect on products produced with the input material subject to supply difficulties. It should then be possible to quantify, with knowledge of consumer demand, the material's new equilibrium price and quantity.

Conventional economic theory assumes that supply disruptions induce efficient firms (i.e. those operating with cost minimising factor input combinations) into 'forced' input substitutions, which increase costs of production. The degree of production essentiality possessed by any material input will, therefore, depend both on the existence of inter-material or intra-factor substitution possibilities (i.e. the degree and depth of substitution respectively) and on consequent production cost increases. Substitutions in terms of recycled materials and product substitution possibilities are relevant in this context. If substitution becomes a physically binding constraint, the monetary value of potential output losses will also be important.

Summary of the conventional approach to the strategic sensitivity of materials

Figure 4.1 summarises the conventional approach to strategic sensitivity. Input and product substitution information would be linked to an analysis of recycling possibilities and to material supply characteristics. The monetary losses to an economy because of restricted consumption and adoption of more costly alternatives, and increased resource costs due to forced substitutions and loss of output would determine the economic magnitude of the strategic sensitivity effect. A comprehensive economic (general

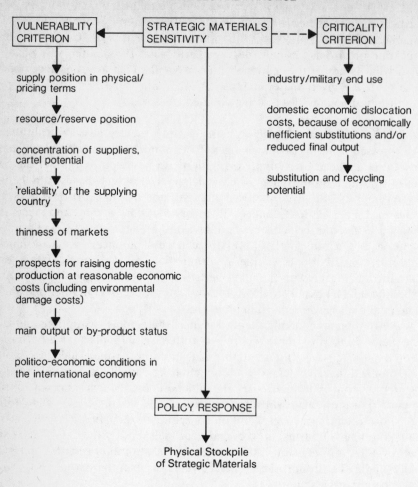

POLICY PRINCIPLES AND PRACTICE

Figure 4.1   Overview of the conventional approach to strategic materials policy

equilibrium) analysis of an economy's susceptibility to potential material supply disruption would need to focus initially on the primary, basic processing and fabricating sectors of the economy. After that, the secondary impacts of the disruption, right through to final industrial and consumption demand, would require quantification.

Hazilla and Kopp (1984a, 1984b) have investigated the demand and substitution possibilities for titanium, vanadium, cobalt, columbium and cadmium in the US primary metals sector. The results of their neo-classical model indicated that columbium and titanium are viable substitutes for cobalt in the production of primary metals. Titanium is also apparently a substitute for vanadium and cadmium, but complementary to columbium (= niobium in Europe). This result is, however, not very realistic. Model simulations suggested that disruption costs associated with enforced factor input substitution were much smaller than the costs of lost output. Substitution was a strong mitigating factor as long as supply disruptions were less than 35 per cent of current consumption levels. Supply shortfalls in excess of 35 per cent of current consumption either could not be fully alleviated physically or imposed prohibitively high costs. These simulation results, however, only represent the partial static equilibrium effects for a single consuming sector.

Despite the apparent lack of any concerted and successful attempt to imitate the OPEC action, potential future cartelisation cannot be completely ruled out. A recent study of selected 'strategic metals' found some grounds for arguing that the pre-conditions for cartel action were present (Radetzki, 1984). According to Radetzki, metals whose primary use is in the production of special steel and steel alloys qualify as strategic metals. Six metals, chromium, cobalt, manganese, niobium, tungsten and vanadium, were analysed because their closest substitutes are also found within the group. This is reflected in very low price elasticities of world demand for the metals, ranging from −0.1 to −0.5. They were also chosen because since 1970 non-OECD production has been increasing for all six metals. Four non-OECD producers in aggregate now control more than 40 per cent of world production. The price elasticities of supplies from outside the potential cartel are also relatively low, on average about 0.7. Nevertheless, if prices rose very substantially, sea-bed nodule deposits could be exploited for their cobalt and manganese. In the short term, however, supply elasticity would be between 0.1 and 0.2, if the international economy was expanding. Manganese and chromium are judged by Radetzki to be most strategically sensitive and the other four metals less so because of greater relative substitution possibilities and price elastic scrap recovery possibilities. The markedly different political/cultural/economic characteristics of the four potential cartel partner countries also remain formidable obstacles to the required level of policy coordination.

Table 4.2 lists some of the main candidate strategic materials as determined by the conventional approach to strategic sensitivity. The traditional policy response in a number of Western economies (the United States, France, Japan and the United Kingdom) has been the establishment of a physical strategic materials stockpile. In the United Kingdom,

Table 4.2   Officially designated strategic (i.e. critical/vulnerable) materials

USA (official)		UK (official)		Private analyst[1]		Private analyst[2]
First tier[3]	Second tier	First tier	second tier	First tier	Second tier	First tier
chromium	diamonds	chromium	antimony	beryllium	germanium	chromium
manganese	beryllium	manganese	cobalt	chromium	cobalt	manganese
cobalt	vanadium	phosphate	molybdenum	columbium	manganese	cobalt
PGMs	graphite	rock	nickel		PGMs	copper
	rutile	PGMs	niobium		vanadium	PGMs
	bauxite		tantalum			gold
	tin		titanium			
	tantalum		vanadium			

Notes: (1) = Weston (1984); (2) = Hargreaves and Fromson (1983); (3) = first and second tier differentiated by the degree of substitution thought feasible.
Sources: US OTA (1983); House of Lords Select Committee (1982) R. Weston (1984).

a stockpile was set up in 1982, although since 1985 official policy has been emphasising the need to dispose of stocks.

A critique of the conventional approach

At first sight, the vulnerability and criticality criteria appear simple and relatively straightforward to apply. However, a considerable amount of ambiguity is present, because a multitude of factors are relevant to the assessment of a given material's strategic sensitivity on this basis. More-over, many of the factors are interdependent and are often difficult to evaluate quantitatively. To make matters worse, the terms 'strategic material', 'criticality' and 'vulnerability' have been adopted as emotionally charged catch-phrases by analysts serving commodity dealers and financial institutions. The conventional view of strategic sensitivity has over-emphasised the availability and supply of raw materials, to the neglect of issues relating to materials technologies.

Aggregate Indexes of Strategic Sensitivity

An important weakness in the conventional treatment of strategic mate-rials has been that analysts have given the impression to policy-makers that fully quantified indexes of strategic sensitivity, based on measures of the magnitude and extent of vulnerability and criticality, can be constructed (Hargreaves and Fromson, 1983; Bridgewater and Nott, 1981). The utility of such aggregate indexes is open to severe doubt. The use of index numbers in such a fashion probably obscures more than it illuminates.

Weaknesses in the vulnerability criterion

The IGS (now the British Geological Survey) has suggested that, in the context of supply vulnerability, it is possible to quantify the degree of concentration of sources of supply (House of Lords Select Committee on Strategic Materials, 1982). The proposed Index of Concentration is expressed in terms of the number of supplying countries and the proportion of the total supplies contributed by each.

While this Index of Concentration is useful in its own right it is only a partial measure of vulnerability. Supply vulnerability will be affected by, for example, the number of mines and production enterprises (together with supporting infrastructure) in supplying countries, and whether social or private ownership patterns prevail. The reliability of countries as suppliers of materials is also important but meaningful quantification of this factor is almost impossible. It requires the incorporation of questions of political stability, national ideology and economic nationalism (for some attempts at quantification, see Hargreaves and Fromson, 1983; Stalker *et al.*, 1984). As the IGS reminded the House of Lords Select Committee on Strategic Materials in 1982, the industrialised Western democracies are not necessarily more reliable as suppliers than other countries: witness the strike by Canadian nickel miners in 1969, which precipitated the most serious metal crisis in the United Kingdom since the Second World War. Further, while a country like Australia is politically stable, the length of the supply route could be cause for concern.

As already noted, sources of vulnerability tend to be interdependent. Materials produced in small quantities, for example, the platinum-group metals, will be most susceptible to large fluctuations in price. Additionally, materials which have a market of only a few tonnes or less are also more vulnerable to supply interruption because they are likely to be produced by a small number of enterprises and also because production capacity can be outstripped by a growth in demand at the mere kilogram level. However, as the strength of linkage between the various vulnerability factors will differ from one specific usage of a material to another, they justify being considered separately. Yet the fact that these factors are not independent of each other complicates the analysis and further frustrates attempts to construct a satisfactory aggregate index of vulnerability.

Weaknesses in the criticality criterion

To depict accurately the full economic cost of a supply disruption, a complete sectoral equilibrium model of the economy would be required. Data constraints and modelling technique limitations currently preclude this possibility. Conceptually, the conventional economic view of material substitution, a vital factor in the degree of criticality, has also tended to be rather limited. It reflects the profession's concern with the role of prices in influencing materials demand and has neglected both functional substitution and design change possibilities. The substitution process will be analysed in more detail in a later section.

The role of materials technologies

The conventional approach to strategic sensitivity has failed to give enough emphasis to materials technologies. The availability of specialist processing facilities and supporting infrastructure have become vital factors in the analysis of materials vulnerability and criticality (Jacobson and Evans, 1984). Thus, for example, the ores of many of the essential materials used in the electrical and electronics industry, such as silicon and germanium, are commonplace and practically worthless as commodities. Extensive processing is required to make them suitable for the manufacture of devices and components. It is perhaps not surprising, therefore, to learn that in the strategic materials debate in the United States there has been a shift from concern over the dependence on imported raw materials to concern over the dependence on competitive materials technology.

Many of the features observed when analysing the usage of materials in the electrical and electronics industry would seem to carry over into other sectors of consumption. A phenomenon that has attracted much attention is the apparent persistent decline in the overall materials intensity of the Gross Domestic Product in industrialised economies (Etheridge, 1981; Evans and Szekely, 1985). Evidence indicating the progressive decline in the consumption of material resources, and of metals in particular, has been reported in both trend projection and input–output studies. The quality of this evidence has been criticised by Auty (1985). He concluded that the factors responsible for changes in materials intensity remain poorly understood.

Both trend projection and input–output models have had to be augmented by a measure of 'expert judgement' in their final forecast stage. The US Bureau of Mines (1986) has conducted a regression analysis in which consumption of selected metals per unit of Gross National Product was regressed on time. The dependent variable (intensity of use) was a ratio of the quantity of metal consumed in a specific industry to the constant dollar output of that industry between 1972 and 1982; and forecasted out to 1993. These forecasts were finally 'adjusted' by a panel of experts. Only 19 per cent of all the metals' intensity of use trends analysed showed increasing use of metal per unit of output.

In the absence of a detailed explanation, the declining intensity-of-use-trend hypothesis has been based on two separate general assumptions:

(a) that the rise in per-capita income levels shifts demand from manu-facturing to service industries, which have a lower materials intensity;
(b) the changes in the intensity of use of materials depend primarily on time and on the pace and type of technological innovation.

For some metals the net impact of technological innovation, both on processing activities and end-product manufacture, seems to be metal conserving. There has been a general trend towards the manufacture of lighter, thinner and stronger metal-based products. Well-known examples are the development of tinplate with thinner coatings of tin, of thinner-walled copper pipes for plumbing applications, of optical glassfibres to replace copper cables and wiring in telecommunications, and of steels with improved strength-to-weight ratios.

Metals-intensive basic manufacturing sectors have also contracted while 'high-technology' sectors, requiring sophisticated processing and yielding an enhanced value-added content, have expanded. This will lead to a decline in overall metals consumption, unless the rate of growth in the 'high-technology' sectors has been sufficiently great to outweigh the fall in intensity of use (this has been the case, for example, in the use of lead in storage batteries). Manufacturers are being presented with a growing choice of materials—some would say a 'hyper-choice' (CPE, 1985)—with each material having properties that are tailored to meet increasingly precise application requirements. In consequence, mineral and energy resources are diminishing in relative importance, while at the same time the enabling technologies are becoming an ever more critical factor in determining strategic sensitivity. An extreme case is provided by the microelectronics industry based on device-grade silicon and gallium arsenide. In 1984, total world market for gallium arsenide wafers, based on less than 20 tonnes of gallium metal, was worth £200 million. This compares with a value of £10,000 million for the 1.8 million tonnes output of stainless steel (Jacobson and Evans, 1984). It is predicted that, with an unusually high annual compound growth rate of 20 per cent, the value of electronic device manufacture alone will soon equal and then exceed that of the entire steel industry (Jones *et al.*, 1986).

Costs and benefits of a long-term physical stockpile

On economic efficiency grounds it is necessary to demonstrate that intervention in the market mechanism (via a stockpile) is likely to produce improvements in economic welfare (net of transactions costs) greater than those that would have occurred under the free market.

Apart from the speculative motive from stockholding, private firms can normally be expected to hold a certain level of stocks because of transactions and precautionary motives. Stocks are required to facilitate the normal business operations and also act as a buffer against unanticipated market fluctuations. In principle, stocks would be accumulated up to the point when the marginal revenue from holding stock just equals the marginal holding costs. Under materials supply crisis conditions, the theoretically most efficient level of stocks would be that which, when released and allocated, resulted in the largest reduction of expected crisis costs (consumer and producer costs) net of stockpiling costs. Efficient private stockpiling would reach an equilibrium level determined by the interaction between the expected material price (falling as stocks are increased, *ceteris paribus*) and the material acquisition price plus marginal storage costs. But the private stockpiling level would diverge from the economically efficient level of stocks needed to satisfy the materials supply crisis if market imperfections were present. These imperfections would include: imperfect information, risk aversion, tariff/trade barriers, and expectations by firms that the government would seek to limit the private gains from stock appreciation in a supply crisis situation. There may well therefore be an economic case for public stockpiling to boost stockholding (Labys, 1980).

Nevertheless, if public stockpiling is undertaken it will then affect private stockpiling behaviour. Private inventories are likely to be reduced because the expected future material price is likely to be less than it would have been in the absence of a government stockpile. Once in place, the potential government purchases and sales of stocks could adversely influence the subsequent pricing and supply of strategic materials. Lack of information on stock release rules would add to the uncertainty of the reaction of private firms to government decisions (Labys, 1986). The end result could well be increased materials price volatility and consequent disruption of production and consumption plans.

More generally, some candidate strategic materials (e.g. germanium, PGMs and columbium) are only produced as by-products of other mining or processing activities. By-product materials have relatively low price elasticities of supply and are sold on narrow markets. The stockpiling of such materials could serve only to make markets even narrower and therefore more prone to speculation. There is also the probability that over time stockpiled materials become technically obsolescent. For example,

US cobalt stocks bought in the 1950s (at 99.5 per cent purity) are today of inadequate quality for many superalloy applications.

The forms in which materials are stockpiled also need to be reconsidered. There is a growing tendency for supplying countries to integrate vertically mining and extraction with secondary processing. Thus, in the case of chromium, South African and Finnish producers are currently extending their operations downstream from ore recovery and ferro-chrome production to manufacturing stainless steel semi-finished products (Rogers, 1985). At the same time, ferrochrome producers in the EEC, Japan and the United States have severely cut back production in recent years due to fierce competition from new smelters in countries with indigenous supplies of chromium, in particular South Africa (Papp, 1983; Rogers, 1984). In consequence, the major alloy-steel consuming countries have become heavily dependent on South Africa not only for chromium but for ferrochrome and high-quality steels and, above all, for the processing facilities and technology involved. The loss of the value-added steel processing and manufacturing activities by the major Western industrial countries to South Africa would appear to be irreversible as that country is now building up a world lead in ferrochrome and steel smelting technology (Rogers, 1985). The stockpiling of upgraded forms of materials would increase acquisition costs but this would be counterbalanced by the stockpiled potential to ease likely bottlenecks in crisis situations.

The lack of warning, characteristic of short-run institutional material scarcity situations, and the time lags inherent in some substitution processes are two further factors which would support the case in favour of a stockpiling policy. Overall, if public stockpiling is undertaken, its performance will be difficult to evaluate in strict economic efficiency terms. In any case, subjective judgements will be required since it is likely that stockpiling policy will be determined on the basis of a range of criteria, distributional, political and economic.

Formulation of a more systematic approach to resource contingency planning

A broad-based mitigation strategy

The conventional approach to the issue of strategic materials supply problems has placed too much emphasis on the availability and supply of mineral ores and not enough on the role played by processing technologies and their associated industrial infrastructure. Further, the traditional policy response strategy in this context has been overly dependent on a single instrument, the long-term physical stockpile. Any new strategy

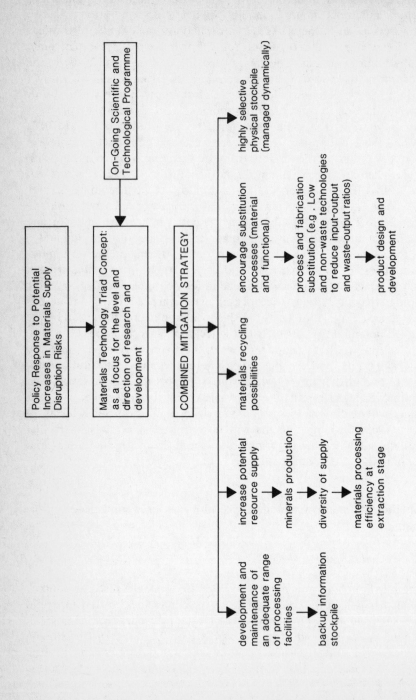

Figure 4.2   Resource contingency planning approach

aimed at reducing the vulnerability of the civil and defence industries in the United Kingdom to problems associated with their materials supplies necessarily must be multi-pronged (Watchman, 1984).

Figure 4.2 summarises the basic elements in a suggested broad-based mitigation strategy which encompasses the so-called 'Materials Technology Triad' (US OTA, 1983). The strategy aims both to increase potential supplies of resources and, through various conservation measures (including secondary materials recycling), effectively to reduce demand for primary materials.

Stockpiling option

Stockpiling could have a role in mitigating the effects of short-term supply shortages. However, to be effective, a stockpile would have to be operated in a dynamic manner, following changes in patterns of usage within the country, including methods of production. There is otherwise the danger, as experienced in the United States, that large quantities of material will be accumulated which, in the course of time, become technically obsolete. A prime example is provided by the stocks of cobalt in the US strategic stockpile which were acquired in the early 1950s. Furthermore, material held in a stockpile must be immediately usable by domestic manufacturing industry. It would, for example, be pointless holding chromite for the purpose of producing stainless steel if facilities were lacking in the country to convert the chromite to ferrochrome. On the other hand, changes in methods of steel production could reduce the utility of a ferrochrome stockpile. A stockpiling policy therefore calls for highly discriminating judgements based on detailed specialised knowledge of the needs of user industries: the possibility of a scheme jointly administered by government and industry is worth considering in the circumstances.

Substitution processes

Material or functional substitution would be the appropriate responses to sustained supply interruptions. It is an important element in any strategy designed to hold the long-run problem of physical resource depletion at bay. Stockpiling augmented by substitution could mitigate short-term supply interruption problems (OTA, 1983). Material substitution may result from the introduction of new technology, from shifts in the composition or quality of final goods, and from changes in the mix of factor inputs used in producing these goods (Tilton, 1983; Schlabach, 1984). It would appear that inter-material competition has become more intense and substitution more prevalent, particularly since the early 1960s. The number of materials has increased and the properties of existing materials have been enhanced in order to penetrate new markets (Tilton, 1983).

The initiating causes and the process of substitution itself are under researched topics. Empirical evidence is limited, but studies examining the use of tin in various applications suggest that three factors—relative materials prices, technological change, and government regulations—are important. Economic models often assume that material prices are the primary driving force behind substitution. The conventional theory assumes that the price variable and material demand are linked together in a lagged and reversible relationship. The nature of the lagged demand response most often assumed is one relevant to situations in which existing technology and equipment permit the use of one material for another in the production process. The absence of a materials balance constraint means that substitution can respond immediately to changes in material prices above a certain threshold level. Further, if and when price falls again the substitution process is reversible.

Thus in Figure 4.3, a desired level of output, given by the isoquant Q_1, can be produced by a range of combinations of substitutable primary and

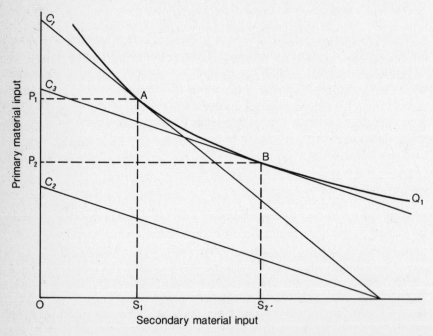

Figure 4.3   Conventional economic view of substitution process

secondary (scrap) material inputs. Giving the existing prices of the primary and scrap inputs, the slope of isocost line C_1 indicates the ratio of the scrap input price to the primary input price. Faced with such circumstances a firm would minimise its costs of production for an input level Q_1 by operating at point A, using S_1 scrap inputs and P_1 primary inputs. Now if the price of the primary input increased because of supply shortage, this would be reflected in a change in the slope of the isocost line. Let the isocost line rotate from C_1 to C_2. In order to continue producing output Q_1 at minimum cost, the firm substitutes, in the short run, increased inputs of scrap, S_1 to S_2, for primary inputs, P_1 to P_2.

It remains to be demonstrated, however, that such situations not subject to implementation lags are the norm rather than somewhat special cases. It seems feasible that the more numerous situations are likely to be those in which equipment must be modified and/or replaced before significant levels of substitution can take place. Substitution would be subject to a lengthy time lag and would not be easily reversible. Often new technology must be introduced before substitution can occur. The time lag in this case is often considerable and the process is irreversible. Some analysts claim to have identified several levels of substitution with consequent 'average' implementation lag times (see Table 4.3). Technology seems to be a dominant factor affecting material substitution and is stimulated only indirectly over the long run by material price changes. Government regulations, particularly increasingly stringent health and safety regulations and environmental protection measures, have also exerted a growing influence on material substitution. Direct stimulation of appropriate 'substituting' technological innovations will require government interventions and a degree of indicative planning. The case has been made

Table 4.3   Levels of substitution and implementation lags

Level	Lag time (yrs.)
Simple (non-interactive) material substitution; physical substitution	1–3
Development of new material or chemical process	3–4
Process/design substitutions (interactive)	4–5
Relatively complex systems changes	7
Complex systems changes	10
Telephone exchange technology	13
Discovery, innovation and extensive application	15

Source: Adapted from Schlabach (1984).

justifying government support for research and development programmes aimed at substituting for critical materials, in the same way that it might be expected to take a lead in instituting a stockpile (Watchman, 1984; Clark and Field, 1985).

Government action could be directed at the provision of better incentives to conduct research and development on new material-saving technologies. The so-called Low and Non-Waste Technology (LNWT) movement has attracted an increased level of industrial and governmental attention over the last decade or so (Pearce and Turner, 1984). Fundamentally, LNWTs are process changes aimed at minimising the input–output and the production waste–output ratios. A number of European governments, as well as the EEC Commission, have instituted policies designed to boost the take-up rate of LNWTs. French industry, for example, invested an estimated 500 million francs in state-subsidised LNWTs in 1984, with governmental agencies contributing some 200 million francs (Industry and Environment, 1986).

Materials recycling

Recycling is usually given a positive, if modest, role to play in mitigating materials shortages. Data on the generation and flow of scrap containing strategic materials are, however, lacking in all countries. There is a need for a regular survey of data on the generation and disposal of scrap containing, in particular, chromium, cobalt, manganese and PGMs.

According to Weston (1984), only antimony and germanium have a high recycling recovery rate. Beryllium, hafnium, mercury, PGMs and titanium (in some uses) do not have easily available substitutes. Only platinum has reasonable extra recycling potential (via catalytic converters in the main). Manganese, cobalt and molybdenum also face substitution constraints and have limited recycling potential. Much here will depend on manganese nodule extraction potential. A US Bureau of Mines analysis of the factors influencing the economic viability of a proposed system to mine and process nodules came to a pessimistic conclusion. The hydraulic dredging and ammonia leach processing system was designed to recover nickel, copper and cobalt from a high-grade zone in the north-east Equatorial Pacific Ocean. After-tax rates of return of 6–7 per cent only were predicted. These rates were well below those required to attract private risk capital. Nodule project economics are most sensitive to variations in metal prices. But there seems little prospect this century of metal prices rising in real terms to levels that would bring internal rates of return of around the required 30 per cent. Government assistance is clearly required in the form of tax concessions or other types of stimulants. There are also no known technological breakthroughs that might significantly improve the economics of nodule projects that would not at the same time improve the economics of exploitation of competitor land-based nickel laterites (Hillman and Gosling, 1985; Johnston and Otto, 1986).

In general, recycling rates in most industrialised economies are quite high (in terms of recovery rates) and research suggests that the least cost opportunities for recycling have by and large already been exploited. The published recycling effort rates reflect the activities of the private reclamation industry which are concentrated on industrial and commercial waste flows (home, prompt and commercial new scrap flows). Typically, these wastes will be generated in large concentrated quantities (high mass), are often of known composition, and will be relatively uncontaminated. These favourable physical factors go some way towards guaranteeing a financial profit for the would-be reclaimer. The physical characteristics of post-consumer scrap (low mass, relatively high contamination, dispersed location) make recycling financially less attractive and have inhibited effort rates. Table 4.4 summarises the recycling potential for a range of strategic materials.

The future position of the recycling industries needs to be reassessed in the light of the recent fall in world growth rates of production which, if sustained, could radically alter the relationship between primary and secondary industries (Radetzki and Van Duyne, 1985). The simplest approach to the forecasting of secondary material consumption has been to relate such consumption either directly to GDP, or indirectly by relating it to some measure of economic activity (e.g. scrap aluminium consumption related to the state of the castings market, which in turn is related to automobile output) (Deadman and Grace, 1979). Such forecasts have proved accurate in the short run, but will need adjustment over the long term because of the effects of technical change (Turner and Deadman, 1983). Whilst such models would predict a fall in the absolute amount of scrap used with an absolute decline in output, a decline in the growth rate of GDP may be consistent with either a rise or a fall in the share of output due to scrap recovery.

Steady-state models of the recycling rate (the share of recovered scrap in total demand for an input) have indicated that both the growth rate of the overall economic system and the average product lifetimes of given products (potentially recyclable) play an important role in determining the extent of recycling's contribution to resource conservation (Banks, 1976; Pearce, 1976; Radetzki and Svensson, 1979). Such models assume a product lifetime of (d) years; and a fixed proportion of scrap (α) recycled and supplied to a free market in which the price of scrap adjusts continuously to equate scrap demand and supply. It is further assumed that scrap and primary material inputs are perfect substitutes.

Table 4.4 Survey of substitution and recycling potential for selected strategic materials

Material	Substitution potential	Recycling potential
Chromium (active free market operates)	Essentially no short-term substitute for chromium in stainless steels and super alloys (only 10% substitution possible); ten-year R & D programme required before advanced materials could replace chromium alloys in certain aerospace and industrial applications; significant functional substitution possible in products such as furniture, automobile trim, kitchen equipment and sinks; aluminium, coated carbon steel and plastics substitutes here.	Scope for post-consumer, chromium-bearing scrap recycling, i.e. obsolete stainless steel, scrap and steel making and chemical processing plant waste; automobile scrap, including catalytic converters good sources of scrap; US recovery rate 10%; rates would rise with increasingly stringent ambient environmental standards regulation.
Manganese (largest producers operate an administered price system but free market for small producers and merchants)	Limited substitution only, via computer controlled feeding of manganese and sulphur additions to some carbon and alloy steels; ferromanganese processing capability important.	Recycling insignificant except as an intrinsic component of steel scrap.
Cobalt (producer prices, but growth in free market trade since Zaïre supply disruption in 1978)	No substitution of cobalt in cemented carbides in machinery and machine tools; and until recently only limited substitution by nickel in super alloys for jet engines. Advanced materials (ceramics, etc.) may in future displace cobalt in some aerospace and industrial applications. Consumption of cobalt in electrical uses is, on the other hand, falling sharply; ceramic magnets and iron–neodymium–boron magnets have been displacing cobalt-containing magnets.	US recovery rate about 10%. Superalloy scrap (< 50%) is recycled for re-use in superalloys, but only home/prompt scrap. Post-consumer scrap is contaminated with carbon and sulphur which limits its use, especially in critical (jet engine) applications. Processes are under laboratory test to recover individual elements from mixed alloy scrap and also to recover cobalt from spent catalysts in the petroleum industry. Paints/ driers involve dissipative uses of cobalt. Financial viability likely to remain a significant obstacle to extra recycling.
PGMs (platinum, iridum and palladium) (producer price, but also free and future market for platinum; former deals also in scrap platinum) One primary ore source otherwise by-product	No substitutes as part of automobile catalytic converters to control exhaust emissions. Some substitution possible via gold and silver for electrical components.	Recycling potential is significant; platinum in industrial catalysts is recycled; chemical catalysts are an increasing recycling activity. Electronic scrap (home/prompt) is recycled but little post-consumer scrap because of collection cost constraints. Automobile catalytic converters should prove to be an increasing source of scrap platinum, although total supply is limited by PGM losses during the converter's operational life and because scrap processing involves losses.

Table 4.4—*cont.*

Material	Substitution potential	Recycling potential
Beryllium (narrow market)	Few if any perfect substitutes in electronics, aerospace and nuclear industry applications.	Very limited, some home scrap recycling but no post-consumer scrap recycling.
Titanium (producer prices, but very small free and scrap market)	No effective substitutes in jet engine, air-frame, space and defence application.	Some uses totally dissipative, i.e. titanium dioxide; some recycling of scrap aerospace construction alloys but small scale; US recycling rate around 0.05%.
Vanadium (co-product) (producer prices for long term contracts; free market in boom conditions)	Molybdenum can substitute for vanadium in its major application, HSLA steels.	Small quantity of spent catalysts containing vanadium are reprocessed; some tool steel and other alloys are recycled for their vanadium content.
Nickel (producer pricing; but active free market and small future's market)	Substitution by plastics in coatings, containers, auto parts and plumbing.	US recovery rate is 23% both prompt and post-consumer industrial scrap; chemical and catalytic applications are dissipative; in steel sector nickel is reclaimed as an alloy component rather than separately.
Columbium (by/co-product) (flexible prices, direct sales)	In stainless steel and HSLA steel application, potential substitutes would have to be used in greater quantity; important microalloying element, no effective substitutes.	Recycling insignificant; present in very small quantities in many alloys, so recovery not feasible.
Germanium (narrow market; direct sales usually)	No substitutes in infra-red optics systems and as germanium dioxide in optical fibres for telecommunications.	Significant recycling (> 50%) of scrap electronic and infra-red sensing devices; new scrap source also because of inevitable production defaults.

Sources: NARI (1982); US Bureau of Mines (1986); Weston (1984).

If the total material demand is growing at a rate $g\%$ per annum, the total demand for material input at time t (M_t) may be written as:

$$M_t = M_t^p + M_t^s = M_0^{e^{gt}}$$

(where M_t^p = demand for primary material; M_t^s = supply of scrap; and M_0 = initial demand).

The supply of scrap M_t^s can be written as:

$$M_t^s = \alpha \, M_t - d = \alpha \, M_0^{e^{g(t-d)}}$$

Hence the steady-state share (β) of scrap in total input demand is:

$$\beta = M_t^s/M_t = \alpha\, e^{-gd}$$

So the higher the growth rate of the economy and the longer the average product lifetime, the smaller is recycling's relative contribution to resource conservation. Both the total stock of scrap potentially available at any given time and the increasing marginal costs of scrap supply (dominated by the collection cost function) serve to limit recycling activity in a growth economy. Alternatively, such models predict a rise in the recycling rate in response to a fall in the growth rate for total material input, provided the scrap recovery ratio and product durability remain unchanged in the event of such a fall.

The steady-state models cannot, however, be used to model the transition phase between two steady-state positions. The assumption of perfect substitutability between scrap and primary inputs also allows no role for changes in relative input prices which are observed in practice. The Radetzki–Van Duyne model (1985) attempts to take account of both these conditions. In general, scrap and primary inputs are imperfect substitutes because of the difficulty and expense of refining and processing scrap contaminated with other elements. The Radetzki–Van Duyne model introduces a free market for scrap in which the supply of scrap depends on both the lagged value of total material output and on scrap prices. The demand for scrap is derived from a standard cost minimisation approach constrained by a CES production function. Primary material price is assumed constant in real terms in the long run on the grounds that improvements in technology will have cost-saving impacts which will offset any increase in primary prices due to resource depletion. The price elasticity of demand for final output is assumed to be zero, avoiding any feedback problems running from changes in input prices and thus demand for final output.

On the basis of these assumptions, steady-state equations may be derived for both scrap price and for the recycling rate. The percentage change in scrap price, $\hat{P}_t$, from the initial steady-state position is given by

$$\hat{P}_t = d\,\Delta g\,/\,[(1 - \beta)(\sigma + \theta)]$$

where σ is the marginal rate of technical substitution between scrap and primary inputs in the production process; θ is the price elasticity of scrap supply (assumed constant); Δg is the absolute difference between two steady-state growth rates. A fall in the rate of growth can be seen to lead to a reduction in scrap prices. Such a fall has an impact on the recycling rate as the percentage change in this rate, between two steady-state positions, β, can be shown to be

$$\beta = -\,d\,\Delta g + \hat{P}\theta$$

Thus a fall in the growth rate increases the recycling rate through the first term, but this increase is moderated through the second term which will be negative. Intuitively, lower scrap prices reduce the incentive to supply and recycle scrap, and the lower the substitutability is between scrap and primary inputs, the greater this moderating effect will be. Similarly, the larger the price elasticity of scrap supply, the greater the moderating effect. Only if scrap supply is completely price-inelastic, or if scrap and primary inputs are perfect substitutes, does the model yield identical results (in terms of recycling rates) to the simpler model outline above. The equations for scrap prices and recycling rate changes given above are valid, strictly speaking, only for small changes in the growth rate. In order to predict the effect when large changes in growth rates are involved, the extra assumption of constancy in the price elasticity of demand for scrap is introduced. Simulation of the resulting equations can then be performed to see how stable the model is in its predictions for the relative price of scrap and for the recycling rate.

Tables 4.5 and 4.6 illustrate two possible cases. Table 4.5 could relate to a product with a short lifetime (paper and board) in which in the base year only about 27 per cent of output is obtained from economy material. Only a small increase in the steady-state recycling rate is predicted, irrespective of scrap supply elasticities or technical substitution possibilities. With such a short lifetime, scrap prices exhibit only minor falls and hence the moderating effect they give to what can anyway be a small rise in the recycling rate is negligible. Table 4.6 illustrates a quite different potential outcome. This could relate to a product with an initial scrap recovery rate M_t^s/M_{t-d} substantially higher than in the Table 4.6 case, and for which the product lifetime is relatively long. Parameter values similar to those in Table 4.6 for d and β_0 were used by Radetzki–Van Duyne to investigate copper and iron/steel recovery in the United States. The longer product lifetime allows for substantial falls in scrap prices in some cases which can materially affect the steady-state recycling rate. Within this model the decline in scrap prices can only moderate and not outweigh the rise in the recycling rate due to the decline in the growth rate. The bigger the price elasticity of supply of scrap, the smaller will be the relative fall in the scrap prices. The smallest effect on the recycling rate of a fall in growth will be found where substitution between scrap and primary inputs is small and the price elasticity of scrap supply is high. In some cases, quite substantial increases in the recycling rate are predicted from this model.

This rise in the predicted steady-state recycling rate represents a satisfactory outlook for secondary industries, even if the future for the primary extractive industries appears less encouraging. This assessment is strengthened further if the comments of Radetzki and Van Duyne on the likely dynamics of prices and outputs between two steady states are

Table 4.5   Short product lifetime case

			low (0.1) Y_0	low (0.1) Y_z			medium (0.5) Y_0	medium (0.5) Y_z			high (1.5) Y_0	high (1.5) Y_z
low (0.5)												
	P	g_0	1	1	P	g_0	1	1	P	g_0	1	1
		g_1	1	0.92		g_1	1	0.95		g_1	1	0.98
		g_2	1	0.84		g_2	1	0.91		g_2	1	0.96
	β	g_0	0.27	0.27	β	g_0	0.27	0.27	β	g_0	0.27	0.27
		g_1	0.27	0.28		g_1	0.27	0.28		g_1	0.27	0.27
		g_2	0.27	0.29		g_2	0.27	0.28		g_2	0.27	0.28
medium (3)												
	P	g_0	1	1	P	g_0	1	1	P	g_0	1	1
		g_1	1	0.98		g_1	1	0.99		g_1	1	0.99
		g_2	1	0.97		g_2	1	0.97		g_2	1	0.98
	β	g_0	0.27	0.27	β	g_0	0.27	0.27	β	g_0	0.27	0.27
		g_1	0.27	0.28		g_1	0.27	0.28		g_1	0.27	0.28
		g_2	0.27	0.29		g_2	0.27	0.29		g_2	0.27	0.29
high (10)												
	P	g_0	1	1	P	g_0	1	1	P	g_0	1	1
		g_1	1	0.99		g_1	1	0.99		g_1	1	0.99
		g_2	1	0.99		g_2	1	0.99		g_2	1	0.99
	β	g_0	0.27	0.27	β	g_0	0.27	0.27	β	g_0	0.27	0.27
		g_1	0.27	0.28		g_1	0.27	0.28		g_1	0.27	0.28
		g_2	0.27	0.29		g_2	0.27	0.29		g_2	0.27	0.29

Notes: Initial scrap recovery rate $M_t^s/M_{t-d} = 0.3$; $d = 2$ years; $g_0 = 5\%$ p.a.; $g_1 = 3\%$ p.a.; $g_2 = 1\%$ p.a.; $\beta = 0.27$.

accepted. A drop in the growth rate is seen to have its immediate and most obvious effect in terms of the creation of excess capacity in the primary industry. In contrast with the assumed constancy in the long-run primary input price, the short-run primary price may fall sharply, reducing scrap use in the short term (consistent with the results of short-run forecasting models). The problem for the secondary industry firms during this period in the transition phase is that they may not be able to stay in business at the lower price levels. Much will depend on the recycling industry's ability to

Table 4.6 Long product lifetime case

			low (0.1)		medium (0.5)		high (1.5)	
			Y_0	Y_{20}	Y_0	Y_{20}	Y_0	Y_{20}
low (0.5)	P	g_0	1	1	1	1	1	1
		g_1	1	0.44	1	0.64	1	0.81
		g_2	1	0.195	1	0.41	1	0.66
	β	g_0	0.22	0.22	0.22	0.22	0.22	0.22
		g_1	0.22	0.30	0.22	0.26	0.22	0.24
		g_2	0.22	0.42	0.22	0.31	0.22	0.26
medium (3)	P	g_0	1	1	1	1	1	1
		g_1	1	0.85	1	0.87	1	0.90
		g_2	1	0.72	1	0.75	1	0.81
	β	g_0	0.22	0.22	0.22	0.22	0.22	0.22
		g_1	0.22	0.32	0.22	0.31	0.22	0.28
		g_2	0.22	0.48	0.22	0.43	0.22	0.36
high (10)	P	g_0	1	1	1	1	1	1
		g_1	1	0.95	1	0.95	1	0.96
		g_2	1	0.90	1	0.91	1	0.92
	β	g_0	0.22	0.22	0.22	0.22	0.22	0.22
		g_1	0.22	0.33	0.22	0.32	0.22	0.31
		g_2	0.22	0.49	0.22	0.47	0.22	0.43

Notes: Initial scrap recovery rate $M_t^s/M_{t-d} = 0.6$; $d = 20$ years; $g_0 = 5\%$ p.a.; $g_1 = 3\%$ p.a.; $g_2 = 1\%$ p.a.; $\beta = 0.22$.

adopt technologies which improve the efficiency with which they process and refine scrap. Technical advances are occurring: for example, selective resin technology could potentially exert a significant impact on secondary metals recovery. The technology involves a wet physical/chemical process. The resins are silica-based, silica being an abundant material. The first application of the technology will probably be in jewellery metal recovery. The existence of a market in scrap will delay the recovery of primary prices and new investment in primary production as the new, lower, steady-state growth continues. Thus on this basis, the transition between two steady-state recycling rates following a decline in growth is unlikely to be a smooth one. The fastest rise in the recycling rate will occur in that period in which new primary capacity remains low.

The central idea which gives the model its special interest lies in the interaction between secondary and primary industries. The results are derived for the case of a perfectly competitive secondary industry. This may not, however, be a realistic assumption for UK secondary industry market conditions (Deadman and Turner, 1981). Both the form of the supply function for scrap and the production function assumptions adopted by Radetzki–Van Duyne also deserve further analysis.

The case for government intervention in order to focus and direct research and development effort is strengthened by the observation that technological change is characterised by a certain randomness and subject to discontinuities. Some substitution trends, in particular materials mixing, increased product durability and miniaturisation are likely to hinder, for example, attempts to extend recycling activities. Industry is continually changing its product output in an effort to minimise costs. Within this general constraint, substitutions also take place because of factors such as energy conservation and environmental/safety regulations. Design changes in order to improve the recyclability of eventually scrapped products, however, have not been so evident (Henstock, 1986) and will require regulatory action. Materials mixing can produce potentially incompatible combinations as far as recycling is concerned, while at the same time producing technically and/or aesthetically superior products. Miniaturisation reduces the amount of recoverable material per unit of scrap and often requires an intricate recovery operation.

Processing facilities and information stockpile

Less dramatic problems such as escalating costs of raw materials can be at least as damaging to the economy in the longer term and thus equally justify contingency plans. A case in point was the oil crisis in 1973, which caught the leading industrial countries virtually unprepared and had a serious impact on their economies. Maintaining and upgrading existing processing facilities may be easy to achieve, but to establish capacity for entirely new domestic production may not often make immediate economic sense. However, the positive knock-on effects in other areas might be considerable. For example, initiating domestic production of device-quality silicon from silica would not only secure strategic supplies and help to reduce the commercial vulnerability of domestic users, but could have a stimulating effect on operations as diverse as silicone production and the manufacture of engineering equipment (Jacobson and Evans, 1984). At the very least, a case can be made for establishing small, strategic processing facilities and keeping these in a 'mothballed' state until such time as they are required.

The stockpile notion can be extended beyond a physical materials bank, to incorporate the concept of a 'technology stockpile', i.e. a bank of information on, for example, process technologies. It would ensure the appraisal of a wide range of options and would be a useful preliminary step in a mitigation strategy aimed at facilitating future substitution processes (Schlabach, 1984). Supporters of the movement for the introduction of LNWTs have explored the idea of a 'Process Encyclopaedia' in some detail. More data on the generation and disposal of scrap containing strategic materials also need to be collected on a consistent and continuing basis.

Thus, to recapitulate, conventional stockpiling is a demonstrably inadequate means of attempting to secure the supply of critical materials for manufacturing industry. For a contingency policy on materials resources to be effective, it requires the adoption of a much broader strategy, encompassing several complementary approaches, including:

(a) the setting-up of a highly selected physical stockpile, closely tailored to the needs of user industries, that would not be confined to mineral ores and primary raw materials, such as ferrochrome; this stockpile would have to be actively managed and continually updated;
(b) the development and maintenance of an adequate range of processing facilities, capable of providing domestic civil and defence industries with materials in forms that meet their manufacturing requirements, and that would be available for use in an emergency. The development and updating of an information stockpile;
(c) the institution of an ongoing scientific and technological programme aimed at increasing substitution possibilities, recycling of scrap and developing other material-conserving solutions.

Establishing the appropriate framework for resource contingency planning

Having recognised the need for a multi-criteria approach to contingency planning of materials resources, one must then consider how to achieve it in practice.

At present, the sort of institutional framework called for, one that is broadly based and at the same time fully integrated, is lacking in the EEC. Even with regard to the limited measure of stockpiling, France is alone in the EEC in having fully adopted such a scheme. Administered by the

Director General of Mines, it is believed that the French government stockpile holds two years' supplies of certain metals and minerals (costing $340 billion), but exact details of its composition have not been disclosed (Marsh, 1983).

The EEC does not have any collective policy on contingency planning of raw materials. In the early 1980s the European Commission presented a report to the Council of Ministers indicting why a policy to safeguard materials supplies is desirable, but this was not taken any further (House of Lords Select Committee Report on 'Strategic Materials', 1982). However, the Commission is active in planning and coordinating a range of activities (including the sponsorship of scientific technological research) that together constitute an embryonic resource planning policy. These activities could be easily integrated into a more comprehensive scheme of resource contingency planning within the EEC.

A framework that might be considered as an appropriate model for Europe is provided by the National Critical Materials Council in the United States, which was established by the National Critical Materials Act of 1984 (Leamy, 1985). Operating within the Executive Office of the President, this body has been assigned the role of coordinating government materials-related policies and research and development programmes on advanced materials. It has the authority to oversee the whole area of materials research and the duty to assess the future needs of both government and industry. Among its specific functions are:

(a) to assess the adequacy of the materials content of educational curricula;
(b) to draw up an inventory of critical materials and to forecast the needs of government and industry for them and, with the collaboration of the Office of Science and Technology Policy and others, to predict possible major problems that may emerge in the future;
(c) to provide Congress with recommendations on changes in policy, regulation and on legislation that may be required.

The National Critical Materials Council has been empowered to establish advisory panels and to convene Federal inter-agency committees to assist it in its work.

What the US National Critical Materials Act does not directly address is a role for the private sector in the formulation and implementation of materials-related policies. By comparison, Japan, Sweden and Switzerland have all developed 'private' stockpiling policies. Sweden maintains a national economic defence stockpile but also encourages private stockpiling by allowing accelerated tax write-offs for reduced inventory valuation (avoiding the taxing of inflationary increases in stock value). Switzerland has both mandatory stocks held by industrial 'consortia' and financed by the government, and voluntary stockpiles, facilitated by government credit (lower interest rates and tax rebates). In a materials crisis situation, the mandatory stocks are released only by government order, but 50 per cent of the voluntary stocks remain with the private holder and are not subject to government disposition. In Japan the private sector is assigned the major responsibility not only for initiatives in research and development on new materials and related technologies but also for securing supplies of raw materials. This position extends to the official strategic stockpile which is currently being built up by the Japanese government in partnership with private industry (*Metal Bulletin*, 27 June 1986). Associations of private firms maintain inventory levels under the guidance of the Ministry of International Trade and Industry.

For the United Kingdom it makes sense for materials policies and, in particular, resource contingency planning to be developed as part of a joint EEC undertaking, building on existing Community programmes.

References

Auty, R., 1985, 'Materials Intensity of GDP', *Resources Policy*, **11** (4).

Banks, F., 1976, *The Economics of Natural Resources*, Plenum Press, London.

Barnett, H., 1979, 'Scarcity and Growth Revisited', in Smith, V.K. (ed.), *Scarcity and Growth Reconsidered*, Johns Hopkins University Press, Baltimore.

_____ 1982, 'Are Minerals Costing More?', *Resource Management Optimisation*, **2** (1).

Barnett, H. and Morse, C., 1963, *Scarcity and Growth: The Economics of Natural Resource Availability*, Johns Hopkins University Press, Baltimore.

Bridgewater, A.V. and Nott, M.V., 1981, 'A Methodological Assessment of Raw Materials in the UK', *Resources Policy*, **7** (4).

Clark, J.P. and Field, F.R., 1985, 'How Critical are Critical Materials?', *Technology Review*, **4** (1).

CPE, 1985, 'L'Hyperchoix des matériaux', Centre de Prospective et d'Evaluation, *Sciences et Techniques*, Special Number, 48–61.

Deadman, D. and Grace, R., 1979, 'Recycling of Secondary Materials: An Econometric Study of the UK Aluminium Industry', *Conservation and Recycling*, **3** (1).

Deadman, D. and Turner, R.K., 1981, 'Comment: Modelling the Supply of Wastepaper', *Journal of Environmental Economics and Management*, **8** (1).

Etheridge, W.S., 1981, 'Demand for Metals', *Materials in Engineering*, **2** (1).

Evans, J.W. and Szekely, J., 1985, 'Newer vs. Traditional Industries: A Materials Perspective', *Journal of Metals*, **37** (12).

Goeller, H.E. and Zucker, A., 1984, 'Infinite Resources: The Ultimate Strategy', *Science*, **223**, February.

Hagland, D.G., 1984, 'Strategic Minerals: A Conceptual Analysis', *Resources Policy*, **10** (3).

Hall, D.C. and Hall, J.V., 1984, 'Concepts and Measures of Natural Resource Scarcity, with a Summary of Recent Trends', *Journal of Environmental Economics and Management*, **11** (3).

Hargreaves, D. and Fromson, S., 1983, *World Index of Strategic Materials*, Gower, Aldershot.

Harris, D.P. and Skinner, B.J., 1982, 'The Assessment of Long-Term Supplies of Minerals', in Smith, V.K. and Krutilla, J.V. (eds), *Explorations in Natural Resources Economics*, Johns Hopkins University Press, Baltimore.

Harris, S.L., 1986, 'Precious Metals Recovery from Low-Grade Resources', *Journal of Metals*, **38** (6).

Hazilla, M. and Kopp, R.J., 1984a, 'Assessing US Vulnerability to Raw Material Supply Disruptions: An Application to Non-fuel Minerals', *Southern Economic Journal*, **51** (2).

——— 1984b, 'A Factor Demand Model for Strategic Non-fuel Minerals in the Primary Metals Sector', *Land Economics*, **60** (4).

Henstock, M., 1986, *Design for Recyclability Summary Report*, *Materials Forum Annual Report*, Institute of Metals, London.

Hillman, C.T. and Gosling, B.B., 1985, *Mining Deep Ocean Manganese Nodules*, US Bureau of Mines, Information Circular 9015, Washington, DC.

House of Lords Select Committee on 'Strategic Minerals', 1982, *20th Report on the European Communities*, HMSO, London.

Industry and Environment, 1986, 'Low- and Non-Waste Technology', **9** (4).

Institute of Geological Sciences, 1985, *World Mineral Statistics (1977–81)*, HMSO, London.

Jacobson, D.M. and Evans, D.S., 1984, *Critical Materials in the Electrical and Electronics Industry*, The Institution of Metallurgists, London.

Johnson, C.T. and Otto, J.M., 1986, 'Manganese Nodule Project Economics', *Resource Policy*, **12** (1).

Jones, S. *et al.*, 1986, 'Future Demand for Gallium Arsenide Semiconductor Devices', *Metals and Materials*, **2** (4).

Labys, W.C., 1980, 'Commodity Price Stabilization Models: A Review and Appraisal', *Journal of Policy Modelling*, **2** (1).

Labys, W.C., 1986, 'Stockpiling Economics', in Beever, M.B. *et al.* (eds), *Encyclopaedia of Materials Science and Engineering*, Pergamon Press, Oxford.

Leamy, H., 1985, 'The National Critical Materials Act', *MRS Bulletin*, No. 1, 21–2.

Marsh, P., 1983, 'The West Builds Up Its Metals Mountain', *New Scientist*, March, 573–7.

Metallgesellshaft, 1982, 1983, 1984, *Metal Statistics*, 69th, 70th and 71st edns., Frankfurt-am-Main.

NARI, 1982, *Recycled Metals in the 1980s*, National Association of Recycling Industries, New York.

Papp, J.F., 1983, 'Chromium', in *Mineral Commodity Profiles*, US Department of the Interior, Bureau of Mines, Washington, DC.

Pearce, D.W., 1976, 'Environmental Protection, Recycling and the International Materials Economy', in Walter, I. (ed.), *Studies In Environmental Economics*, Wiley, New York.

Pearce, D.W. and Turner, R.K., 1984, 'The Economic Evaluation of Low and Non-Waste Technologies', *Resources and Conservation*, **11** (1).

Radetzki, M., 1984, 'Strategic Metal Markets: Prospects for Producer Cartels', *Resources Policy*, **10** (4).

Radetzki, M. and Van Duyne, C., 1985, 'The Demand for Scrap and Primary Metal Ores After a Decline in Secular Growth', *Canadian Journal of Economics*, **18** (2).

Radetzki, M. and Svensson, L., 1979, 'Can Scrap Save Us From Depletion?', *Natural Resources Forum*, **3** (1).

Ray, G.F., 1984, 'Mineral Reserves: Projected Lifetimes and Security of Supply', *Resources Policy*, **10** (2).

Rogers, M., 1984, 'The Chromium Industry in South Africa and Zimbabwe, 1984', unpublished report, University of Oxford.

——— 1985, 'Chrome and Ferrochrome: Firmly in the Hands of the Few', *Metal Bulletin Monthly*, No. 175, 15–19.

Schlabach, T.D., 1984, 'Substitution: Technology', *Conservation and Recycling*, **7** (1).

Stalker, K.W. *et al.*, 1984, 'An Index to Identify Strategic Metal Vulnerability', *Metal Progress*, No. 11, 55–65.

Tilton, J.E., 1983, *Material Substitution: Lessons from the Tin-Using Industries*, Resources for the Future, Washington, DC.

Turner, R.K. and Deadman, D., 1983, 'The UK Wastepaper Industry and Its Long Term Prospects', *Journal of Industrial Economics*, **32** (2).

US Bureau of Mines, 1986, *Domestic Consumption Trends, 1972–82, and Forecasts to 1993 for Twelve Major Metals*, Washington, DC.

US OTA, 1983, *Strategic Materials: Technologies to Reduce US Import Vulnerability*, United States Congress, Office of Technology Assessment, Washington, DC.

Watchman, J.B., 1984, 'The Nature of the Critical and Strategic Materials Problem', AGARD (NATO), CP–356, 1.1–1.11.

Weston, R., 1984, *Strategic Materials: A World Survey*, Croom Helm, London.

Chapter 5

The Sustainable Use of Natural Resources in Developing Countries

David Pearce

The problem

There is now an overdue recognition that the economic fortunes of many developing countries are inextricably bound up in the state of their natural environments, particularly with the quality and quantity of soil, water and biomass resources. Over-use of these resources, combined with only limited appreciation of their complex interdependence, has resulted in depletion of what are, in essence, renewable resources. Use rates have been based on non-sustainable practices, i.e. harvest rates have exceeded the sustainable yields of the resources. The results are soil erosion, water pollution and reduced water supplies, deforestation and other biomass loss and diversion, and desertification.

The economic significance of natural resource degradation (NRD) shows up directly in terms of losses of inputs to well-being as with reduced woodfuels supply, increased time costs in woodfuel collection, increased prices of marketed biomass fuels, similar impacts on water supply, reduced nutritional intake (e.g. via reduced cooking activity). But the impact extends to national and regional economies through reduced agricultural yields, added impetus to rural–urban migration, externalities in the form of reduced hydroelectricity output, and depletion of natural assets which are the basis of both indigenous and export industries such as timber. The key concept is 'sustainability'. Changes in resource management practice toward sustainable resource use could at least contribute to the preservation of the renewable resource base, and hence to the direct well-being of the population and to the future of the macroeconomy. Those changes

* This is a modified version of a much longer paper presented to the Economic and Social Science Research Council Workshop on Environmental Economics, University of East Anglia, July 1986. I am indebted to participants of the workshop for comments on that version. I am also grateful to Jerry Warford and Dennis Anderson of the World Bank for other comments, and to Norman Myers for many discussions on the general issues. The paper was prepared with the assistance of a Personal Research Grant from ESRC's Environment and Planning Committee.

have to take place at both the microeconomic level—the household and farm—and at the macroeconomic level—in terms of overall economic policy. Moreover, the policy measures need not be complex or expensive. Comparatively simple, low-cost but pervasive measures can be undertaken, notably in respect of price reform.

Against this background, this chapter outlines some of the issues arising from NRD in developing countries. A greatly expanded treatment will be available elsewhere (Pearce and Warford, forthcoming).

The severity of natural resource degradation

There are numerous surveys of what is happening to the renewable resource base in developing countries (Holdgate *et al.*, 1982; Repetto, 1984; World Resources Institute/IIED, 1986; Myers, 1984; Global 2000, 1980; Simon and Kahn, 1984). Differing views about the seriousness of the situation partially reflect differing quantitative assessments of *physical* magnitudes, as with the dispute over rates of conversion and loss of tropical moist forests (Melillo *et al.*, 1985). But underlying the debate on the severity of NRD are also different 'world-views' about the evolution of primarily agriculture-based economies. In somewhat caricature terms, those who deny the severity of the problem (the 'cornucopists') also tend to argue that some NRD is an inevitable part of the transition from more to less primitive agricultural technologies. In ecological terms, this is a shift from one ecological equilibrium to another, deliberately brought about because the existing equilibrium is characterised by levels of well-being that are 'too low'. Those who express the greater concern point to the existence of limits to the application of changed technologies and farming systems set by the ecological characteristics of the regions suffering the most: models of development applicable to temperate systems are not applicable to tropical or semi-arid zones. In terms of ecological change, the existing state is one of disequilibrium—an imbalance between the demand for and supply of natural resources. Moreover, while disequilibrium is a process of change, there is no guarantee that the transition path is to a new ecological equilibrium in which standards of well-being are higher.

It seems not unfair to say also that the differing views reflect the anticipated policy implications of measures of NRD severity. Interventionist policy is eschewed by the cornucopists. It tends to be advocated, or at least reluctantly acknowledged, by the alternative view. In between is a school of thought that acknowledges the severity of NRD, but points to comparatively simple policy measures which rely substantially on modest intervention and use of market incentives (Repetto, 1986).

Typically absent in the debate, however, are criteria for *measuring* the severity of NRD. Two are highlighted here: the 'carrying capacity' approach and the use of general economic indicators.

Measuring carrying capacity—the capability of the land, forest cover and water resources to support human populations—is hazardous. Moreover, it is not always an appropriate concept since it concerns the capability to support the *maximum* population rather than the 'optimal' one (Mahar, 1985; Ho, 1985). Nonetheless, it is suggestive as a first indication of resource constraints. Table 5.1 shows some calculations for the population carrying capacity of crops, livestock and woodfuels in the Sahelian and Sudanian zones of West Africa. It will be observed that existing populations already exceed sustainable levels in the Sahelian and Sahelo–Sudanian zones, and that the woodfuels resource constraint 'bites' before the crop plus livestock constraint in all regions. The carrying capacity approach provides some quantitative confirmation of even casual observation, but it also suggests that, in this case, action on woodfuel supply is even more important than general agricultural policy, although they interact through the external benefits of trees on crops (windbreaks, erosion reduction) and livestock (through fodder supply).

Table 5.1   Carrying capacity in the Sahelian/Sudanian zones

| | Population per km^2 | | | |
| | Sustainable | | Actual | |
	Crops + livestock	Woodfuels	Rural	Total
Saharan	0.3	—	0.3	0.3
Sahelo–Saharan	0.3	—	2.0	2.0
Sahelian	7.0	1.0	7.0	7.0
Saharan–Sahelian	15.0	10.0	20.0	23.0
Sudanian	22.0	20.0	17.0	21.0
Sudanian–Guinean	35.0	20.0	9.0	10.0

Source: Steeds (1985)

Two 'back of the envelope' calculations illustrate the potential importance of extending measures of NRD severity to include economic magnitudes. In the first we look at one effect of deforestation in poor countries, which is the diversion of dung supplies to the fuel sector. As woodfuel supplies decrease, households collect dung which would otherwise have been left as soil fertiliser. The 'present value' of the dung as fuel to the household is higher than its value as soil nutrient—the latter will show up as a stream of future benefits, the former as an immediate benefit. The present thus appears to be quite explicitly traded against the future, but the context is one where there is no choice anyway since there are neither fuel nor fertiliser substitutes to which households can gain access. Based on earlier work by Newcombe (1984) on dung 'diverted' to fuel use in Ethiopia and fertiliser–crop response rates, the monetary value of lost agricultural productivity in Ethiopia due to dung diversion could be as much as $600 million per annum, or about 30 per cent of value added in the agricultural sector. Such a calculation is crude, but it is illustrative of the kind of economic loss due to just one aspect of NRD.

The second example concerns sedimentation of hydro-reservoirs due to soil run-off in excess of anticipated rates. There are many sources of such sediment and it seems fair to say that the scientific state of the art does not permit us accurately to allocate 'receipts' of sediment to sources which include deforestation, poor farming practice, and road building (Southgate *et al.*, 1984; Southgate, 1986). However, one survey of two hundred major hydroelectric dams built since 1940 indicates that, at a 1 per cent constant sedimentation rate per annum, the 'live' storage capacity of these dams will be reduced by one-third in the year 2000 (Sfeir-Younis, 1985). The 1 per cent rate is in fact conservative in terms of actual rates of sedimentation. Hydroelectricity in 100 developing countries contributed some 445,000 gigawatt hours (gWh) of electricity in 1980. Applying the 30 per cent loss figure, then, would suggest a loss of 148,000 gWh by the year 2000. Taking an 'alternative cost' approach (which understates the value of the electricity in terms of willingness to pay for it), and valuing the oil that would be needed to produce this much electricity at $12 per barrel, the total electricity loss is $3 billion distributed across the various countries. Again, the approach is indicative only, but it suggests that sedimentation, which is in part due to NRD, is extremely costly.

A final indicator of 'severity' relates NRD more directly to measures of gross national product (GNP). Economists have for some considerable time expressed concern about various arbitrary features of national income accounting. More recently, they have attempted methodological and practical modifications to the accounts to attempt to reflect some aspects of NRD (Peskin, 1981; Norgaard, 1985). For example, countries heavily reliant upon natural resources are depreciating a capital stock which is not (typically) accounted for in measures of income and wealth. Preliminary estimates by Repetto (1986) suggest that, applying average rental values (broadly, the difference between prices and costs of production) to timber logged in Indonesia, forest depreciation cost some $3.6 billion in 1982 alone. This may be related to a GNP of some $90 billion, i.e. a 4 per cent difference between gross and 'net' national product (in fact NNP will be less still because of the need to allow for the depreciation of manufactured capital as well). This comparatively simple procedure could obviously be used across a whole range of countries, incidentally also providing a database of 'rents' which can then be related to tax takes by individual governments.

Depletion of an exhaustible natural resource such as coal or oil is typically regarded as having two cost components. These are the direct costs of extraction and the 'user cost' element, where the latter refers to the foregone benefits in the future of using up a unit of the resource now. Indeed, expressed in terms of the marginal unit of use, the optimal price of an exhaustible resource is equal to its marginal extraction cost plus the marginal user cost. Practical algorithms for computing the user cost component (also known as the 'depletion premium') are given in Munasinghe and Schramm (1983) and Schramm (1985).

For *renewable* resources, however, user cost appears irrelevant since the use of a unit of the resource now does not preclude a unit of use later, given that the resource renews itself. There may, however, be a rise in harvesting costs as the stock of the resource decreases, an effect termed the 'marginal stock effect' by Clark (1976). In our case, however, we are interested in non-sustainable use rates, harvests in excess of sustainable yield (where the latter will also vary with the stock level). In these circumstances there is a user cost because non-sustainable management of a renewable resource will reduce the future availability of the resource. As noted above, there are also additional costs in the form of externalities such as river, reservoir and estuary sedimentation, soil erosion, desertification, etc. Moreover, it is now accepted that all these effects render ecosystems less resilient to exogenous 'shocks' such as climatic changes. What was previously a normal reaction to, say, a monsoon period, becomes potentially catastrophic as soils are unable to contain the water and are washed away, nutrients are leached, and so on.

All this suggests that the 'marginal opportunity cost' of non-sustainable resource use is made up of the direct harvesting costs, a user cost element, the externalities and some expected value of added 'disaster' cost. A more formal analysis is given in the Annexe to this chapter, and is extensively dealt with in Pearce and Markandya (1987a). MOC then becomes a measure of the severity of NRD—the higher MOC, the more serious the situation. The current state of the art in both modelling the physical relationship between resource sectors and in 'monetising' the linkages is not such that we have much hope of quantifying MOC, although progress in monetising environmental damage in developed economies suggests that this situation may change rapidly (Pearce and Markandya, 1987b). As such, MOC is best thought of as an aid to identifying the relevant factors in the resource depletion problem, and as a checklist when judging the importance of depletion.

The severity of NRD can thus be indicated in various non-exclusive ways. The traditional approaches based on projections of supply and demand for, say, woodfuels retain their use, although they have typically not allowed for any feedback effects of rising costs of harvesting. A crude first indicator is also given by the carrying capacity concept which can provide a broad basis for priority action. The indicators favoured here relate to known economic magnitudes such as GNP, using the overall framework for analysis provided by the marginal opportunity cost concept.

The 'causes' of resource degradation

Unravelling the factors giving rise to NRD is complex. If NRD is seen as a transitional cost in the evolution of whole economies, and of the agrarian sector in particular, then the entire development process generates resource depletion. NRD is then a problem only if the feedback effects from NRD to development are themselves understated or unanticipated. The alternative view confirms that feedback effects are important, but further argues that the particular path of development in which resources are used non-sustainably is itself going to be short-lived. This is the view taken here.

The proximate causes of resource loss are, then, forest clearance for agricultural land use, non-sustainable woodfuels harvesting, over-intensive rates of animal stocking, farm practice—including choice of inappropriate crops and rotational patterns—exogenous climatic impacts, and population pressure. Population growth will itself force the marginalisation of many peasants and farmers as extensive margins of cultivation are increased to ecologically fragile lands, e.g. hills and mountainsides. Allen and Barnes (1985) show that this appears to be the process by which deforestation occurs, for example. Population change accompanied by increased urbanisation also generates high demands for urban fuels such as charcoal, supplies of which come from rural districts as peri-urban sources are exhausted. Lastly, population growth generates a higher demand for woodfuels and non-cash crops simply by virtue of extra mouths to be fed. Offsetting these effects may be some of the dynamic impacts that population pressure has in 'forcing' switches in agricultural technology (Boserup, 1965, 1981). But for countries suffering severe NRD it seems more likely that the relevant ecosystems cannot support significant changes in land productivity (Ho, 1985). That is, the stages of agricultural development will be limited by climate, intrinsic soil quality, topography and varying erosion rates arising from changes in agricultural technology. The other factor generating NRD will be the extent to which losses of the factors giving rise to resource regeneration—fallow periods, applications of animal waste as fertiliser, shelterbelt effects of trees, and so on—are compensated for by manufactured inputs such as fertiliser. Whole social processes and plain economic limitations will drive a wedge between these rates of factor use, causing NRD. The idea that NRD is thus 'automatically' compensated for in some evolutionary model of agricultural change is therefore naïve.

Quite where the analysis of causation stops is an open issue. For example, population growth appears to have been regulated in many traditional societies in accordance with the available supply of resources (Repetto and Holmes, 1983; Wilkinson, 1973). The implicit suggestion is that modern-day population growth could be, in part at least, a conscious response to resource loss as parents 'invest' in children as a labour supply and as a source of security in old age (Cassen, 1976). Others express severe doubts as to whether this kind of life-cycle rational decision-making can be said to be applicable in context where so many other exogenous influences change so rapidly (Ghatak, 1986). Rather, it is the factors impinging on and breaking down the self-regulating features of traditional resource-use practice that causes population growth to take place in an apparently non-rational manner.

Much the same goes for the widespread argument that what 'causes' the resource problem is common ownership of land, the so-called 'tragedy of the commons' (Hardin, 1968). The idea is that each user of commonly owned land will maximise his own self-interest, ignoring the effects of his actions on other users (the 'crowding' externality) and the user cost of consumption (the 'intergenerational' externality). This common property argument is taken to be an instance of 'market failure', but not in the context of what markets fail to achieve. Rather, it is taken to be an instance of the failure of markets to develop properly.

While such a model has wide currency in economics, it is worth noting that even in the contexts for which it was developed (usually fisheries) there is a stable equilibrium in which the resource is used sustainably. It is true, however, that the equilibrium stock is lower than would be the case if the resource was singly owned, thus increasing the risk of extinction. More relevant, however, is the fact that the institutional structure presumed in the commons model is inapplicable as a general statement about resource ownership effects in developing countries. Common ownership frequently involves highly organised controls on the use of the resource, with sanctions by the community against individual 'maximisers'. As Bromley (1985) notes:

Long established norms and conventions dictate both the rules for controlling the rate of use and the rules for changing these rules. This institutional structure has evolved over long periods of time and has as its central motivation the assurance of survival of the group

In short, many common property regimes are regimes designed for permanent livability.

This contrasts somewhat with the view that NRD is best solved by the conferment of property rights based on individual ownership (Ault and Rudman, 1979). A good deal of the confusion stems from a failure to distinguish between 'open-access' resources (*res nullius*) and 'common property resources' (*res communis*). The latter tend to be characterised by institutional control structures, the former by the absence of such structures. There can be little doubt that open-access resources will have very high risks of extinction through over-use. Conferment of some form of property right may then be a first step in reversing or containing NRD in that context. This is also likely to be true where land is occupied but without title. Such land is clearly neither open access nor common property, but it is characterised by risks of expropriation. Thus, Feder (1986) has found that capital formation on land with security of tenure in Thailand is higher than on land characterised by lack of title. Interestingly, however, this study, along with others, suggests that the link between capital formation and security of tenure is via the ability of the tenured farmer to use his land as collateral in securing credit.

All in all, then, causal analyses which place responsibility for NED on the lack of property rights have some validity, but blanket judgements that it is the presence of common property which causes NRD are frequently wrong and invariably simplistic.

One further 'model' of the NRD process deserves some mention since it has secured more than moderate currency. This approach suggests that NRD is actually 'optimal', reflecting conscious decisions to extinguish the resource over some lifetime planning period. Morey (1985) has used an optimal control approach to suggest that this may be the case with desertification, for example. The analytic basis for this approach comes from the more general theory of resource-use optimisation. It is quite feasible to secure a result that a given resource should be 'run-down' to extinction (Plourde, 1970; Clarke, 1976; Hartwick and Olewiler, 1986). The necessary conditions are that the price of the resource is high, discount rates are high, and that harvesting costs should in general be unrelated to the remaining stock. It is difficult to accept the non-dependence of cost on the stock size in the case of developing countries, but the implicit value of a resource such as woodfuel will be high, and discount rates will appear to be high. The problem is that the discount rates of the resource users are not 'given'. They are themselves the result of the resource-degradation process which compels actions to be taken which imply high discount rates. Thus, in the face of woodfuel shortages, the diversion of dung to fuel and away from soil fertiliser is 'rational', given that the fuel shortage affects tomorrow's welfare whereas the condition of the soil affects next season's welfare. *Ex post* discount rates are higher than *ex ante* discount rates, but it is the latter that have relevance to social decisions about optimal rates of resource depletion. In short, high apparent discount rates are not explanations of the NRD process: they are simply restatements of it.

The discount rate issue and the various views on the role of private property rights may be classified as instances of market failure in one form or another. The more conventional definition of market failure would include the failure to account for externalities even in a system of well-defined property rights. Upstream pollution of downstream waters would be an example.

The literature on the 'political economy of government', however, also points to a wide area of 'government failure' in the efficient use of resources. Such failures include intervention in markets, marketing controls, land-use controls, inappropriate tax policy and the general failure of bureaucracies to conceive of and implement rational resource policies. Some examples are reasonably clear-cut in their implications for resource depletion. These would include the failure to price fuels in an appropriate manner. Regardless of the overall level of prices, *relative* prices matter; otherwise there will be a tendency to exploit the lowest priced resource first regardless of its true scarcity. One might begin such an analysis by calculating what relative prices should be on the basis of thermal equivalence 'at the pot', i.e. in terms of heat delivered to the point of final use. Table 5.2 shows relative prices for various fuels in different countries, using electricity as the 'numéraire'. These may be compared to the thermal equivalence 'equilibrium' values. It will be observed that LPG (bottled gas used mainly in towns) is grossly underpriced in three of the four countries, as is kerosene (used for lighting and some cooking). Charcoal is underpriced in two of the four countries and fuelwood (wood burned directly for cooking) in three of the four. It is no accident that the underpricing of fuelwood and charcoal is associated with severe woodfuels depletion in the relevant countries. Woodfuel prices in Ethiopia are higher than the equilibrium prices, partly reflecting the already depleted state of forests there, but also reflecting deliberate government policy. In all cases where prices diverge from the equilibrium prices, government intervention in the various markets through price controls and subsidies explain the variation.

Table 5.2 is illustrative only. Desirable relativities would also reflect factors such as convenience as well as the externalities involved in the use of each fuel. In short, relativities should reflect marginal opportunity costs in the sense described above. Because of the complexity of estimating MOC at this stage, it is not possible to indicate more clearly what the appropriate relativities should be. Absolute levels would be established by 'anchoring' at least one of the prices to the cost of importing the fuel (the 'border price') which is itself the opportunity cost for a traded commodity (Pearce and Markandya, 1987a).

As a general proposition, the pattern of resource prices in many

Table 5.2   Illustrative relative fuel prices, 1980

	Haiti	Senegal	Indonesia	Ethiopia	Equilibrium
Fuelwood	14	6	4	29	20
Charcoal	17	8	40	83	30
Kerosene	35	28	8	58	67
LPG	57	6	14	80	88
Electricity	100	100	100	100	100

Source: Interdisziplinare Projekt Consult (1985).

developing countries bears little relationship to the pattern that one would expect, even judgementally, if they were based on a concept of marginal opportunity cost. Instead, subsidies are widely applied to 'sensitive' fuels, i.e. fuels consumed by politically important classes, who may be the rural and urban poor, but are often the urban middle-income groups. This tends to explain subsidies to LPG, for example. Subsidies to diesel fuels are perhaps more widely 'class-based', given the role that diesel plays in urban transport and in mechanised farming. It does seem fair to say, however, that pricing policies do not give high importance to the interests of the rural poor.

Similar findings relate to taxation policies affecting natural resources. Failure to tax the proceeds of resource exploitation results in less of the economic rent accruing to governments and more being available to other 'rent-seekers'. ('Rent' in this context is the difference between the value of the resource output and the costs of extraction or harvesting). Rents are allocated according to the distribution of political power among rent-seekers, so that the actual allocation need not correspond at all to what is required by conventional economic efficiency requirements, and certainly not what is required if the social costs of resource depletion are taken into account (Colander, 1984). Rent-seeking is thus likely to accelerate deple-tion profiles and encourage non-sustainable harvesting of renewables, although the presumption that a high proportion of rent going to govern-ments will result in some approximation of 'optimal'-use rates cannot go unquestioned. Nonetheless, the evidence suggests that governments take a remarkably small porportion of rents. In the Philippines, for example, Repetto (1985) finds that the government took only 10–14 per cent of rents from all timber sales. Other effects follow. The same rent-seekers will work towards the adoption of projects in which available rents, and their potential share of them, are likely to be large. In irrigation projects this is likely to be large, publicly controlled projects in which irrigation charges are kept low (so as to maximise the rents of users, i.e. the difference for them between the value of benefits and the user charges) and water is expropriated by farmers in the head reaches of the system (Repetto, 1986).

If rent-seeking is likely to encourage unsustainable use patterns, other influences are less clear. Exchange rate controls may lead to under- or overvaluation. Overvaluation will discourage exports and may have the incidental effect of preserving resources. Undervaluation is likely to encourage exports of cash crops such as rubber which in turn are grown on deliberately cleared forest land. It seems fair to say that, while the effects of exchange rate distortions on agricultural productivity have been investigated in some detail, the link to natural resources has not been made. Gains in productivity could, for example, be achieved at the cost of longer-term resource conservation.

The essential feature of this discussion is that economies in which a large number of efficiency distortions exist will be characterised by a generally wasteful use of natural resources. In so far as these inefficient use rates contribute to harvest levels in excess of sustainable yield, the distortions are themselves generating resource depletion. This conclusion, is, then, suggestive as to the types of incentive required to correct NRD. focusing on economic distortions is not an alternative to the wider 'social' explanations of NRD based in analyses of unequal access to political and economic power. In many ways, the rent-seeking model reflects these underlying social inequalities. The reason for eschewing any extended discussion of the social basis of NRD, apart from limited space, is that we are concerned with feasible, reasonably short-term incentive measures, rather than with wholesale changes in social processes that may take long periods of time. A 'political economy' explanation of NRD, from a Marxist standpoint, is given in Blaikie (1985); see also the discussion in Chambers (1983).

Incentives for resource economy

The identification of the dominant 'causes' of NRD suggests the kinds of incentives needed to counteract it. Dealing with the underlying 'big' causes such as overpopulation and unequal access to land requires major policies with long time lags between policy design, implementation and effect. This does not make the policies unimportant. They have to proceed, but they need not be exclusive of other, less complex and probably more immediately effective policy. General macroeconomic policy could be strengthened by more positive action on distortionary prices. There must be no presumption that the implementation of prices based on standard efficiency measures will be adequate: efficiency has to be interpreted to be inclusive of all the components of social opportunity cost. But the evidence suggests that aiming at conventional efficiency prices (border prices for traded goods and marginal supply costs for non-traded goods) will move economies in the right direction as far as reducing NRD is concerned.

One of the chief ways in which such a price policy would help NRD is through the general 'conservation' effect of proper resource pricing. As noted previously, absolute prices tend to be held down through subsidy policies, thus encouraging wasteful use of energy and water. Relative prices tend also to be distorted because of policies of protecting particular social groups, and these distortions then fail to signal real resource scarcity. Similar comments apply to exchange rates and to intertemporal prices in the form of discount rates.

By the same token, fiscal policies which seek to appropriate more of the rent from existing resource developments for government should reduce resource-depleting, rent-seeking behaviour. But this argument is contingent upon rational resource-depletion decisions by government and this will not be warranted if government itself is a 'rent-dissipater', as has so often been the case. The political economy of government suggests that government cannot be viewed as a neutral instrument of benign policy on behalf of the population—it has its own goals and objectives. This in turn raises the issue of 'privatisation' of resource-using activities. It must be accepted that government failure may be as important as market failure in this respect, but at least some privatisation experiments suggest a more resource-conserving picture because of the need to set use charges at cost-related levels. How far this holds for land ownership itself is, as we have seen, not straightforward. Private ownership is likely to be preferred to no ownership or to ill-defined ownership, but there remains no incentive to internalise the externalities in any private ownership system. With many forms of common property that internalisation takes place because of institutional requirements that the individual serve the overall community interest.

The incentive problem is thus both simple and complex. It is simple in suggesting that more explicit use is made of the self-interest of the individual and the common interest of the local community. It is complex in that devising practical measures for resource conservation may well require a detailed understanding of social norms and practice. In other words, incentives are likely to vary from one community to another. One example is the role which women play in resource use. Given that women in most African communities are responsible for cooking, fuelwood collection, water gathering, and are often the head of the farming household, any policies designed to augment tree-planting, improve water supplies, and secure more efficient stoves and fires must be targeted on them. While recognition of such target groups exists in many small-scale policy ventures, it is surprisingly absent in larger-scale investment policy, perhaps itself a reflection of the weak rent-acquiring powers of this important social group.

Conclusion

Even this limited discussion should suffice to indicate the scale and pervasive nature of the resource degradation process. The natural environment cannot be treated as a dispensable feature of economic change. It is part of the process of economic development and resource degradation is a means of retarding that development. The focus here has been on the direct economic importance of renewable resources in terms of conventional measures of economic well-being such as GNP. The analysis of the process of NRD and its causes point the way to some comparatively modest and cost-effective measures at least to slow down that degradation. When other resource values are added—genetic diversity, wildlife, global ecosystem functioning—the need to act rapidly and effectively on the renewable resource base of developing countries is strengthened further. But in terms of persuasive policy now, the economic value of these resources can and should be demonstrated.

Annexe

Marginal opportunity cost

This annexe sets out the components of marginal opportunity cost (MOC). Fuller detail is to be found in Pearce and Markandya (1987b). The equation below shows how MOC is comprised:

$$MOC_i = MC_i + MUC_i + \Sigma\, MEC_{ij}$$

MOC is the marginal opportunity cost.
i is the ith resource.
MC is the direct cost of harvesting the resource.
MUC is the marginal user cost, i.e. the foregone marginal benefit by using up the resource now.
MEC is the marginal external cost imposed on another sector, j, by depleting a resource in sector i. Thus, this would include the effect of deforestation on soil erosion, or soil erosion on sedimentation and so on.

MUC   is analysed in detail in Munasinghe and Schramm (1983) and Schramm (1985).

References

Allen, J. and Barnes, D., 1985, 'The Causes of Deforestation in Developing Countries', *Annals of the Association of American Geographers*, **75** (2).

Ault, D. and Rudman, G., 1979, 'The Development of Individual Rights to Property in Tribal Africa', *Journal of Law and Economics*, **22** (1).

Blaikie, P., 1985, *The Political Economy of Soil Erosion*, Longman, London.

Boserup, E., 1965, *The Conditions of Agricultural Growth*, Aldine, Chicago.

———— 1981, *Population and Technological Change*, University of Chicago Press, Chicago.

Bromley, D., 1985, 'Common Property Issues in International Development', *Bostid Developments*, **5** (1).

Cassen, R.H., 1976, 'Population and Development: A Survey', *World Development*, **4** (11/12).

Chambers, R., 1983, *Rural Development: Putting the Last First*, Longman, London.

Clark, C., 1976, *Mathematical Bioeconomics*, Wiley, New York.

Colander, D.C. (ed.), 1984, *Neoclassical Political Economy: The Analysis of Rent-Seeing and DUP Activities*, Ballinger, Cambridge, Mass.

Feder, G., 1986, 'The Economic Implications of Land Ownership Security in Rural Thailand', unpublished, Department of Agriculture and Rural Development, World Bank, Washington, DC.

Ghatak, S., 1986, *An Introduction to Development Economics*, 2nd edn., Allen and Unwin, London.

GLOBAL 2000, 1980, *Report to the President*, US GPO, Washington, DC.

Hardin, G., 1968, 'The Tragedy of the Commons', *Science*, **162**.

Hartwick, J. and Olewiler N., 1986, *The Economics of Natural Resource Use*, Harper and Row, London.

Ho, T.J., 1985, 'Population Growth and Agricultural Productivity in Sub-Saharan Africa', in Davis T.J. (ed.), *Population and Food: Proceedings of the Fifth Agricultural Sector Symposium*, World Bank, Washington, DC.

Holdagte, M., Kassas, M. and White, G.F., 1982, *The World Environment 1972–1982*, Tycooly, Dublin.

Interdisziplinare Projekt Consult, 1985, *Energy Pricing in Developing Countries*, Report to GTZ, Frankfurt-am-Main.

Mahar, D. (ed.), 1985, *Rapid Population Growth and Human Carrying Capacity: Two Perspectives*, World Bank Staff Working Paper 890, Washington, DC.

Melillo, J., Palm, C., Houghton, R., Woodwell, G., and Myers, N., 1985 'Comparisons of Two Recent Estimates of Disturbances in Tropical Forests',

Environmental Conservation, **12** (1).

Morey, E., 1985, 'Desertification from an Economic Perspective', unpublished, Department of Economics, University of Colorado.

Munasinghe, M. and Schramm, G., 1983, *Energy Economics, Demand Management and Conservation Policy*, Van Nostrand Reinhold, New York.

Myers, N., 1984, *The Primary Source*, Norton, New York.

Newcombe, K., 1984, *The Economic Justification for Rural Afforestation: The Case of Ethiopia*, Energy Department Paper No. 16, August, World Bank, Washington, DC.

Norgaard, R., 1985, 'Linking Environmental and National Income Accounts', Paper to Environmental Accounting Workshop, UNEP/World Bank, Paris, September.

Pearce, D.W. and Markandya, A., 1987a, 'The Costs of Natural Resource Depletion in Low Income Developing Countries', in Bromley D. and Bishop, R. (eds), *Natural Resources and Development*, University of Wisconsin Press, Madison.

_____ 1987b, *The Benefits of Environmental Policy*, OECD, Paris.

Pearce, D.W. and Warford, J., 1987, *The Economics of Natural Resource Degradation in Developing Countries*, forthcoming.

Peskin, H., 1981, 'National Income Accounting and the Environment', *Natural Resources Journal*, **21**.

Plourde, C.G., 1970, 'A Simple Model of Replenishable Resource Exploitation', *American Economic Review*, **60**.

Repetto, R., 1984, *The Global Possible: Resources, Development and the New Century*, Yale University Press, New Haven, Conn.

_____ 1985, *Creating Incentives for Sustainable Forest Development*, World Resources Institute, Washington, DC.

_____ 1986, *Appropriate Incentives in Public Irrigation Systems*, World Resources Institute, Washington, DC.

_____ 1986, *Natural Resource Accounting in a Resource Based Economy: An Indonesian Case Study*, World Resources Institute, Washington, DC.

_____ 1986, *World Enough and Time: Successful Strategies for Resource Management*, Yale University Press, New Haven, Conn.

Repetto, R. and Holmes, T., 1983, 'The Role of Population in Resource Depletion in Developing Countries', *Population and Development Review*, **9** (4).

Schramm, G., 1985, *Practical Approaches for Estimating Resource Depletion Costs*, Energy Department, World Bank, Washington, DC.

Sfeir-Younis, A., 1985, 'Soil Conservation in Developing Countries', unpublished MS, World Bank, Washington, DC.

Simon, J., 1986, *Theory of Population and Economic Growth*, Blackwell, Oxford.

Simon, J. and Kahn, H., 1984, *The Resourceful Earth*, Blackwell, Oxford.

Southgate, D., 1986, *The Economics of Soil Conservation in the Third World*, Report to World Bank Projects Policy Department, July.

Southgate, D., Hitzhuhen, F. and MacGregor, R., 1984, 'Remedying Third World Soil Erosion Problems', *American Journal of Agricultural Economics*, **66** (5).

Steeds, D., 1985, *Desertification in the Sahelian and Sudanian Zones in West Africa*, World Bank, Washington, DC.

Wilkinson, R.G., 1973, *Poverty and Progress*, Methuen, London. World Resources Institute/IIED, 1986, *World Resources 1986*, Basic Books, New York.

Chapter 6

Alternative Approaches to the Valuation of Environmental Resources

Chris Nash and John Bowers

Introduction and summary

Environmental effects of projects may be very wide-ranging, encompassing effects on production of other commodities utilising environmental resources, on health, amenity and recreational facilities. In some cases, these effects are immediate and well known; in others, they are long-term and subject to great uncertainty. In this chapter, a variety of techniques for valuing such effects are reviewed, of which the most important are revealed preferences, alternative costs and stated preference (or contingent valuation) techniques. The use of option values as a way of taking account of long-run uncertainties is discussed. Finally, current practice in two sectors in which cost–benefit analysis is routinely used — land drainage schemes and transport projects — is briefly reviewed. It is concluded that significant methodological progress has been made in both the development of hedonic price models and of stated preference techniques in the last ten years. Nevertheless, we are far from a situation in which reliable money valuations can be placed on environmental effects and the normal practice in cost–benefit analysis is either to ignore environmental factors or to use a mixture of quantitative and qualitative descriptions in non-money terms. Where irreversible effects of uncertain consequences are involved, it appears that all the literature can do is to warn that a positive benefit/cost ratio does not necessarily mean that the project should go ahead. In these circumstances, cost–benefit analysis should only be used subject to predetermined environmental constraints.

The problem in dealing with environmental effects of projects is threefold. Firstly, environmental effects often have no natural units of measurement. This is particularly true of effects on amenity, which range from air pollution and noise (where a variety of physical indices are available, and the issue is finding one which most directly relates to people's perception of amenity value) to visual amenity (where measures of landscape value are highly subjective). Secondly, valuation usually poses problems. This is because environmental effects are typically both externalities and public goods: they are not sold in any market, and the classic 'public good' problem arises in any attempts to ask for valuation directly. Thirdly, and most seriously, forecasting environmental effects is frequently a matter of great complexity and uncertainty. Understanding of ecosystems is limited, and the project evaluator who expects an ecologist to be able to provide precise forecasts of the long-term environmental effects of his project is likely to be disappointed. One possible effect is extinction of particular environmental resources, be they direct inputs to production processes, types of landscape or plant or animal species. This offers particular problems for assessment since — unless they can be re-created — extinction involves removal of the option of using the resource at any time in the future for production, recreation or scientific or medical research. Of course, extinction is rarely the product of a single project, but rather that of many projects conducted simultaneously in a number of places. Thus there is a need — by no means confined to environmental factors — to reconcile the methods used for appraising individual projects with the need to take a strategic view of the consequence of the totality of all such projects.

The layout of this chapter is as follows. In the next section, we consider some broad methodological issues regarding the treatment of environmental effects in cost–benefit analysis. We then discuss in turn the methodologies available for handling the immediate environmental costs and benefits of projects, and the uncertain longer-term factors. The issue of 'option values' is of course central to the latter task. Finally, we undertake a brief review of the current treatment of environmental effects of projects in practice. Given the enormous literature on the subject, we cannot hope to be comprehensive, but we hope to have covered the main issues and debates and to be able to reach some broad conclusions on the current state of the art.

Some methodological issues

A social cost–benefit analysis is concerned solely with the forecasting and evaluation of the effects of a project upon people whose utility is affected by it. In other words, it starts from the basic value judgement that it is the preferences of individuals that count. Moreover, individuals are assumed to regard environmental resources as commodities, which they would be willing to trade against material possessions. Clearly, then, we are discussing valuation in a limited framework. Animal rights, or a belief in the sanctity of nature, have no place in this discussion. However, such value judgements could be introduced into a cost–benefit analysis in the form of constraints, or environmental standards, which must be met if a project is to proceed at all. Alternative reasons for introducing environmental standards in appraisal might be as a way of dealing with the strategic issues and uncertainties involved in appraising environmental effects. We shall have more to say on this in a later section.

Where valuations are to be based on individual preferences, it would be helpful if economists were in agreement on exactly what is to be measured. Unfortunately, they are not. One school of thought insists that cost–benefit analysis is to be confined to the application of the compensation test. In this case, it is clear that it is the 'willingness to pay' of gainers and the 'required compensation' for losers that are to be measured. Satisfaction of the compensation test enables one to state that if an optimal redistribution of income were possible, and if this redistribution did not change the outcome of the compensation test, then the project should go ahead.

If these conditions are not seen as realistic, then more knowledge of the social welfare function is required, in order to be able to weight costs and benefits according to their distributional impact. This requires that monetary valuations be seen as cardinal utility indicators. The usual procedure is to take either the willingness to pay or the required compensation and to weight it by an estimate of the social marginal utility of income of the person or groups in question. In this case, there is no unanimity on which of the two measures to take; in general, they will only coincide for marginal changes where the income effect may safely be ignored.

In practice, it appears that five different methodologies have been suggested as ways of placing money values on environmental effects. These are as follows:

(a)   *The revealed preference approach*: This relies on finding situations in which consumers have a choice between incurring money expenditure or suffering the ill-effect in question (or not experiencing the effect in the case of positive externalities). For valuing effects experienced in and around the home, the hedonic model of house prices has been very widely used. Wage rate differentials may be used to value environmental effects at work. Where experiencing the effects involves a specific journey for the purpose, demand curves may be estimated by the 'Clawson' technique.

Despite its popularity, this approach has some significant shortcomings. It requires that those under investigation face, and perceive themselves to face, a real choice—failure to allow for constraints on choice or misperception of alternatives can seriously bias the results. Relevant factors must either be measurable in quantitative terms or as dummy variables. Multicollinearity frequently exists between a host of explanatory variables, and mis-specification leading to bias is always a potential problem. Above all, large sample sizes with adequate variation in the explanatory variables are needed, and the results still typically remain imprecise.

(b)   *The alternative cost approach*: A seemingly much simple approach to this problem is to ask what expenditure would be necessary to remove the ill-effect in question. This has been much used in studies of pollution, and is obviously appropriate where the expenditure in question is actually incurred, and does completely remove the externality. Unfortunately, neither of these conditions often holds true. Take the case of double-glazing to remove noise nuisance. Where people are not actually willing to pay the cost of double-glazing, this may overstate the cost of noise to themselves. Indeed, even when they are willing to pay the cost, this may be partly for the other benefits of double-glazing such as heat insulation and security. On the other hand, insulation does not completely solve the problem since it is only effective when the windows are closed and one is inside the building. Thus we do not even know the direction of the bias involved in using double-glazing costs as an estimate of the social cost of noise.

This approach does become much more applicable, however, when environmental constraints are perceived to apply. For here, the expenditure to satisfy the constraint must be incurred if the project is to go ahead. A particularly interesting application of this idea is suggested by Klaassen and Botterweg (1983). They argue for a binding constraint on developments in designated conservation areas in The Netherlands that they should cause no further deterioration in the natural environment. Thus, any habitats lost by developments in one location must be wholly compensated for by development of 'shadow projects' to recreate such habitats elsewhere. An example is given of the creation of a new sand-bar with dunes off the Voorne coast to replace the area lost by the construction of Europoort near Rotterdam. If the environmental constraint is binding, then we have an environmental standard akin in all practical effects to safety standards in structure design. The cost of the shadow project becomes part of the cost of the primary project on which CBA is conducted. If the primary project passes the test and is undertaken, then the shadow project must be undertaken too. If the shadow project is not treated as an environmental standard, then there is no reason to think that its cost bears any particular relationship to the size of the environmental effect it relates to.

(c)   *'Stated preference' techniques*: Many academic economists have been highly suspicious of attempts to produce valuations of effects by means of survey techniques instead of prices in actual markets. The enormous expenditure on market research using these techniques suggests that commercial organisations have few such inhibitions. The advantages of the approach are that it can be used to specify choices between exact sets of circumstances which do not necessarily exist in practice. Because a whole list of rankings of alternatives can be obtained from a single interview, the approach tends to be less costly than revealed preference studies: the transfer price or contingent valuation technique (which asks explicitly for the price at which the respondent would switch from one choice to another) is particularly efficient as it provides a direct measure of the value in question at the individual level. Sample sizes can be correspondingly smaller (Gunn, 1981).

Two main disadvantages of the approach have tended to restrict its use in economic research in the past.

First, there is a belief that people will be unable to answer hypothetical questions accurately. This problem is minimised by making the hypothetical situation as familiar as possible, although this militates against use of the technique in the very circumstances of a currently non-existent situation in which revealed preference techniques are also impossible. It is important to note, however, that complete accuracy in the responses is not required as long as they are unbiased.

Second, there is a fear that people may deliberately or unintentionally bias their responses to hypothetical questions. The most familiar reason for this is 'stragetic' or 'policy response' bias, where the person interviewed seeks to conceal his true preferences in a way which influences the outcome to his own advantage. A succession of studies starting with Bohm (1978) has suggested that this is not, in practice, a great problem. Schulze, d'Arge and Brookshire (1981) also identify 'information bias' and 'instrument bias' as potential sources of problems. The former refers to the fact that a respondent to a hypothetical question may not have adequate information, for instance, on the full range of alternatives open to him. The latter refers to the problem that respondents may have views, for example, about the desirability of raising a particular tax, or that the final answer in a bidding exercise may depend upon the starting-point. Thus the answer obtained may depend on the precise wording of the questions put.

Obviously, all sources of bias can be minimised by careful survey design. Evidence from the transport field suggests that the most accurate and unbiased responses are obtained from repeated rankings of options involving alternative levels of three or four attributes, where the attribute levels are so designed that they both reveal accurately the valuations in question and avoid the most obvious temptations to introduce strategic bias (Bates, 1984). By contrast, the contingent valuation method—as practised in most studies of environmental effects—asks for a single money value for the willingness to pay for a specified benefit or the required compensation for a specified cost. The reason for this is obvious: it would be difficult to devise ranking games which trade off different degrees of environmental intrusion for different levels of, say, taxation and accessibility. Nevertheless, the contingent valuation technique does appear likely, a priori, to be prone to biases. More will be said on the practical experience of the technique in the section on 'Immediate Environmental Effects'.

As with revealed preference techniques, there are severe difficulties in applying stated preference techniques to effects which cannot be measured in quantitative terms and which are not of a simple 'present/not present' nature (for instance, deterioration of the quality of a view). Various devices, ranging from photographs through tape recordings or films to complete 'environmental simulators' have been used to try to overcome this problem.

(d) *Expert opinion*: Sometimes, usually when all else fails, valuation is based on the expressed opinion of people with supposed expertise in the subject at hand. For instance, it has been suggested that the required compensation for injury or death could be based on court awards. Justification of this approach requires that the experts in question be adopting the same value judgements as the project analyst regarding what it is that they are trying to measure, and that they really do have some expert knowledge which makes their estimate of some value. Just because they are required to make such judgements in practice does not necessarily mean that they are able to do so with an acceptable degree of accuracy.

An interesting case of expert valuation arises from the habitat protection provisions of the Wildlife and Countryside Act 1981. The Nature Conservancy Council is empowered to make payments to landholders for loss of income resulting from restrictions on land use, the restrictions and payments being embodied in a management agreement between the parties. The willingness of the Conservancy to enter such an agreement has been taken in some recent appraisals of land drainage projects as indicating that the scientific value of the site, in the view of the Conservancy as the expert body, is at least equal to the cost of the management agreement. Statements by the relative minister that sufficient funds will be available to meet the costs of management agreements could be taken to mean political support for this valuation.

(e) *Political weights*: A further alternative, usually also of the last resort, is to try to obtain 'political' valuations, either by obtaining a direct political decision, or by imputing values from past decisions. As a direct substitute for 'willingness to pay'-type data, this would seem to have little justification. On the other hand, it may be that there are some issues on which people believe that 'moral' preferences should rule, rather than the 'personal' preferences revealed in the market (Harsanji, 1955). Perhaps political leaders are the appropriate people to judge on this issue. Examples of the use of political weights in Great Britain are both the equity value of time and the value attached to pain, grief and suffering in road investment appraisals.

Immediate environmental effects

In this section of the chapter, we consider the literature on the valuation of 'immediate' environmental effects. What we mean by this is effects which are both 'immediate' in time and where the causal chain by which the effect is produced is reasonably well understood. Longer-term, more complex and more uncertain effects are postponed to the following section. Obviously, this distinction is by no means clear-cut, but we consider it to be a useful way of dividing the literature.

Immediate environmental effects may be further categorised as effects on (a) production of other goods; (b) health; (c) amenity; or (d) recreation. Again, these somewhat overlap, particularly in the case of effects on recreational facilities, which may be seen as a combination of effects on production of services and on amenity. However, the distinction is useful in terms of the techniques of analysis typically in use. We consider the evidence on each of these factors in turn, before considering in subsection (e) the comprehensive valuation of natural environments.

(a)   *Production of other goods*: This is the most obvious external effect. Examples are the effect of air or water pollution on crop yields, fisheries, building or plant maintenance costs, or water purification (see, for instance, the reviews by Pearce (1978a) and Turner (1978). Whilst forecasting the magnitude of the effect is a major problem, valuation is usually quite straightforward, since most of the other goods concerned are marketed. However, the usual problems regarding the need to adjust market prices for taxes, subsidies and other distorting factors exist; these are often quite complex, particularly in the common case where subsidised and protected agricultural production is involved (Bowers and Cheshire, 1983), or where tax provisions encourage excessive exploitation of natural resources (Krutilla and Fisher, 1975).

(b)   *Health*: Forecasting the effects of environmental changes on health is similarly a problem. Since pollution, ill-health, poor housing, low socio-economic status and poor medical services are often associated with each other, the use of single equation regression techniques with aggregate data is fraught with danger of specification error leading to biased coefficients. Gerking and Schulze (1981) show how these problems could produce a wholly spurious relationship.

Early work on the valuation of ill-health (and ultimately premature death) concentrated on an accounting approach, which sought to add up the 'cold-blooded' costs of loss of output and provision of health care. What this left out, of course, was the willingness to pay of the victim, his relatives and friends to avoid the pain and suffering of ill-health or death.

'Revealed preference' and 'stated preference' techniques have been used to try to fill this gap; both have their drawbacks. Revealed preference studies have sought real situations in which one incurs an increased probability of sickness or death in return for some other benefit. The usual context has been one of road safety, where driving faster or crossing in a dangerous location saves time (Melinek, 1974; Gosh, Less and Seal 1975). The main problem here is that one needs to know what people's perceptions of the increased risk really are, and whether indeed they perceive it at all or consider the choices open to them. Additionally, the technique is a roundabout one, which presumes that we know sufficiently accurately the person's value of travel time savings.

Discontent with such approaches has led to the use of 'stated preference' techniques in this area. Respondents are asked to choose between coach or air services with different fares and different probabilities of accidental injury or death, other factors being held constant. The approach over-comes both objections to the revealed preference approach, and there seems no particular reason to expect strategic, instrument or information bias to be a problem. Whilst the accuracy with which people can respond to a hypothetical question on a sensitive issue involving very small probabilities must be open to doubt, inaccuracy in itself is not a great problem as long as responses are unbiased. Certainly, a recent unpublished study on behalf of the British Department of Transport has produced sensible answers, using techniques based on the earlier work of Jones-Lee (1976). There is still of course a need to add in costs not borne by the respondent— National Health Service costs, impact of loss of output on others, grief and pain experienced by others.

(c) *Amenity*: Loss of amenity can arise due to noise, air pollution or visual pollution. It can occur at any location—home, work or other—or while travelling by any mode—foot, bicycle, car or public transport. However, most empirical work has been directed to effects either at home or during recreational activities. The latter literature will be considered in the next section.

The emphasis on loss of amenity at home may arise partly because this is seen as the most important location to consider; it also certainly reflects the prevalence of the use of house prices as the basis for valuation. The starting-point for this work was the observation that relative property prices reflect a capitalised valuation of all the advantages of occupying a particular house—physical characteristics, location relative to workplaces, shops and other facilities; and environmental characteristics. Thus, if the effect on house prices of an increase in noise or air pollution could be predicted, *ceteris paribus*, that would be treated as a valuation of the disamenity involved.

Unfortunately, this argument only applies in its crude form if all consumers have the same willingness to pay for the characteristic in question. Otherwise, there is an unknown loss of surplus involved. However, more recent house price work, building on the model of Rosen (1974), has overcome this problem. Rosen shows that the implicit prices of characteristics, derived from a hedonic price equation relating house prices to characteristics, may be used in a second-stage model of the demand for and supply of these characteristics. In general, demand and supply equations need to be estimated simultaneously, but if it is reasonable to assume that the housing stock in the area in question is inherited, and thus determined exogenously, then one may obtain an inverse demand function for characteristics by regressing the implied price for each characteristic for each house on the levels of all characteristics and on the relevant socio-economic determinants of demand. However, there remains some controversy as to whether the assumptions necessary for the model to hold are sufficiently close to reality for the results to be reliable. Key assumptions are:

(i)   that the housing market is in a competitive equilibrium;
(ii)   that moving house is the only way of adjusting the characteristics of the house one lives in;
(iii)   that perceptions of environmental quality are identical between individuals.

All of these are known to be violated in practice. The role of and imperfections in sources of finance, misperceptions and imperfect knowledge and exogenous constraints may lead to serious distortions in the market. Kerry Smith (1977) concludes that we do not yet know how important violations of these assumptions are.

Most of the empirical evidence on the effect on house prices of noise and air pollution is from the United States, and beyond the fact that most of the studies do find a significant relationship, it is hard to generalise on the nature of the results. Walters (1975) asserts that in the case of noise there appears to be a consistent relationship whereby an additional unit of noise nuisance leads to a 0.4–0.7 per cent reduction in house prices. Pearce (1978b), however both challenges Walters's interpretation of the five studies he reviewed and adds a further three to produce a range of 0.2–0.7 per cent. More recent work, using the full Rosen model to estimate the inverse demand curves for attributes, has concentrated on air pollution (Nelson, 1978; Harrison and Rubinfeld, 1978). An interesting exception is that of McLeod (1984), who has used that model to examine the effects of proximity to a neighbourhood park, proximity to a local highway, and presence of a river view in an area of Perth, Western Australia. He finds all these factors to be significant, with a river view commanding a premium of no less than 28 per cent. But without a quantitative measure of the quality of a river view, we cannot say how this premium would be affected by various degrees of visual intrusion. Price (1978) suggests that such a quantitative measure will have to rely on expert judgement. Other factors may also affect the interpretation. Thus a safe view, one where there is no risk of its being blocked by subsequent building would presumably command an 'option value' premium over the same view subject to risk. The use of stated preference techniques for the valuation of disamenity in the home is less well-developed than in the context of recreational facilities, although one of the earliest forms of trade-off analysis—the priority evaluator—was applied to just such a trade-off between access and amenity (Hoinville and Prescott-Clark, 1972). However, Schulze, d'Arge and Brookshire (1981) report a study in which both contingent bidding and the Rosen house price model were applied to the same set of houses in Los Angeles. The former gave an average bid of just under $30 per month for a 30 per cent improvement in air quality, whilst the latter gave a figure of $40. The similarity of these results suggests that one may be able to apply whichever approach appears the most practicable for the problem to hand.

(d) *Recreation*: Projects may create or destroy facilities for recreational activities such as rambling, fishing, nature study or hunting, or they may simply change the value of these environmental services by introducing or eliminating noise, air or water pollution, visual intrusion or changing the population of fish, birds or animals in the area. Evaluation of such effects has been an area of extensive application of both surrogate market and stated preference techniques.

The usual surrogate market approach derives from Clawson's (1959) observation that the price of admission to a recreational facility may be regarded as the sum of any actual admission or parking charges and of the cost of getting there. Thus, the price varies widely over the population according to their location relative to the facility. Observation of trip rates at varying distances from the facility permits a demand curve to be estimated directly from cross-section data.

This sounds very straightforward. However, the literature now contains a host of criticisms of the technique, particularly at its most simplistic. The most important points are:

(i)   Assumed motoring speeds and costs and values of travel time are often a major determinant of the final valuation of benefits. Ideally

these need to be collected directly in the survey or estimated
within the model (Common, 1973; Cheshire and Stabler, 1976).
This is often difficult due to multicollinearity.

(ii)   Households do not only vary in proximity to the site in question,
but also in proximity to substitute and complementary sites. Thus,
the relative quality and cost of using these facilities needs to be
introduced into the demand equation (Everett, 1979). This in turn
raises a need to measure quantitatively the quality of alternative
sites; this is in any case necessary if the technique is to be capable
of producing *ex ante* evaluations of changes in the environment
of sites, or the creation of entirely new ones. A common way
round the problem is to make a heroic assumption that the site will
be of identical value to an existing one (see Krutilla and Fisher,
1975).

(iii)   Many visitors to recreational facilities are combining the journey
with other visits, or simply with a ride in the country (Cheshire and
Stabler, 1976). Thus the imputed value is that of the joint
consumption of these activities.

More recent studies have tried to correct for these problems, but in a
rather arbitrary fashion. For instance, Everett (1979) found that most
people enjoyed the journey to Dalby Forest, so he assumed a zero value of
travel time. This is no solution—the true figure could be positive, zero or
negative. He found that 79 per cent of visitors had come solely to visit the
forest, whilst the rest were 'meanderers', so he simply halved the value
attached to the latter visits. He was particularly concerned with the
valuation of wildlife, so he asked respondents to allocate a score between 0
and 10 to their interest in wildlife. Their consumers' surplus was allocated
to wildlife in proportion to this score.

Given these problems, it is not surprising that this should have been a
fertile area for the application of stated preference techniques to value
directly changes in the quality of sites, such as a reduction in the frequency
of wildlife encounters or the destruction of a view. Perhaps more surprising
is the fact that all the previously published studies of this type of which we
are aware come from North America. As an example of the sort of
quantitative results obtained, Brookshire, Ives and Schulze (1976) found
that visitors to Lake Powell would be willing to pay $700,000 per annum (in
1974 prices) to prevent construction of a power station nearby, an average
of $2.77 per family group.

Schulze, d'Arge and Brookshire (1981) review studies valuing the loss of
amenity due to strip mining, reduction in the quality of a lake environment
due to construction of a power station, loss of long-distance views due to
air pollution, intrusion into a forest area by the development of geothermal

energy resources, and the valuation of changes in the frequency of wildlife encounters. A major concern of their review was with the evidence of bias in these studies. No evidence of significant strategic bias was found in any of the five studies that tested for it. By contrast, information bias was found in one study out of three, starting-point bias in one study out of four, and instrument bias in two out of three. Clearly, survey design is therefore very important, and the findings regarding instrument bias (which imply that respondents' declared willingness to pay depends, for instance, on whether the method of payment is property tax or a sales tax) are worrying. The presence of starting-point bias in one case is also of concern; the simple way round the problem is to permit open-ended responses, but other writers conclude that this leads to a less accurate response. It must also be said that some of the tests of bias are themselves weak and open to question. Nevertheless, the results may be regarded as reasonably encouraging, and do suggest that a well-designed stated preference experiment can provide at least order-of-magnitude estimates of recreational and amenity costs and benefits.

(e)   *Comprehensive valuation of natural environments*: Natural environments may be valued for any or all of the above four reasons. In this section we discuss some attempts that have been made at their comprehensive valuation.

There is a considerable volume of literature seeking to value natural environments as the capitalised stream of anticipated user benefits. Much of this work relates to the United States and is frequently concerned with wetlands. It has involved a number of the approaches discussed above. The UK counterpart to this literature is the cost–benefit analyses carried out by and for Water Authorities and Internal Drainage Boards of land drainage schemes. Many UK wetlands are at best semi-natural environments subject to some form of pastoral agriculture and the net output of the unimproved agriculture appears as the opportunity cost of land improvement. Since US wetlands are typically not of this form, user benefits are less obvious.

Several studies have viewed wetlands as inputs in production functions for fisheries. Batie and Wilson (1979) relate food supplies for oyster fisheries linearly to the acreage of adjacent saltmarsh and use wetland acreage as a factor input in a Cobb-Douglas production function for oyster catches. Wetland value is then discounted total factor product. A similar but more sophisticated study is Lynne, Conray and Prochaska (1981) on the role of wetland areas in the blue crab fisheries of the Gulf of Florida. This study models the population dynamics of the blue crab and makes the maximum sustainable yield population a function of the area of wetland available. In conjunction with fishing effort variables this determines yields.

A more wide-ranging approach to valuation is Gupta and Foster (1975) on the benefits of freshwater wetlands in Massachusetts. The authors identify four categories of benefit: wildlife services; visual–cultural (encompassing recreational, educational and aesthetic benefits); water supply; and flood control. The first two categories are measured by finding the prices that government agencies pay to purchase land for conservation. The maximum price paid is assumed to prevail for the highest quality land and prices for lower grades are obtained by scaling according to an 'expert' index of quality: an index based on ecological criteria for wildlife and one based on assessment by landscape architects for visual–cultural services. With wildlife services it is assumed that State and Federal agencies recoup their expenditure by the sale of sporting licences, so that purchase price is capitalised returns from lease of sporting rights. Consumer surplus is thus omitted. The valuation of wildlife sites from their sporting value is well developed and with a large literature (see, for example, Hammack and Brown (1974) and is an element in the famous Hell's Canyon Study (Krutilla and Fisher 1975), but it clearly only encompasses one of the benefits yielded by wildlife.

The land prices used by Gupta and Foster are those paid by town councils for wetlands as public open space. Purchases have to be approved by a simple majority of the electorate but are grant-aided by the Federal or State authorities. If total expenditure gross of grant equals the present value of consumer benefits, this can only be by accident.

For the remaining two categories of water supply and flood control, Gupta and Foster resort to the cost of alternative provision with the difficulties and objections already discussed. This approach is also used for another alleged user benefit of wetlands, the control of non-point pollution (essentially the run-off of agricultural chemicals). An appraisal of this literature is Park and Batie (1979), where the suggested alternative is the modification of agricultural practices and the wetland value is thus the present value of foregone agricultural net product. Apart from the usual points that the benefit of wetland for water quality control may exceed or fall short of the cost of alternative provision and the difficulties of measuring the social value of agricultural output, considerable doubt exists on whether wetlands do perform a pollution control function. If they do, their ecosystems are likely to be modified thereby.

There is a growing literature on the valuation of non-marketed user benefits of nature reserves and similar natural environments, many of which are assessed and surveyed in Shaw and Zube (1980). The Clawson technique is obviously as applicable here as with any other form of recreation and no more need be said on the subject. The alternative is stated preference techniques aiming by questionnaire to determine individuals' compensating and equivalent variations for wildlife sites and wildlife resources. This is one of the techniques for determining sporting values of wildlife reserves but it has also been used for consumer benefits of observation of natural history (e.g. Shulze, d'Arge and Brookshire, 1981; Walsh, Loomis and Gillman, 1984). The literature has identified some sources of benefits other than anticipated consumer surplus. Apart from option value discussed in the next section, an existence value has been identified—a willingness to pay for the knowledge that an environment is protected even though use is not anticipated. Whether this source of benefit is really distinct from other consumer benefits is questionable, given that even though the individual may have no expectation or intention of actually seeing a blue whale or the Camargue he may expect to view these things on television. It seems highly likely that existence demand is stimulated by television, but is the existence demand a demand for a consumer benefit via this medium? The other value identified is the bequest value defined as a willingness to pay for the satisfaction derived from endowing future generations. This is clearly a user benefit and one that has long been recognised in economics.

More unorthodox approaches have also been tried. An unusual and original way of assessing wetland value, and applicable equally to any other form of habitat, is that of Gosselink, Odum and Pope (1974), who estimate the 'life-support' value of marshes. The approach is to calculate the energy output from primary production in an acre of marshland and to scale this by the ratio of GNP to energy consumption—the inverse of the average amount of energy produced per dollar of GNP—then to discount to determine present value. Using this methodology the authors estimated a price per acre of marshland of $82,000 at 1970 prices. In a critique of this approach Shabman and Batie (1978) apply the technique to the valuation of lay land in Virginia. They reach a value of $6,969 per acre at a time when the price of farmland including buildings was $556 per acre! The 'life-support' proponents are aware of this problem. In defence of a similar high valuation of an acre of forest Odum and Odum (1972) state:

This value may be regarded as somewhat inflated by egocentric man, since he might not consider all the work done by a forest as useful to man. However we believe it comes closer to the real value than conventional cost-accounting which values forests only in terms of yield of wood . . . and ignores its life-support values. [p. 184]

Shabman and Batie show that the calculation is based on some fundamental misunderstandings of the nature of markets and principles of economics. It would make sense only in a world where the objective was to maximise output of energy regardless of whether it could be utilised and where all other inputs including labour were treated as free goods.

Uncertainty and long-term environmental effects

Where projects entail the destruction or substantial modification of natural environments, the analyst is presented with a peculiarly intractable problem whose essentials may be adumbrated as follows:

(i)   Eco-systems are complex and their dynamics imperfectly understood. Hence the longer-term consequences of modifications of natural environments are often unknown. An analogous case in the field of health concerns the long-term effects to the individual and even, genetically, to future generations, of exposure to chemicals or radiation.

(ii)   With current technology effects are irreversible.

(iii) Apart from short-term user benefit the value of retention of existing ecosystems and the existing degree of ecological diversity to human populations is unclear. Man is currently and has long been a major modifier of the biosphere.

(iv)   But in any case, there is a severe practical problem in determining the value of any particular community of plants and animals to the system as a whole.

Consider a project that will destroy an example of a scarce habitat containing a community of plants and animals some of which are confined to that habitat type. In destroying that example of habitat, the risk of the loss of the habitat type as a whole with the consequential loss of the species that are specific to it is thereby increased, unless those species are able to adapt to new habitats at a sufficiently rapid rate. The risk of extinction is negatively related to the number of surviving examples of the habitat and to the risk of destruction of each example provided these latter risks are independent, which, whether the source of risk is 'natural' or the result of human action, they may not be. In Western Europe the problem is probably more frequently posed as one of the area of habitat type rather than the number of isolated examples of it. The minimum area required for viability is frequently not known but 'island effects', the fact that below a threshold size an isolated habitat may deteriorate to extinction even though it is protected from man-made threats to it, are recognised. In the case of tropical forests it has been argued (Myers, 1984) that the specificity of habitat types is such that almost all acts of felling result in the extinction of plant and animal species, some probably never to be known to science. Threats from habitat loss can exist even for species which are mobile and utilise a range of, for them, interdependent habitats. Thus the Nature Conservancy Council argued in a public inquiry on a reclamation of part of the Wash that the reclamation placed at risk species of Arctic breeding waders, whose breeding habitat was abundant but which depended for survival on a limited amount of temperature inter-tidal feeding zones during winter or migration periods.

But if it can be predicted with reasonable confidence that a project would render extinct certain plants and animals, how should this be viewed? What is the value of their continued existence, over and above any direct 'user benefits' of the type discussed in the previous section? Within the confines of cost–benefit analysis, and ignoring ethical arguments about the right of animals and plants to exist, there are two arguments. The first concerns the importance of the genetic pool. It is argued (Myers, 1984) that natural plants and animals provide a major source if not *the* major source of developments in pharmaceuticals, in the development of new foods, and in the sustainment of productivity in agriculture, by providing sources of pesticides and agents of biological control and species for cross-breeding to improve existing strains. One example cited frequently concerns the discovery of a perennial corn in Mexico which if successfully introduced commercially would result in large savings in ground preparation and reseeding in cereal production (Vietmeyer, 1979). A more mundane and domestic example is that a producer of grass seeds is paying premium rates to take hay from a nature reserve, which provides a source of seeds of scarce grass types that it needs for its research and development of higher yielding agricultural varieties.

The second argument is that species are useful as components of ecosystems providing basic physical and biological support for life; controlling quality of the atmosphere and climate, water quality, waste-disposal and maintaining of soil quality. This second argument is unlikely to be significant for scarce species or ecosystems, although it may be relevant to the rapid depletion of currently abundant habitats such as tropical rain forests (Myers, 1984).

The central argument is, therefore, that there is a finite probability that a particular species dependent on a particular range of habitat types may prove the source of a major development in human welfare. Its elimination may thus deprive humanity of the opportunity of some technological breakthough in the treatment of disease, or the production of the means of life. The size of this probability, that future generations will have need of the genetic material embodied in any particular species or community of species threatened with extinction, is unknown, of course, but presumably is very small. The risks are probably higher in tropical rain forests than in any other type of habitat since they contain such a large proportion of the earth's life forms—40 per cent of all species inhabiting 7 per cent of the earth's surface—and, if the various studies are properly representative, have provided the natural source for a large proportion of the major developments in pharmaceuticals, agriculture, chemicals, etc.

(Presumably, the risk of loss of useful genetic material per hectare destroyed is greater for tropical forest than for any other type of habitat. Whether the risk of loss per species destroyed is greater for tropical forests is unclear. It may be that the West has 'mined' its genetic materials so that what remains unexploited is unlikely ever to be of use while tropical forests contain virgin veins. From a national rather than a global viewpoint, of course, the poverty of species in temperate regions gives each a scarcity value.)

The theoretical basis for valuing these possibilities rests in the notion of option value. It is now well established that where development is irreversible, uncertainty over the future value of undeveloped land— provided there is a finite probability that land in its undeveloped state will yield more utility than it would when developed—will lead rational utility maximising individuals to conserve more undeveloped land, that is to develop at a slower rate, than would be the case if that uncertainty, or the irreversibility, were removed.

The implied premium attached to retaining the option to future benefits from undeveloped land is called the option value. A positive option value will exist even with risk neutrality, provided that more information about benefits can be expected to accrue with the passage of time and that information is not dependent on current decisions on whether or not to develop.

As originally presented (Weisbrod, 1964), the notion of option value was no more than a risk premium, which could arise from a large variety of forms of uncertainty other than the specific technological uncertainty discussed earlier in this section. Thus both the size and the sign of an option value would depend on the cause of the uncertainty and on the degree of risk aversion of the individual in question. Schmalensee argues that when the issue is uncertainty about future tastes, option value may be positive or negative, but the best one can do in practice is to assume it to be zero (Schmalensee, 1972). Freeman (1984) shows the issue to be basically one of whether the marginal utility of income is higher or lower in the state of the world in which the option to consume the good is exercised. For cases of demand resulting from uncertainty about future incomes or the prices of related goods, he suggests that option values are most likely to be large in cases of uncertainty about future income, in which case the option value for someone who is risk-averse is negative. However, this is assuming that the good will only be consumed in the case in which future incomes are high. Many of the cases for option values discussed in the environmental economics literature concern options which will only be exercised in the face of some calamity resulting in low incomes. Thus, for instance, a risk-averse individual who was uncertain as to whether his income would ever permit him to visit a tropical rain forest would have a negative option value for the consumption benefits of such a visit—his willingness to pay for the option would be below his expected consumer's surplus. Conversely, a risk-averse individual considering the availability of a new resource (e.g. a strain of rice) which he would only need at a time of acute famine would have a positive option value. In other words, this definition of option value stresses the importance of preserving resources which may be needed if future events turn out badly (in terms of reduced incomes or lack of availability of alternative resources), rather than resources which will only be needed if incomes rise sufficiently to generate the demand. To this extent, the emphasis in practical research on option values on recreational rather than production benefits may be misplaced. However, in terms of the tractability of the problem, it is easy to see how this emphasis has come about.

Where the uncertainty concerns the supply of an environmental resource, the value of which is certain, there seems to be greater unanimity that a risk-averse individual will have a positive option value (Smith, 1985). Thus projects which put at risk the survival, for instance, of species of known recreational or scientific value should not necessarily go ahead even if the expected value of their benefits exceeds the expected value of their costs.

The above conclusions relate to a world in which a single decision for or against conservation has to be made at a given point in time. The notion of option value as being associated with the benefits of keeping options open lends itself more naturally to a framework of sequential decision-taking in which decisions may be deferred. In this alternative interpretation, optional value (often termed a quasi-option value) represents a conditional value of information: 'the gain from being able to learn about the future that would be precluded by development if one does not develop initially' (Fisher and Haveman, 1985). While this will be positive even with risk neutrality, its absolute size will vary with the degree of risk aversion, with the time horizon over which decisions are taken, with the nature and degree of time preference, and with the probability density function of outcomes, i.e. with the perceived probability of land in its undeveloped state becoming more valuable than land which has been developed.

The expositions of the concept in the literature relate to simple, two-period decision frameworks with known probability density functions. This is of course far removed from the problem as we have explained it. It is not clear when, if ever, the additional information will be forthcoming, nor what possible use the genetic material affected could have, far less the probability of it being needed. In these circumstances there would appear little possibility for the estimation of option value via desktop study. Various writers (Fisher and Haveman, 1985; Henry, 1974) have produced tables showing how option value could be calculated and how it would vary with given parameter values, but these are simply arbitrary numbers.

One possible means of valuation of option values would be a market solution, by identifying the industrial companies who in, for instance, pharmaceuticals, food technology, or pest control conduct research on genetic materials; and discovering what they would be prepared to pay to conserve genetic pools in the form of natural and semi-natural habitat. In a stimulating article, Brown and Swierzbinski (1985) show that under any market structure private producers will conserve less than the socially optimum volume of genetic material. Most would be conserved under conditions of monopoly, but even then under most assumptions too little will be conserved.

In practice, attempts at measuring option value have used the contingent valuation approach. A pioneering study was that of Greenley, Walsh and Young (1981), which considered willingness to pay to prevent pollution of a river by mining activity for a given time period. The sum of option, bequest and existence values was found to exceed direct user benefits. Unfortunately, no serious attempt was made to control or test for strategic bias and there was clear evidence of instrument bias, hypothetical payment being four times as high in the form of a sales tax as in water charges. Furthermore it has been questioned (Freeman, 1984) whether the authors' questionnaire properly distinguished option value from expected consumer surplus, the combination of the two being normally termed 'option price'.

A more rigorous study was that of Brookshire, Eubanks and Randall (1983). This explicitly sought to measure an option price for the possibility of hunting grizzly bears and bighorn sheep in Wyoming. Since the contingent valuation method was applied to the sale of licences to hunt, this was effectively converted to a private good, thus minimising strategic bias. A substantial willingness to pay was estimated, but no attempt was made to partition this between expected consumer surplus and option value.

Such an attempt was made in the study by Walsh, Loomis and Gillman (1984). They asked a sample of 218 households what they would be willing to pay to preserve, or to extend to a specified degree, the wilderness status of an area of Colorado. They then asked respondents to allocate this sum between expected consumer surplus, option value, existence value and bequest value. Again, the sum of the last three was of the same order of magnitude as direct user benefits; option value alone was more than 25 per cent of the user benefit figure. Obviously this approach has the merit of avoiding double-counting, but it does seem to require a thorough understanding by those being surveyed of some subtle distinctions.

These studies are all attempting to measure private rather than social option values. If private individuals possess a higher degree of risk aversion than is appropriate for society the estimates will be biased upwards.

Conversely, if the social discount rate is less than private discount rates they will be biased downwards. It is also clear that the option values calculated do not relate to the risks of foregoing major advances in human welfare as a result of loss of genetic capital or threat to welfare from disruption of life-support services; rather they relate to the more limited notion of option value of Weisbrod, and are measures of the willingness of consumers to pay to preserve the option of known consumption possibilities. Nonetheless, this element represents a substantial supplement to consumption benefits of wildlife sites even though these are typically small compared with development benefits.

Where the sites concerned have other producer benefits another element of option value might also be estimated. An interesting article by Hodge (1984) relates the necessary premium of development over preservation benefits to the probability of changes in relative prices attached to development and preservation and shows that, even with no expected change in price relatives, a fairly modest degree of variability around the mean yields a substantial option value. For a social discount rate of 5 per cent and a 20-year decision period the premium of development over preservation benefits necessary to make development the preferred option is about 25 per cent. An identification of alternative uses of wildlife sites and an investigation of the likely variance of prices and production costs for these options might thus be a useful exercise. It would provide only a component of option value in the sense that the genetic pool arguments rest on possible uses currently unknown. These contingencies can only be dealt with in the current state of knowledge by administrative rules designed to protect the genetic stock from possible losses. The Wildlife and Countryside Act 1981 is such a system, although it does not contain an absolute block on damaging development where state agencies or state departments are involved in development. The proposals for shadow projects discussed above (Klaassen and Botterweg, 1983) would provide a stronger safeguard. An attempt at identifying all the options that would be closed by a proposed irreversible development, while limited clearly by current knowledge, might be a move in the direction of more rational decision-making.

Methods used in practice

The studies referred to in previous sections have largely been in the nature of methodological research rather than designed to provide relevant inputs for practical decision-taking. How much have such techniques contributed in the practical appraisal of projects? The answer seems to be not much.

Two areas in which cost–benefit analysis is routinely applied to projects with significant environmental impact are land drainage schemes and transport infrastructure projects. In the former, the principal quantified factors are capital and operating costs and the value of agricultural output. In the latter, the factors are capital and operating costs, time savings and savings in accidents. In neither case are environmental effects valued in money terms.

The most common approach in drainage projects is still to ignore environmental effects (Bowers, 1983). Sometimes a separate environmental impact assessment (EIA) is undertaken. Whereas in the past there has been no British requirement for this, there is now an EEC directive (not yet implemented in Britain) similar to that in the United States requiring EIAs to be undertaken for specified types of project. An EIA is generally a mixture of qualitative and quantitative information. The latter may be cardinal (number of species on a site) or ordinal (grades of agricultural land).

Obviously, a well-designed environmental impact assessment provides valuable information for the decision-taker. However, the approach relies heavily on ad hoc judgement both in the selection of effects for inclusion and in weighing their relative magnitudes. Little guidance is provided on how these effects can be traded off against quantified costs and benefits in the appraisal.

Within the transport sector, one major study which did attempt to go beyond this was that of the Third London Airport (Commission on the Third London Airport, 1971). The study included a mixture of valuations from surrogate markets (house price depreciation), stated preference techniques (on the compensation necessary for loss of one's home), and alternative costs (e.g. fire insurance values). Unfortunately, at the time of the study these techniques were less well-developed than they are today, and the crudity of many of the applications served to provoke strong attacks on the application of cost–benefit analysis to such issues (Self, 1970). Thus when environmental issues again came to the fore in the appraisal of trunk-road schemes, what was recommended was not an attempt to include these factors in the formal cost–benefit analysis. Rather, an assessment of alternatives using a 'framework' of some eighty different pieces of information, in a variety of units and including some verbal description (Leitch, 1977), is now required for all trunk-road schemes. These include an NPV computed from the time, accident and operating cost savings of the scheme as against capital and maintenance costs.

As with a separate environmental impact assessment, the problem remains of how the decision-taker is to trade off the various effects measured in a variety of units. There is a danger that the EIA is seen as a hurdle through which the project must pass, rather than as contributing to an understanding of the relative value of different projects. For instance, in the case of road schemes, a 1977 Department of Transport discussion paper stated: 'Although there is often some implicit regard for environmental factors in choice of alternative schemes it is rarely that the location, suitably landscaped, which optimises operational benefit is not chosen (at least not deliberately)' (Jefferson, 1977). Despite the subsequent introduction of the Leitch framework, it is our impression that the computed NPV remains overwhelmingly important at the scheme selection state, and that the full framework is seen as relevant—if at all—only in choosing between options for a particular scheme. It is noteworthy that DTp can sanction implementation of a scheme with a positive NPV which has environmental disbenefits, whilst it needs Treasury approval before it can proceed with a scheme with a negative NPV but environmental benefits. The same is true of the Ministry of Agriculture, Fisheries and Food with respect to land drainage projects.

Conclusion

The valuation of environmental effects in cost–benefit analysis has made great progress in the last ten years. This progress has come from two main sources. The first is the development of more rigorous empirical models of surrogate markets, building on the theoretical foundations laid by Rosen (1974). The second is the progress in refining and testing stated preference techniques in a wide range of areas. Within a limited range of circumstances, both techniques now seem capable of providing reasonable valuations. Nevertheless, we are still a long way from being able to provide accurate and consistent monetary estimates of all the items of environmental costs and benefits that are likely to be of importance in practical studies.

But it is in dealing with uncertainties in forecasting effects that the greatest problems remain. Even in fairly direct effects, such as forecasting the effect of changes in air pollution levels on mortality, we have had to report uncertainty as to whether a statistically significant relationship exists. Forecasting the effect, for instance, of destruction of habitats and the likelihood that species lost would have been of substantial benefit in medical or agricultural developments, is simply beyond our capabilities. Whilst the method of 'option values' measurement has been developed to the stage where it may be used to provide a rough estimate of private willingness to pay to retain the option of future user benefits, we know of no way of measuring option values in this broader context. Thus the literature can do little more than warn that one should be very wary of undertaking projects with irreversible effects of this type, even when a conventional cost–benefit analysis would indicate that it is desirable to proceed with the project. In these circumstances, it would seem appropriate to require that cost–benefit analysis be used to choose between alternatives only within a choice set bounded by some sensibly chosen environmental constraints.

References

Bates, J. 1984, 'Values of Time from Stated Preference Data', Planning and Transportation Research and Computation, Summer Annual Meeting.

Batie, S.S. and Wilson, J.R., 1979, 'Economic Values Attributable to Virginia's Coastal Wetlands and Inputs in Oyster Production', Research Division Bulletin No. 150, Dept. of Agricultural Economics, Virginia Polytechnic Institute and State University, Blacksburg, Va.

Bohm, P., 1978, 'Estimating Demand for Public Good: An Experiment', *European Economic Review*, 3.

Bowers, J.K., 1983, 'Cost–Benefit Analysis of Wetland Drainage', *Environment and Planning*, Series A, 15 (2).

Bowers, J.K. and Cheshire, P.C., 1983, *Agriculture, the Countryside and Land-Use: An Economic Critique*, Methuen, London.

Brookshire, D.S., Eubanks, L.S., and Randall, A., 1983, 'Estimating Option Prices and Existence Values for Wildlife Resources', *Land Economics*, 59 (1).

Brookshire, D., Ives, B. and Schulze, W., 1976, 'The Valuation of Aesthetic Preferences', *Journal of Environmental Economics and Management*, 3 (4).

Brown Jr., G.M. and Swierzbinski, J., 1985, 'Endangered Species, Genetic Capital and Cost-Reducing R & D', in Hall, D., Myers N. and Margaris, N.S. (eds), *Economics of Ecosystem Management*, Dr. W. Junk Publishers, Dordrecht.

Cheshire, P.C. and Stabler, M.J., 1976, 'Joint Consumption Benefits in Recreational Site Surplus: An Empircal Estimate', *Regional Studies*, 10.

Clawson, M., 1959, *Methods of Measuring Demand for and Value of Outdoor Recreation*, RFF Reprint No. 10, Resources for the Future Inc., Washington, DC.

Commission on the Third London Airport, 1971, *Report*, HMSO, London.

Common, M.S., 1973, 'A Note on the Use of the Clawson Method for Evaluation of Recreation Site Benefits', *Regional Studies*, 7.

Everett, R.D., 1979, 'The Monetary Value of the Recreational Benefits of Wildlife', *Journal of Environmental Management*, 8.

Fisher, A.C. and Haveman, W.M., 1985, 'Endangered Species: The Economics of Irreversible Damage', in Hall, D., Myers, N. and Marjaris, N.S. (eds), *Economics of Ecosystem Management*, op. cit.

Freeman III, A.M., 1984, 'The Sign and Size of Option Values', *Land Economics*, 60 (1).

Gerking, S., and Schulze, W., 1981, 'What Do We Know About Benefits of Reduced Mortality from Air Pollution Control?', *American Economic Review*, **71**, Proceedings of the 93rd Annual Meeting of the American Economic Association.

Gosh, D., Lees, D. and Seal, W., 1975, 'Optimal Motorway Speed and Some Values of Time and Life', *Manchester School of Economic and Social Studies*, 43.

Gosselink, J.G., Odum, E.P. and Pope, R.M., 1974, 'The Value of the Tidal Marsh', Centre for Wetland Resources, Louisiana State University, Baton Rouge, La.

Greenley, D.A., Walsh, R.G. and Young, R.A., 1981, 'Option Value: Empirical Evidence from a Case Study of Recreation and Water Quality', *Quarterly Journal of Economics*, (4).

Gunn, H., 1981, 'Value of Time Estimation? Working Paper 157, Institute for Transport Studies, University of Leeds.

Gupta, T.R. and Foster, J.H., 1975, 'Economic Criteria for Freshwater Wetland Policy in Massachusetts', *American Journal of Agricultural Economics*, **57** (1).

Hammack, J. and BrownJr., G.M., 1974, *Waterfowl and Wetlands: Toward Bioeconomic Analysis*, Baltimore, Johns Hopkins University Press.

Harrison, D. and Rubinfeld, D.L., 1978, 'Hedonic Housing Prices and the Demand for Clean Air', *Journal of Environmental Economics and Management*, **5**.

Harsanyi, J.C., 1955, 'Cardinal Welfare: Individualistic Ethics and Interpersonal Comparisons of Utility', *Journal of Political Economy*, **73**.

Henry, C., 1974, 'Option Values in the Economics of Irreplaceable Assets', *Review of Economic Studies Symposium on the Economics of Exhaustible Resources*, Special Issue.

Hodge, I.D., 1984, 'Incertainty, Irreversibility and the Loss of Agricultural Land', *Journal of Agricultural Economics*, **35** (2).

Hoinville, G. and Prescott-Clarke, P., 1972, 'Traffic Disturbance and Amenity Values', *Social and Community Planning Research Document* 214, London.

Jefferson, J.R. (Chairman), 1977, 'Route Location with Regard to Environmental Issues: Report of a Working Party', Discussion Paper No. 10, *Monetary Evaluation, Department of Transport, London*.

Jones-Lee, M., 1976, The Value of Life: An Economic Analysis, Martin Robertson, Oxford.

Klaassen, L.H. and Botterweg, T.H., 1983, 'Project Evaluation and Intangible Effects: A Shadow Price Approach', *Études du Cémagref*, **7**.

Krutilla, J.V. and Fisher, A.C., 1975, *The Economics of Natural Environments*, Resources for the Future Inc., Washington, DC.

Leitch, Sir George (Chairman), 1977, *Report of the Advisory Committee on Trunk Road Assessment*, HMSO, London.

Lynne, G.D., Conray, P. and Prochaska, F.J., 1981, 'Economic Valuation of Marsh Areas for Marine Production Processes', *Journal of Environmental Economics and Management*, **8**.

McLeod, P.B., 1984, 'The Demand for Local Amenity: A Hedonic Price Index Approach', *Environment and Planning*, Series A, **16**.

Melinek, S.J., 1974, 'A Method of Evaluating Human Life for Economics Purposes', *Accident Analysis and Prevention*, **6**.

Myers, N., 1984, *The Primary Source: Tropical Forests and Our Future*, W.W. Norton and Co., London.

Nelson, J.P., 1978, 'Residential Choice, Hedonic House Prices and the Demand for Clear Air', *Journal of Environmental Economics and Management*, **5**.

Odum, E.P. and Odum, H.T., 1972, 'Natural Areas as Necessary Components of Man's Total Environment', *Transactions of the North American Wildlife and Natural Resources Conference*.

Park, W.M. and Batie, S.S., 1979, 'Methodological Issues Associated with Estimation of the Economic Value of Coastal Wetlands in Improving Water Quality', Sea Grant Project Paper VPI-SG-79-09, Dept. of Agricultural Economics, Virginia Polytechnic Institute and State University, Blacksburg, Va.

Pearce, D.W., 1978a, 'Air Pollution', in Pearce, D.W. (ed.), *The Valuation of Social Cost*, George Allen and Unwin, London.

———— 1978b, 'Noise Nuisance', in Pearce, D.W. (ed.), ibid.

Price, C., 1978, *Landscape Economics*, MacMillan, London.

Rosen, S., 1974, 'Hedonic Prices and Implicit Markets', *Journal of Political Economy*, **82**.

Schmalensee, R., 1972, 'Option Demand and Consumer Surplus: Valuing Price Changes Under Uncertainty', *American Economic Review*, **62** (4).

Schulze, W.D., d'Arge, R.C. and Brookshire, D.S., 1981, 'Valuing Environmental Commodities: Some Recent Experiments', *Land Economics*, **57** (2).

Self, P., 1970, 'Nonsense on Stilts: The Futility of Roskill', *Political Quarterly*, July.

Shabman, L.A. and Batie, S.S., 1978, 'Economic Value of Natural Coastal Wetlands: A Critique', *Coastal Zone Management Journal*, 4 (3).

Shaw, W.S. and Zube, E.H., 1980, 'Wildlife Values Centre for Assessment of Non-Commodity Natural Resource Values', Report No. 1, University of Arizona, Tucson, Ariz.

Smith, V.K., 1977, 'Residential Location and Environmental Amenities: A Review of the Evidence', *Regional Studies*, **11**.

Smith, V.K., 1983, 'Option Value: A Conceptual Overview', *Southern Economic Journal*, **49** (3).

Smith, V.K., 1985, 'Supply Uncertainty, Option Price and Indirect Benefit Estimation', *Land Economics*, **61** (3).

Turner, R.K., 1978, 'Water Pollution', in Pearce, D.W. (ed.), op. cit.

Vietmeyer, N.D., 1979, 'A Wild Relative May Give Corn Perennial Genes', *Smithsonian*, **10** (1).

Walsh, R.G., Loomis, J.B. and Gillman, R.A. 1984, 'Valuing Option Existence and Beques Demands for Wilderness', *Land Economics*, **60** (1).

Walters, A.A., 1975, *Aircraft Noise and Prices*, Oxford University Press, London.

Weisbrod, B.A., 1964, 'Collective-Consumption Services of Individualised Consumption Goods', *Quarterly Journal of Economics*, **78** (3).

Part 2
Sustainable Growth and Development Practice

Chapter 7

Towards a Second Green Revolution: From Chemicals to New Biological Techniques in Agriculture in the Tropics for Sustainable Development

S. Ghatak*

Introduction and summary

In Charles Darwin's characterisation of the association between species and environment, the economic and technological nexus figured prominently. The survival of species is conditioned by the flexibility and appropriateness of biotechnology (BT) for different environmental conditions. Given that natural mutation processes were continually producing new genetic variations in living matter, i.e. new bio-technology, 'there was a natural sorting out of the fittest for each environmental niche' (Evenson, 1984). However, mankind over centuries has created a social and economic system of plant and animal husbandry. The natural system has therefore been altered to create more wealth and 'welfare'. As new types of crops developed, pests and parasites had to find new environments in which to survive.

The process of developing new crops has been related to research and development (R. & D.) expenditure (see Table 7.1). Developed countries (DCs) have large comparative advantages in most crop and animal production. For most crops at the beginning of the 1950s (when many Asian and African countries began to acquire political freedom), yields per acre of land were higher in temperate zone countries. This was due to two main reasons: (a) a higher proportion of spending on agricultural R. & D. (i.e. R. & D. expenditure as a proportion of the total value of the agricultural product); (b) a significant difference in the use of agricultural chemicals (like fertilizers, pesticides, insecticides and herbicides) in producing crops between the DCs and less developed countries (LDCs). In fact, even in the 1950s, despite the availability of a menu of advanced agro-technologies, little of it was transferred to the LDCs.

* I thank Professor M.S. Swaminathan, Kerry Turner, Derek Deadman and Fawzi Khatib for all their help. The remaining errors are mine.

Table 7.1   Relation of world expenditures on agricultural research to the value of agricultural product by income group

Group	Per capita income (US dollars)	1971 total	(Public)[†]	1974 total	(Public)[†]
		Percentage of total and public research expenditures to value of agricultural produce*			
I	1,750	2.48	(1.44)	2.55	(1.48)
II	1,001–1,750	2.34	(1.76)	2.34	(1.83)
III	401–1,000	1.13	(0.86)	1.16	(0.92)
IV	150– 400	0.84	(0.71)	1.01	(0.84)
V	150	0.70	(0.65)	0.67	(0.62)

Source: Adapted from Boyce and Evenson (1975).

*   Total expenditures include: (1) national public agriculture; (2) national public agriculture-related; (3) industry; and (4) international. Excludes People's Republic of China.
†   National public agriculture (national public agriculture-related is not included).

In this chapter, I will first examine the causes of the Green Revolution (GR) in LDCs. Next, I will analyse the need for new technology in tropical agriculture for achieving 'sustainable growth'. Accepting the techno-centrist world-view as set out in Chapter 1, the concept of sustainable growth will be examined closely within a simple theoretical model. Next, the case for using the BT in tropical agriculture will be analysed. An attempt will be made to evaluate the economic use of azolla production in a developing country (i.e. the Philippines). Then I will discuss the use of BT in underdeveloped agriculture within an Integrated Pest Management programme. The case of using herbicides will also be considered. Some alternatives to chemical plant protection will be discused. Finally, some constraints on the application of BT in underdeveloped agriculture will be indicated.

The Green Revolution in LDCs

The mid-1960s ushered in the period of Green Revolution (GR) in many LDCs in Asia and Latin America. The reasons for the GR are well documented (see Ghatak, 1986; Ghatak and Ingersent, 1984; Mellor, 1976; Ranadhawa, 1974; Hayami and Ruttan, 1984). Both demand and supply factors played important roles. On the demand side, population growth, rising income and demand for food were important in increasing the pressure on land. On the supply side, natural disasters like drought and flood, and the lack of modern inputs and water supply, simply aggravated the all-too-familiar problems of decline in food supply, distribution, poverty and famine (Sen, 1981). In the end, 'necessity became the mother of invention'. The new technology that was successfully used in tropical agriculture encompassed: (a) 'miracle' seeds, thanks to Borlaug and his team of researchers (e.g. IR-8 in wheat and rice, and dwarf varieties to withstand different types of environment stress); (b) chemical fertilisers (particularly nitrogen, phosphorous and potash); (c) pesticides and insecticides to offer protection from the attack of brown hopper pests; (d) machinery, tractors and harvesters. The yield curve in the agricultural sectors of less developed countries began to shift upwards in the late 1960s and early 1970s.

However, it was soon realised in the industrialised countries that all the 'know-how' of the DCs ('all the King's men and all the King's horses'), including most kinds of agro-technology—better seeds, modern agrochemicals and capital equipment—could not simply be transferred without adjustments to alien environments. The process of growth in tropical agriculture had been accelerated temporarily but had not always been *sustained* as the law of diminishing returns began to set in. The initial impact of the intensive use of better seeds, chemical fertilisers and pesticides on specific crop yields began to falter during the 1970s (Ghatak and Turner, 1981).

The need for new technology for sustainable growth in tropical agriculture

To sustain a rise in food consumption for the masses in the face of a growing population, it became necessary to increase food production not only of principal crops like wheat and rice but also of other types of tropical crops. It is, of course, possible to import food from DCs, but given the balance-of-payment constraint on most non-oil LDCs such imports of food, at the expense of other types of imports critical to the growth of the manufacturing sectors of the LDCs, is not always socially and/or economically desirable. Hence it has become imperative for most LDCs to achieve a sustained growth in agriculture. The desire to attain economic independence is an essential ingredient in a policy designed to achieve sustainable growth in agriculture.

It is important to mention here that the desire to attain sustained growth in tropical agriculture in the face of a population explosion has led to overgrazing, deforestation, desertification and soil erosion in many LDCs. Indeed, if the short-run drive to increase agricultural production causes severe ecological imbalances like soil erosion (through deforestation) in the long run, then such an attempt is very likely to be self-defeating and certainly not sustainable. Hence, from the technocentrist position the search for new technology including BT becomes both urgent and necessary if the conflict between the short-run growth objective and the long-run ecological disorder is to be mitigated. It is indeed a pity that the rain forests of Brazil, Malaysia and India have been considered as 'terrestrial whales'. Their output has been harvested with no consideration given to sustainable yield potentials. Rather, extraction has been driven by the desire to maximise the return to capital in the short or medium term (Ghatak, 1986; also Dasgupta, 1982).

It is, however, necessary to clarify the concept of *sustainable growth* at this stage of our analysis. I shall presently argue that the concept implies living within means. It is also an inter-temporal and relative concept. Whether the growth level of a variable can be sustained or not depends significantly on what happens to a few other related factors. It will also be argued that the growth in tropical agriculture may not be sustainable if it violates seriously the principle of equity (in an intra-generational context). In this sense, the concept of sustainability in production and consumption is not independent of problems related to the justice or 'fairness' of income distribution patterns. Finally, it will be argued that the use of new technology which includes BT is crucial to usher in the second Green Revolution. But public policy should play an important role in regulating the transfer of technology to the LDCs and in minimising the inequality in the distribution of new resources. At the same time, for LDCs interested in the sustained development of agriculture, it is crucial that they spend more scarce resources on programmes designed to boost research and development work in tropical agricultural crops.

In the Tropics, farmers (particularly small and marginal ones) should also be encouraged to adopt the new BT to sustain a target level of growth of agricultural income and output. This requires appropriate economic and social reforms to provide the right incentives to farmers and is influenced by whether or not they behave 'rationally', i.e. responding 'correctly' to appropriate socio-economic signals. However, even a strongly growing economy may not be sustainable over time if it creates extreme polarisation within the society which can eventually lead to violent conflagration. The 'Green Revolution' could easily turn 'Red'. Such conflagration might not occur in the classical Marxist–Leninist way, but it would be a violent and chaotic revolution all the same. It is thus necessary to minimise the degree of inequality in the distribution of gains from the introduction of new technology.

The concept of sustainable growth in tropical agriculture

Despite some recent attempts to analyse the concept of sustainable growth (presumably in the macro-sense of some measure of output or consumption), it is not very clear whether such a concept can be easily and readily defined (see Redclife and Porritt, 1986, and Chapter 1 in this volume). In theory, such a concept should imply the steady-state value of a target variable, e.g. real growth rate of output or consumption. It is useful to add a *time dimension* to the growth of the target variable. Let the target variable be the growth rate of agricultural output in the Tropics: $= -(\dot{y}/y)$. Then, if *over time* such a rate can be maintained, growth can be sustainable. But to achieve such a rate it may be necessary to shift from one production function to another (i.e. from $m \rightarrow n \rightarrow p$). It is interesting to point out that a sustainable growth rate is not always the combination of the highest points on the production function if a specific rate of rise of z

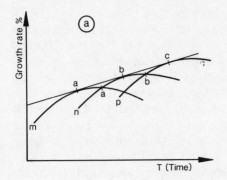

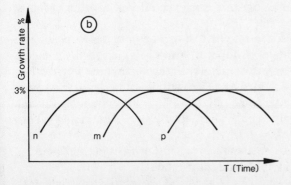

Figure 7.1   Sustainable growth

values is to be maintained (see Figure 7.1(a)). However, Figure 7.1(b) shows that with a given menu of technology a sustainable growth could be the locus of the optimum points of production.

Whether such growth rates of agricultural output as given by the short-run production function can be *sustained* nor not depends, *inter alia*, on: (a) the *availability* of a menu of technology; (b) the use of efficiency of that technology; (c) the price (absolute and relative) of such technology as compared to the rates of return; (d) risks and uncertainties arising out of market and climatic conditions and reflected in the mean and variance of yields and incomes from crop production; (e) the existence of a favourable 'environment'—physical, financial and managerial—for resource use. Violation of any or some of these conditions will prevent the attainment of sustained growth in production. (We will see later that a *sustainable* growth rate of consumption will also depend upon the movement of other macro-variables, e.g. population growth and income distribution.)

To illustrate how the growth rate of agricultural production may not be sustainable in tropical agriculture, cases of actual differential agricultural growth rates in India and Japan will be cited (see Ishikawa, 1967, 1977). Consider the impact of the use of chemical fertilisers on rice production per acre in Japan and in two Indian states as depicted in Figures 7.2(a) and 7.2(b). The growth of crop output in both West Bengal and Tamil Nadu in the late 1960s and early 1970s, when the GR began to spread, rose and then fell sharply. In Figure 7.2(b) in two Japanese districts, the growth rates of crop output are shown to be clearly sustainable. The reason is simple. The mere availability of 'miracle' seeds plus fertiliser is unlikely to achieve sustained results without the availability of a timely and adequate water supply. Further, the simple transfer of technology into an alien environment without due regard to economic and institutional constraints is unlikely to stimulate sustainable growth. In this sense, there is no such thing as a Japanese or an American lesson, as the success of new technology is conditional upon the existence of an appropriate host environment.

The choice of a target growth rate that should be potentially sustainable is a matter of national strategy. All that we can say is that such a choice is usually constrained by a number of factors. In the context of the growth of tropical agriculture, it is very likely that growth of crop output at a steady rate may not be sustainable if some other conditions do not hold. Indeed, the important target variable could alternatively be a sustainable rate of growth in farm income.

The problem of attaining a sustainable rate of growth of farm income can be stated with the aid of the following simple model.

We know that farm income (Y) is given by the product of yield (Q), acreage (A) and farm price (P). Thus, we have

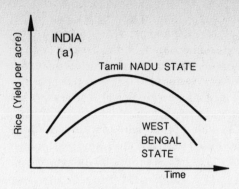

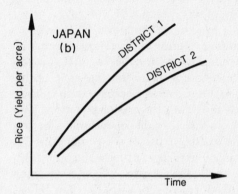

Figure 7.2   Impact of chemical fertilisers on rice production in India and Japan

$$Y = Q \cdot A \cdot P \tag{1}$$

Differentiating (Y) with respect to time (t), we obtain

$$\frac{dY}{dt} = AP \frac{dQ}{dt} + PQ \frac{dA}{dt} + QA \frac{dP}{dt} \tag{2}$$

or

$$\frac{1}{Y} \cdot \frac{dY}{dt} = \frac{1}{Q} \cdot \frac{dQ}{dt} + \frac{1}{A} \cdot \frac{dA}{dt} + \frac{1}{P} \cdot \frac{dP}{dt} \tag{3}$$

Equation (3) can be written in terms of proportional growth rates (in lower-case letters) as follows:

$$Y = q + a + p \tag{4}$$

Equation (4) implies that the rate of change in farm income is equal to the rate of change in yield (productivity), acreage and price.

Consider the case of a stagnant agrarian economy in the Tropics (where $q = 0$). Now, a sustained rise in farm income can emanate from only two sources: (a) a rise in the area under cultivation; (b) a rise in farm prices. Condition (a) is difficult to satisfy in land-scarce tropical countries (e.g. Bangladesh, India, Sri Lanka, etc.). Even in land-abundant countries, (e.g. some African states), the poor quality of the land must act as a real constraint. The fulfilment of condition (b) may not always be acceptable because of its adverse impact on real wages, costs, profits and the growth of industrialisation in dual economies.

The above analysis simply underlines the dilemma that policy-makers face in many LDCs. It also emphasises the need for increasing productivity of land by using the available modern inputs (i.e. $q > 0$).

While the more efficient use of 'miracle' seeds, chemicals, fertilisers and water will enable the tropical agriculture to grow in the future, it is not at all certain that the technology which accounted for the first GR (or 'the seed fertiliser revolution') will be adequate to meet the challenge of the 1980s. The first challenge continues to pose problems because of the falling arable land/man ratio in many South and South-East Asian countries. The second, newer challenge emanates from the inevitable operation of the law of diminishing returns on the use of existing types of seeds or fertilisers. The major problem, in terms of technical fixes, is to develop the 'new BT'. Technology is required which could be used in adverse and varied weather conditions. I will now discuss some major reasons for using the 'new BT' in tropical agriculture in order to achieve a sustainable growth in yield for agricultural crops.

Use of BT in tropical agriculture

The age-old scenario of underdeveloped agriculture in LDCs may not at the outset appear to present a very favourable opportunity for the use of modern biotechnology. However, the increasing application of such techniques will have a very important impact on food production and consumption in developing countries. The major changes during the second GR phase might be as follows:

(1) The use of biotechnology is likely to *raise* the trend lines of growth of many types of agricultural products. It is true that yields of some specific types of food grains, e.g. wheat and rice, have increased significantly in a number of Asian countries. It seems that an increasing use of BT will enable these countries to achieve growth rates which are sustainable in the

short and medium term if (a) such technology is available at a reasonable price; (b) new BT may permit the development of varieties of maize, corn, soyabeans, wheat, etc. widely applicable in the African countries (see Kloppenburg and Kenney, 1984). Public policy may play an important role (via the manipulation of subsidies and taxes) in spreading the use of BT in LDCs as it did in the spread of the first GR.

(2)   The techniques of BT, including those of genetic engineering and tissue culture, are being applied in DCs in an effort to improve cereal crops. Genetic engineering also provides a method of raising food production in tropical agriculture by altering the genetic make-up of plants. It can include nitrogen-fixing genes into cereal crops and thus make them less dependent upon chemical fertilisers. Enhanced resistance of plants to insects will lower pesticide needs for a given amount of food production. The nutritional level of foods can be increased by including synthetic DNA to produce essential amino-acids such as lysine and methiomine. Genetically engineered crop varieties adapted to low levels of fertility or tolerant of saline conditions could raise productivity in large areas of marginal land in Africa and Asia where traditional high-yielding varieties are not suitable.

Many multinational corporations (MNCs) have acquired seed companies recently (Buttel and Barker, 1985; Barker and Kloppenburg, 1985). The logic of such purchases lies in the crucial role of seeds in the food chain, in good profitability prospects, and in the fostering of a better environmental image (compared with, say, direct involvement in pesticides production). Further inducement of commercial investment in plant breeding in the West is provided by effective legal protection. The world consumption of seed stood at £28 billion in 1982 (Dunnill and Rudd, 1984). The close association between seeds and agro-chemicals has been acknowledged by the MNCs. It is also acknowledged that although plant tissue culture and subsequent recombinant DNA techniques will have a significant effect on the growth of crops, conventional plant-breeding skills are still important in field evaluation, as are the marketing strategies of companies. It is thus important for the governments of LDCs to devise appropriate 'codes of conduct' for the MNCs when they transfer and distribute the agricultural BT to the Third World.

(3)   To achieve a stable (and sustainable) level of food consumption, it is important to strike the right balance between food production and consumption. The use of tissue culture for micro-propagation of plants can allow the production of large numbers of essentially identical superior specimens (Bhalla and James, 1986). However, consistent embryogenesis in cell-suspension culture and the handling of many propagated plants may

cause problems. Subsequent planting requires special techniques which may be important in terms of the prior screening of chemicals for agricultural use since pesticides and other new chemicals influencing nitrogen fixation must all be properly tested.

(4)   The use of hydroponics in *semi-arid agriculture* needs to be strongly emphasised, given the present environment in sub-Saharan Africa. Its increasing use will largely depend upon greater international cooperation and judicious use of government fiscal policy.

(5)   A mixture of different kinds of BTs can increase crop yields substantially. It can also raise the ratio of edible material to waste matter (National Academy of Science, 1976, 1982). The growth of BT has enabled the 'fermentation industry' to use agricultural waste materials to produce vitamins, vaccines, alcohols, organic acids and single-cell protein (SCP) or fodder protein. It has been argued that the use of SCP instead of grain in animal (and also human) feeds would mean that large amounts of grains and legumes, hitherto consumed by animals and human beings, can be released (Bhalla and James, 1986). The economics of SCP production is quite interesting. It is estimated that the price of SCP compared to conventional protein (i.e. milk, eggs, meat) is quite low. It is also argued that 'one SCP plant making 100,000 tons per year can produce about as much protein as that which could be extracted from 120,000 hectares [300,000 acres] of soyabeans, or as much beef [cattle] as could be reared on 2 million hectares [5 million acres] of grazing land' (Heden, 1979). However, it is worth noting that 'SCP is not a panacea that by virtue of its greater efficiency will displace conventional agricultural and animal sources of protein. The methods of the past will continue to be needed . . . Improvements of the old ways and adoption of the new will go hand in hand, complementing each other' (World Bank, 1981).

The use of waste materials in the aquaculture of algae or plants is presently being investigated. The combination of waste materials and micro-organisms can also be utilised productively, e.g. production of fodder yeast on spent liquor (Bhalla and James, 1986).

Applications of biotechnology to agriculture

The following applications of BT in tropical agriculture need to be specially emphasised to foster and enhance:

(1)   desirable agricultural traits in plants, e.g. better disease resistance, salt tolerance;

(2) plants with increased levels of modifications of storage compounds, e.g. high polyunsaturated oils;
(3) pest control, e.g. microbial insecticides, fungicides;
(4) plant genetic manipulation and breeding, e.g. plant growth regulators (such as gibberellins) for modifying leaf abscission, loosening fruit, improving photosynthesis and affecting ripening;
(5) hydroponics in semi-arid agriculture (the technique of growing plants in dilute aqueous nutrients without soil);
(6) Desirable traits in animals such as, for example, better disease resistance, better feed conversion;
(7) animal feed and growth promotion via single-cell protein and/or amino acids;
(8) further development and use of vaccines to combat disease such as foot and mouth and pig scours;
(9) production of azolla, an aquatic fern that lives symbiotically with nitrogen fixing blue-green algae, which can be utilised as a green manure and/or intercrop with rice (e.g. in China and Vietnam). Evidence suggests its growth path is as follows:

$$A_t = A_m[1 + c^{-(a+bt)}]$$

where A_t = the bio-mass per hectare at time t
A_m = the asymptotic maximum attainable bio-mass
a, b = parameters which define the initial stock and the growth rate.

Azolla's use has been recommended in order to insulate rice production from the effects of possible energy (and fertiliser) price shocks and balance-of-payments crises in LDCs. But one study suggests that where urea is available (at world prices) adoption of azolla is unlikely as the cost of producing nitrogen through azolla is higher than the price of nitrogen. Azolla as a *green manure* is also rather cost-inefficient under nearly all types of irrigation. Only with very good irrigation is the effective cost of nitrogen from the azolla intercrop less than the cost of nitrogen from urea (see Tables 7.2 and 7.3). However, given the water control regulations, azolla will tend to benefit farmers who already have high-quality irrigation. The income distribution implications are therefore likely to be regressive (Rosergent et al., 1985).

A different evaluation of azolla use as a green manure in rice production, however, shows considerable biological and economic benefits (see Kikuchi et al., 1984). Under favourable experimental conditions, a layer of azolla covering a 1-hectare rice field releases 20–30 kg of organic nitrogen. Azolla can also be cultured more than once. The application of azolla raised yields of rice by 0.4 to 1.5 tons per hectare over control plots (see

Table 7.2 Estimated costs of azolla production in the Philippines

	Cost (Philippine $)
A. Nursery bed (40m²) Azolla starter inoculum, land preparation, seeding, fertiliser and insecticide applications	23.50
B. Multiplication bed (600m²) Land preparation, fertiliser and insecticide applications, seeding	29.90
C. Azolla in rice field (1 hectare)	827.00
1. As green manure: land preparation, seeding, fertiliser and insecticide applications, plus opportunity cost of land	
2. As intercrop seeding: fertiliser and insecticide application, incorporation of azolla in soils	167.00
Total cost per hectare	
Azolla as green manure	880.40
Azolla as intercrop	220.40

Source: Adapted from Rosergent *et al.* (1985).

Table 7.3 Expected nitrogen contribution and effective cost of nitrogen from azolla used as intercrop and green manure, by quality of irrigation

Quality of irrigation	Expected nitrogen contribution and cost of azolla							
	Wet season				Dry season			
	Intercrop		Green manure		Intercrop		Green manure	
	(kg/ha)	($P/ha)	(kg/ha)	($P/ha)	(kg/ha)	($P/ha)	(kg/ha)	($P/ha)
Good	38	5.45	65	13.34	37	5.60	64	13.55
Average	33	6.29	57	15.22	27	7.68	46	18.85
Poor	32	6.48	55	15.77	10	20.73	17	51.02
Rainfed	29	7.15	50	17.35				

Note: For comparison, the cost of chemical fertiliser including the costs of transportation, application, and credits are $P6.23 and $P9.95 per kg per ha of nitrogen supplied by urea and ammonium sulphate respectively.

Source: Adapted from Rosergent *et al.* (1985).

Table 7.4   Economic return (cost-saving) of azolla use per hectare per season, South Cotabato, Philippines*

	Quantity	Value[†] ($US)
1. N fertiliser saved[‡]	50–19 kg	82.35–12.35
2. Herbicide cost saved		2.94
3. Weeding labour cost saved[§]	33 h	7.41
4. Fertiliser application labour saved[§]	7 h	1.52
5. Azolla application labour added[§]	3 h	0.70
6. Net return (cost-saved)		43.52–11.64
(#1 + #2)/current input (%)		33.8 –11.8
#6/non-land cost[Ω] (%)		11.6 – 3.1
#6/output[¶] (%)		5.4 – 1.5

*   For assumptions on maximum and minimum, see text.
† $US 1 = $P8.50.
‡   Nitrogen price = $0.65 kg/N.
§   Wage rate = $0.22/hour, for the 1980 2nd crop.
Ω   Sum of current input, capital, and labour.
¶   A projected rice yield of 4.47t/ha for no-azolla plots and a price of $0.18/kg unhusked rice are assumed.

Source: Adapted from Kikuchi *et al.* (1984).

Table 7.4). It has also been shown that the economic return from azolla adoption, including *cost savings in chemical fertilisers* and *weed control*, is more than 10 per cent of the total non-land cost of rice production in areas where environmental conditions favour azolla growth (see Table 7.4). Some major constraints on the adoption of azolla are:

(a) the phosphorus content of the soil;
(b) the danger of insect and pest attacks which can raise the cost of pest control;
(c) increase in the wage cost due to a rise in labour requirement.

From the basis of the evidence available so far, we can thus conclude that the potential economic and social benefits of azolla use will be high in those LDCs where the opportunity cost of labour in terms of foregone marginal productivity of labour and real wage is low. The adoption of azolla could therefore depend considerably on the level of real wages and the cost of pest control.

Insecticide resistance, integrated pest management (IPM) and the use of BT in tropical agriculture

The agricultural use of synthetic insecticides generally protects crops but imposes strong selection pressures that can result in the development of resistance. The chief resistance mechanisms are enhancement of the capacity to detoxify metabolically insecticides and alterations in target sites that prevent insecticides from binding to them. Insect control methods must incorporate strategies to reduce resistance development and conserve the utility of the insecticides. The most promising approach, the integrated pest management (IPM), includes the use of chemical insecticides in combination with improved cultural and biologically based techniques.

Three major factors, genetic, biological and control-related, can influence the rate of resistance development in agricultural pest insects. Genetic manipulation of some insects is theoretically possible, but practically difficult, though insect biology can be manipulated. For instance, pheromone lures can be used to attract susceptible insects to dilute a resistant gene pool. Control-related factors (those directly related to insecticide use) are linked to the generally available methods to reduce the insecticide selection pressure, the most important factor in delaying resistance.

The careful selection and exact application of chemical insecticides, and their integration with other control methods consistent with the principles of the IPM, hold promise for effective resistance management (Brattensten *et al.*, 1986). The use of selected insecticide *mixtures* can reduce resistance development as it is more difficult for an insect to develop several adaptations simultaneously. Needless to say, mixtures should be used with caution, particularly in tropical agriculture.

Apart from mixtures, insecticide synergists showed good promise as their use inhibits enzymes involved in insecticide detoxification. But their actual application did not achieve the results expected because:

(a) their range of activity is too narrow and they are less effective against the general population than against metabolically resistant strains;
(b) the additional cost is also a major barrier to their use in tropical agriculture;
(c) it is difficult to choose a synergist to delay resistance, since different field populations of the same species demonstrate highly volatile responses to a given synergist.

To promote the utility of the insecticide and the susceptible gene pool, spray applications should be made only when economically determined threshold infestation levels are present. Such a threshold changes consider-ably depending on crop growth stage. Crop, insect pests and region can be determined only by constant monitoring of population densities.

The use of herbicides in agriculture

Several types of herbicides are now in use in agriculture in both DCs and LDCs. Paraquat is perhaps one of the world's most widely used herbicides. Following its introduction in 1962, it has benefited farmers in many countries and is now an important part of many crop production systems. Its use in the production of many crops (e.g. coffee, cotton, tea, maize, sugar cane, rice, oil palm and rubber, vegetables and bananas) has led to substantial rises in yields without much damage to the environment (see Table 7.5). The use of herbicides like paraquat have been of great economic significance because of the substantial time and labour savings

Table 7.5   Effect of herbicide treatment on coffee yield

Treatment	Mean yield (kg/ha)
Hand cultivation	1,585
Paraquat 0.2 kg/ha	1,803
Paraquat + hand cultivation	1,816
Paraquat + diuron	1,749
Paraquat + simazine	1,867

Source: Adapted from Mitchell (1974).

Table 7.6   Cost savings in weed control in rice and rubber crops

Pre-planting weed control in rice	Unit cost ($US/ha)	Time (days)	Weed control in rubber	Control (days)	Labour (hrs./m./acre)
Buffalo power	114	26–56			
Buffalo + mechanisation	89	25–30	Hand weeding	40–55	21
Paraquat	68–75	5–10	Paraquat	55–60	0.64

Source: Adapted from Paterson (1978) and Seth and Kapper (1968).

made in a possible range of farming systems (see Table 7.6). It has also promoted the growth of 'no-till' farming (direct drilling involving the elimination of ploughing and cultivation procedures prior to crop establishment) which, in addition to the already mentioned benefits, can lead to significant energy savings as well as reduced soil erosion and loss of moisture from soil.

When applied as an overall spray to emerged weeds, paraquat:

(a) is effective on a broad spectrum of weeds, e.g. grass and broadleaf species;
(b) can be quickly applied compared with most mechanical and manual methods of weed control;
(c) is rainfast, so that once the spray has dried on the leaf surface its activity will continue irrespective of the ensuing weather;
(d) is fast acting, so that treated plant tissue shows signs of cellular disruption within hours and is killed within three to seven days;
(e) becomes inactivated on contact with soil, and so is without herbicidal effect on crops established subsequently or on nearby untreated crops;
(f) is relatively safer in protecting the environment as long as it is used as directed.

In tropical, arid climates, the no-till technique promoted by the use of herbicides provides a water reserve which can carry a crop through periods of short-term drought and prevent the development of moisture stress. It is now acknowledged that the main direct cause of soil erosion is the application of unsuitable methods of land cultivation. Water erosion in many parts of the world is now much more serious than that caused by the wind. Water erosion can be significantly reduced by following the major principles:

(a) by maintaining the permeability of the soil surface;
(b) by reducing the rate at which water can flow over the soil surface, i.e. limiting run-off.

The growth of 'no-till' farming in which paraquat has played an important role has aided the application of these principles, thereby much improving the prospects of soil conservation in the future.

Economists tend to estimate the *social* costs (C) and benefits (B) of projects by looking at the net present value (*NPV*—discounted benefits and costs) of any project via the following formula:

$$NPV = \sum \frac{B_i - C_i}{(1 + r)^t}$$

where r = rate of discount and t = time.

If the *NPV* > 0, the project is accepted. If *NPV* < 0, the project is rejected.

An accurate estimation of a global sum of discounted benefits and costs of herbicide use in tropical agriculture is not practicable. The valuation of net benefits is also likely to be influenced by the nature of objectives and constraints, say, in a labour-surplus or a labour-scarce underdeveloped 'dual economy'. It is also clear, however, that although the use of herbicides, as the foregoing analysis shows, has its advantages, it has also quite a few disadvantages in labour-*surplus* underdeveloped economies. Policy-makers in such economies are unlikely to be persuaded by the benefits of considerable labour-saving devices, given the very low level of real wages for agricultural labourers and the presence of a considerable amount of 'open' and 'disguised' (i.e. marginal productivity of rural labour is very low or equal to zero) unemployment. Indeed, the objective function could easily be to maximise employment and consumption in such economies. It is possible to hypothesise a positive correlation between growth of consumption and productivity in LDCs as additional consumption is likely to increase the standard of nutrition, labour efficiency and thus productivity to a certain degree. Such a relationship can be approximated by a logistic curve. If this line of argument is valid, then it is rather unlikely that on economic grounds the use of herbicides will be extensively adopted in tropical 'labour-surplus' agriculture (Ghatak, 1986).

Alternatives to chemical plant protection: biological control

Alternatives to chemical plant protection are now increasingly available, thanks to research and development activities in the field of biological controls. Strictly speaking, biological control means the use of one organism to control the population density of another, and it has a long history which dates back to ancient Egypt where cats were kept to control mice.

Given the considerable loss of food crop in tropical agriculture due to the attack by insects, at least five methods could be suggested to control the insect population biologically:

(a) by specific natural enemies, usually parasites;
(b) by non-specific natural enemies, usually predatory species;
(c) by the sterile-male method;
(d) by micro-organisms;
(e) by use of specific hormones

As regards the use of (a) and (b), the problem is that neither parasites nor predators will thrive unless there are already large numbers of the target insect in occupation of the crop. This implies that a farmer must wait until much damage has been done before the pests can be eliminated. This is a special problem with annual food crops (e.g. cereals) where huge losses can be suffered in the short run. The technique has more promise when used on long-term crops like timber. The other problem is that the predator or parasite that is introduced is likely to tackle only one insect pest and will be impotent against, for instance, fungal diseases.

Method (c) involves sterilizing the males of a species (e.g. American screw-worm) by means of gamma rays so as to reduce the population in the following generation. The technique has been successfully tried in the Caribbean, Central America and Southern United States. However, it has been difficult to repeat the success with other insect pests.

Insect population can also be checked by attacks from viruses and bacteria (micro-organisms). But there is a serious difficulty in releasing into the environment large quantities of micro-organisms whose future behaviour is hard to predict and rate of multiplication difficult to control. Also, the release may kill off beneficial insects like honey bees.

Biologically formed substances can sometimes be used to control insects, e.g. juvenile hormones can keep some insects in the larval stage so that they never hatch out and they never multiply. Pheromones (sex attractants) concentrate on freshly hatched males so that the grower knows that an infestation is imminent and can deal with it in time. These techniques have proved useful in giving early warning and are capable of development as parts of IPC management.

Constraints on the application of new (BT) technology

There are various likely constraints on the adoption of new BT in LDCs:

(a) *Product quality*: a new product may be preferred by consumers in DCs but not by consumers in LDCs (see Bhalla and James, 1986).
(b) *Skill requirements*: many LDCs do not have adequate skill and expertise to develop and apply the BT for promoting tropical agriculture.
(c) *Systems dependence*: new technology is very information- and R. & D.-intensive. Such sophisticated technology is highly dependent on costly auxillaries such as sensors, software and peripherals if it is to be truly effective. These forms of systems dependency may significantly constrain the adoption of new technology in LDCs.
(d) *Factor costs and market size*: high capital and development costs will be problematic for smaller firms in LDCs where the average size of the firm is relatively small.

Table 7.7   Research and development costs in the pharmaceutical and agro-chemical industries (1977 prices)

	Pharmaceutical	Agro-chemical
Research and development spending (as % of sales)	10–11%	9.7%
Average cost of research for and development of a new product (new single entity)	$7,500,000	$5,500,000
Number of compounds screened per product introduced	6,000 to 7,000	7,430

Source: Adapted from Marmet (1977).

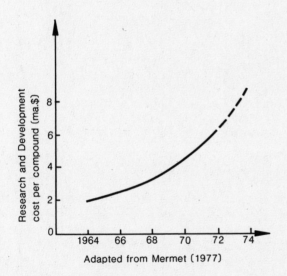

Adapted from Mermet (1977)

Figure 7.3   Research and development cost constraint

(e) *High R. & D. costs and long lead times of around seven years*: both factors obstruct LDCs in the development of the BT relevant for tropical agriculture (see Table 7.7 and Figure 7.3). Here it is imperative to explore the possibilities of international cooperation.

(f) *Income and employment implications*: an important negative impact of BT R. & D. in DCs is the development of derived products like enzyme-based sugar syrups and fructose sweeteners from maize. Such product development can pose considerable problems for those LDCs

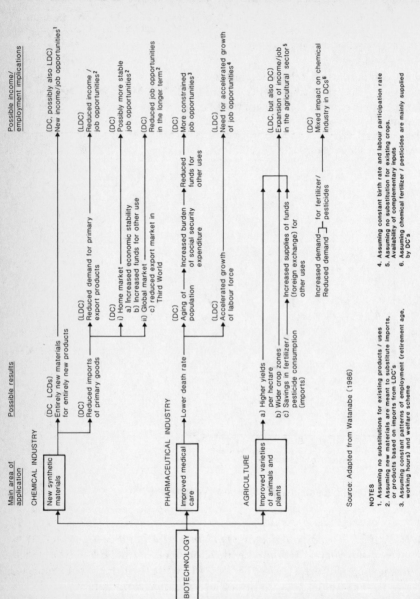

Figure 7.3 Possible employment and income effects of new biotechnology

which produce and export sugar cane and sugar beet. In practical terms it means loss of employment and income for producers of sugar cane and sugar beet. It is obvious that the new BT will have a far greater impact on the employment in the agricultural sector of the LDCs in comparison with the DCs (see Figure 7.4). Agriculture accounts for a very low proportion of employment and income in most DCs. Hence, the impact of the development of new BT on developed agriculture is likely to be marginal. However, as traditional varieties of agricultural products are replaced by new ones in LDCs, due to the advent of BT, the important factor to look at will be the relative labour intensities of new and old crops. Evidence suggests that the replacement of bananas by oil palms has caused considerable unemployment in Costa Rica as the same plantation now needs about one-third less manpower (Izurieta, 1984). The aggregate employment effect of the oil palm will depend on whether the country can produce and sell enough palm oil to offset reduced employment in the banana plantations without causing negative impact on the production and labour intensities of other crops. However, the growth of the oil-palm sector can boost employment in the secondary and tertiary sectors (Watanabe, 1986).

It is now acknowledged that many basic institutional conditions for a successful GR are missing in Africa. The mere availability of HYV seeds, chemical fertilisers and pesticides (the so-called 'technical package') is unlikely to achieve much in the African or Caribbean countries as the weak structure of organisation could easily fail to deliver the goods. Even if genetic engineering reduces water and fertiliser needs for producing a certain amount of crops, a sound infrastructure in the tropical agriculture for seed distribution, product marketing and dissemination of related skills would still be required to achieve desired objectives. As Watanabe observes: 'The same factor seems to have had much to do with the shift of palm oil production from Nigeria to Malaysia' (Watanabe, 1986).

Conclusions

In this chapter I have mainly discussed the problem of the use of old and new BT in order to achieve sustainable growth in yields of tropical foodcrops. It is important to note that the process of sustained intertemporal growth in yield needs continuous expenditure on R & D for new agro-technology. Clearly, a strong political will to promote such technology is a vital ingredient to maintain dynamic and sustained growth. It has been argued at the outset that growth without equity is unlikely to be sustainable in the long run. Hence, it is imperative to take proper steps to distribute justly any gains from increased productivity arising out of the use of new BT. It is equally important to induce the largest number of farmers to adopt the new technology through the creation of an appropriate economic and social environment. Such inducements will probably require substantial land and other types of institutional reform, and the development of suitable infrastructure which will facilitate an easier transfer of agricultural technology to the LDCs. Evidence suggests that the scope for raising crop productivity in many tropical areas of Africa, Asia and Latin America simply by better allocation of 'old' BT is considerable (Borlaug, 1983). Hence, in such countries, it is necessary to use the new BT as a complement to the 'old' BT, after carefully assessing their relative costs and benefits. Such calculations should also include the income and employment effects of different technologies. The prospects for some fermentation agro-industries which use BT are looking increasinglfy attractive because of the rising costs of oil and non-microbial protein. In the case of other BT used in tropical agriculture, e.g. azolla, it has been shown that the economic case for its use is not always overwhelming and the impact of its use on income distribution may not be more egalitarian. Hence, caution is needed before advocating the use of BT to tropical agriculture. LDCs in the tropics differ considerably in their level of economic development, growth of skill and infrastructure and resource endowments. Finally, it is useful to promote greater international cooperation (both public and private) in R. & D. in tropical agriculture not only to meet the challenge of new and rising demand for different types of agricultural products, but also to avoid waste of resources. Such cooperation should also enable us to minimise the technology gap between the rich and poor countries. If the fruits of such R. & D. could be quickly disseminated at a reasonable price, particularly for the large majority of small farmers in the Tropics, the problem of the growing polarisation between the 'haves' and 'have-nots' could also be minimised. Perhaps it is worth remembering that 'small is not just beautiful' in underdeveloped agriculture; it has proved to be quite efficient there as well.

However, it is imperative to develop the necessary cooperation between the DCs and LDCs at different levels, even for selfish reasons which dictate promotion of national interests, as the forces of inertia are immense and deeply entrenched in systems of value and socio-political structures (Rees, 1985). As Machiavelli reminded us in 1513:

There is nothing more difficult to carry out, nor more doubtful of success, nor more dangerous to handle, than to initiate a new order of things. For the reformer has enemies in all who profit by the old order, and only lukewarm defenders in all those who would profit by the new order. The lukewarmness arises partly from fear of their adversaries who have law in their favour; and partly from the incredulity of mankind, who do not truly believe in anything new until they have had actual experience of it.

[Machiavelli, *The Prince*]

References

Barton, J.H., 1984, *The Effects of New Biotechnologies on the International Agricultural Research System*, USAID, Washington, DC.

Bhalla, A.S. and James, J., 1986, 'New Technology Revolution: Myth of Reality for Developing Countries', in Hall, P. (ed.), *Technology, Innovation and Economic Policy*, Philip Allan, Oxford.

Borlaug, N., 1983, 'Contributions of Conventional Plant Breeding to Food Production', *Science*, **222**, 671–5.

Boyce, J.K. and Evenson, R.E., 1975, *Agricultural Research and Extension Programmes*, Agricultural Development Council, New York.

Brattensten, L., Holyoke, C., Leeper, J.R. and Raffa, K., 1986, 'Insecticide Resistance: Challenge to Pest Management and Basic Research', *Science*, March.

Buttel, F. and Barker, R., 1985, 'Emerging Agricultural Technologies, Public Policy and Implication for Third World Agriculture: The Case of Biotechnology', *Americal Journal of Agricultural Economics*, **67**, December.

Buttel, F., Kenney, M. and Kloppenburg, J., 1985, 'From Green Revolution to Biorevolution: Some Observations on the Changing Technological Bases of Economic Transformation in the Third World', *Economic Development and Cultural Change*, **1**.

Cramer, Hans-Hermann, *Plant Protection in Modern Agriculture*, GIFAP, Brussels.

Dasgupta, P., 1982, *Control of Resources*, Bazil Blackwell, Oxford.

Dunnill, P. and Rudd, M., 1984, *Biotechnology and British Industry*, SERC, London.

Evenson, R.E., 1984, 'Benefits and Obstacles in Developing Appropriate Agricultural Technology', in Eicher, K. and Staatz, M.J. (eds), *Agricultural Development in the Third World*, Johns Hopkins University Press, Baltimore.

Ghatak, S., 1981, *Transfer of Technology to Developing Countries: The Case of the Fertilizer Industry*, JAI Press, Hartford, Ct.

_____ 1985, 'Limits to Project Evaluation Under Structural Changes in Developing Countries', paper presented to the Annual Conference of Agricultural Economics Association, Edinburgh.

_____ 1986, *An Introduction to Development Economics*, 2nd edn, George Allan and Unwin, London.

_____ 1987, 'Agriculture and Economic Growth: A Survey', in Gemell, N. (ed.), *Surveys in Development Economics*, Basil Blackwell (forthcoming), Oxford.

Ghatak, S. and Ingersent, K., 1984, *Agriculture and Economic Development*, John Hopkins Press, Baltimore, and Harvester, Brighton.

Ghatak, S. and Turner, R.K., 1981, 'Benefits and Costs of Pesticide Use and Some Policy Implications for Less Developed Countries', in Chatterji, M. (ed.), *Energy and Development in the Developing Countries*, John Wiley, Chichester.

Graff, G., 1982, 'Plant Tissue Culture', *High Technology*, September.

Griffin, K., 1974, *The Political Economy of Agrarian Change*, MacMillan, London.

Heden, C.G., 1981, 'The Political Impact of Microbiology in Developing Countries', UNIDO, IS.261, November.

—— 1979, 'Microbiological Science for Development: A Global Technological Opportunity', in Ramesh, J. and Weiss, C. (eds), *Mobilising Technology for World Development*, Praeger, New York.

Hayami, Y. and Ruttan, V., 1984, 'The Green Revolution: Inducement and Distribution', *The Pakistan Development Review*, **XXIII**, 1.

Hughes, K.A. and Barker, C.J., 1977, 'Tractor Fuel Requirement of Two Tillage Systems and Zero-Tillage', *New Zealand Journal of Experimental Agriculture*, **5**.

Imperial Chemical Industries (ICI), 1984, *Herbicides in the Middle East and Mediterranean Countries*, Plant Protection Division, several issues.

—— 1986, *Paraquat: Benefits in International Agriculture*, Plant Protection Division.

Ishikawa, S., 1967, *Economic Development in Asian Perspective*, Kunkoniya Tokyo.

—— 1977, 'China's Food and Agriculture: A Turning Point', *Food Policy*, **2**.

Izurieta, Carlos A., 1984, 'Technological Change in Palm Oil in Costa Rica', in Bhalla, A. *et al.* (eds), *Blending of New and Traditional Technologies*, Tycooly International, Dublin.

Jennings, P.R., 1974, 'Rice Breeding and World Food Production', *Science*, **213**, 1085–8.

Johnston, B.F. and Cownie, J., 1969, 'The Seed-Fertilizer Revolution and Labour-Force Absorption', *American Economic Review*, **51**.

Kikuchi, M., Watanabe, I. and Haws, D., 1984, 'Economic Evaluation of Azolla Production', *Organic Matter and Rice*, International Rice Research Institute, Manila, Philippines.

Kloppenburg, J.J. and Kenney, M., 1984, 'Biotechnology, Seeds and the Restructuring of Agriculture', *The Insurgent Sociologist*, **12**.

Marmet, J., 1977, 'Problems Faced by the Pesticide Manufacturer in Relation to Social and Economic Aspects of Crop Production', *Pesticide Science*, **8**.

Mellor, J., 1976, *The New Economic of Growth: A Strategy for India and the Developing World*, Cornell University Press, Cornell, Ithaca.

Mitchell, H.W., 1974, 'Weed Control Methods Over a Four Year Period in Kenya: Coffee', in *Proceedings of the Fifth East African Weed Control Conference*, Nairobi.

National Academy of Sciences, 1976, *Technology Assessment Activities in the Industrial, Academic and Government Communities*, Washington, DC.

—— 1982, *Diffusion of Biomass Energy Technologies in Developing Countries*, Washington, DC.

Paterson, E.C., 1978, 'Paraquat Usage in Rice in SE Asia' (mimeo).

Pearce, D.W. and Nash, C., 1982, *Social Appraisal of Projects*, Macmillan, London.

Ranadhawa, N.S., 1974, *Green Revolution*, Allied Publishers, India.

Redclift, M. and Porritt, J., 1986, 'Why Bankrupt the Earth?' An Exploration Into International Economics and Environment, paper presented to The Other Economic Summit Conference, 17–18 April 1986, London University (mimeo).

Rees, J., 1985, *Natural Resources: Allocation, Economics and Policy*, Methuen, London and New York.

Rosergent, M.W., Roumasset, J.A. and Balisacen, A.M., 1985, 'Biological Technology and Agricultural Policy: An Assessment of Azolla in Philippine Rice Production', *American Journal of Agricultural Economics*, **67** (4).

Repetto, R., 1985, 'Overview', in Repetto (ed.), *The Global Possible: Resources, Development and the New Century*, World Resources Institute, Yale University Press, New Haven, Conn.

Sen, A.K., 1981, *Poverty and Famines: An Essay on Exchange Entitlement*, Basil Blackwell, Oxford.

Seth, A. and Kappor, J., 1968, 'Chemical Control from Planting Onwards', *Planter*, **44** (513), (Kuala Lumpur).

Swaminathan, M.S., 1982, 'Biotechnology Research and Third World Agriculture', *Science*, **218** (3).

Watanabe, I., 1986, 'Employment and Income Implications of New Biotechnology: A Speculative Note', *Economic Bulletin for Europe*, **38** (1).

World Bank, 1981, *World Development Report, 1982*, Oxford University Press, Oxford.

_____ 1982, *World Development Report, 1983, 1984*, Oxford University Press, Oxford.

Chapter 8

Pollution Control Objectives and the Regulatory Framework

J. Rees

Introduction

Over the last decade study of policy formulation, implementation practice and decision-making within regulatory authorities has, to use Majone and Wildavksy's (1979) words, become a growth industry. It is now widely accepted that the pollution control process is not a rational sequential system, with a neat hierarchy of stages leading down from a consistent clear statement of policy objectives to the implementation of appropriate strategies designed to ensure their achievement (Figure 8.1). Such rationalist conceptualisations are misleading in their treatment of the nature of policy, its loci of formulation, the decision-making processes at work within regulating agencies and the behaviour of the regulated. (Amongst the burgeoning literature on 'policy as practice' see, for example, Bardach, 1978, 1979; Dunsire, 1978; Jenkins, 1978; Levitt, 1980; Bacharach and Lawler, 1981; Barrett and Fudge, 1981; Mazmanian and Sabatier, 1981; Peacock, 1984).

Few analysts now deny that procedural planning and management models are poor descriptions of actual decision-making behaviour within regulatory authorities. Likewise, it is widely accepted that the regulated do not respond like blind automatons to regulatory mechanisms; they neither react to price signals in the prescribedly rational manner of 'economic man', nor do they simply obey the rules of conduct contained in direct regulations. Both the regulated and 'field' staff within regulatory bodies will have an input into the definition of the problem which regulation seeks to address, the formulation of policy statements, the creation of appropriate administrative arrangements, and the decision about feasible intervention techniques. Moreover, they will subsequently attempt to 'bend' the process of implementation to serve their own interests, respond to short-term political, social or economic pressures, and to ensure that the outcomes conform more closely to their own value systems. However, acceptance that policy formulation and implementation is an imperfect, dynamic and interactive process has, for the most part, not been reflected in economic appraisals of pollution control objectives and regulatory

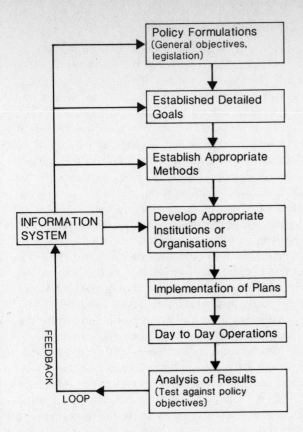

Figure 8.1   The 'rational' policy process

strategies. The analytical implications which stem from implementation research remain poorly explored and largely unintegrated with the mass of literature which debates the goals of environmental policy and the relative merits of alternative administrative structures and regulatory mechanisms. There is still a strong rationalist strain in much of the literature; the messy reality of human institutions is either ignored entirely or is dismissed through the assumption that the management system *ought* (and can be made) to conform to the structured planning-and-control model.

Blind optimisation

The former tactic of ignoring the institutional context within which all pollution control actually takes place is employed (explicitly or more often implicitly) by both physical scientists and many theoretical economists, although of course their views on what constitute an ideal world and optimal outcomes differ radically. Quite properly, criticism has been directed at tunnel-vision science or pseudo-science, where the identification of actual or potential change in environmental systems, the analysis of physical cause–effect relationships, or even the lack of knowledge about ecosystem dynamics is assumed automatically to justify further controls over economic activity. Basically, such critiques contain three fundamental points. First, minimisation of environmental change, minimisation of potentially polluting discharges, minimisation of survival risk, and maximisation of future options or other ecologically based management goals are rejected as the legitimate sole objectives of public policy, since they neglect the resulting socio-economic consequences (Lecomber, 1979; Dasgupta, 1982). Second, the relevance is questioned of control measures which ignore political, legal, economic or administrative feasibility. And third, the efficacy of physically based control strategies is limited by the lack of understanding of, and attention paid to, human response.

The equivalents of these three criticisms can equally be directed towards theoretical economic appraisals of resource issues, as indeed they have been for well over twenty years. Doubts have been raised about the methodological soundness of conventional treatments of pollution control which assume that allocative efficiency is the only legitimate management goal; neglect the distributional, administrative and legal constraints on the feasibility of employing 'optimal' economic incentive systems; and apparently refuse to deviate from the assumption that the pollution control system is populated by economically rational entrepreneurs and regulators, operating without technical, perceptual, organizational and capital availability constraints. Although clearly not all economists have remained deaf to their detractors, it is startling how little the analysis has been adapted to take account of the methodological criticisms. The literature is still replete with papers which refine and re-refine models of efficient pollution regulation, seemingly oblivious to whether the analysis addresses a relevant problem, is based on a politically acceptable policy goal and provides solutions which are implementable, effective or desirable.

Indeed, if anything, the number of such papers has increased over the last five years in response to the political demands for less direct regulation in the environmental field. An example of this type of study is provided by Spulber (1985). In a paper on effluent regulation and long-run optimality, 'firms are assumed to be identical and to behave competitively'

(p. 104); the concern of the regulators is determined to be 'not only with the implications of public policy for the discharges from a representative firm but also with the total pollution observed at the long-run market equilibrium' (p. 103), or alternatively 'to choose industry output, inputs, and the number of firms in a partial equilibrium setting so as to maximize social welfare' (p. 104). Not once in the paper is there even a hint of the ideological assumptions underlying the way welfare maximisation is defined; throughout it is taken for granted that economic efficiency is the sole management objective; nowhere is it acknowledged that the social damage function is not a single, static and easily established entity; and throughout it is seemingly assumed that the model of economic behaviour employed has descriptive value in explaining the behaviour of the regulators and the regulated.

There is, of course, nothing wrong with abstract model building and mathematical gymnastics as long as the practitioners do not regard the results as immediately applicable and policy relevant. But all too often, the abstractions, behavioural assumptions and value judgements are hidden in apparently unequivocal, incontrovertible advice to policy-makers. Spulber, for instance, concludes by reaffirming

the importance of directing public policy toward pricing the use of the environment. The policy instruments which achieve long-run optimality in a competitive market with small firms are the effluent tax and the tradeable effluent permit. Direct intervention . . . will create further distortions in the allocation of resources. [p. 116]

At the moment the fashion pendulum has swung back, in the face of the supposed costs, inefficiencies and 'manipulability' of direct regulation, towards the use of price incentives. However, there is clearly a danger that incentive schemes, advocated on the basis of some abstract model of the economy, will fail to achieve the predicted results, even if they were implemented 'perfectly'. Performance failure is even more probable when the reality of charging practice is taken into account, so setting the seeds for the sort of backlash against economic concepts which occurred during the early 1970s, when it was common in the environmental literature for analysts to throw the baby out with the bath water and to reject as irrelevant the whole package of established economic notions, analytical techniques and management tools (Kapp, 1970, 1972). This would be regrettable since economic incentives have a role to play within a package of management tools; this role can, however, only be judged on what implementable charging schemes actually achieve and not on some assumed properties of 'ideal' pricing systems.

Naïve faith

A second group of analysts avoids confrontation with the reality of policy formulation, implementation and decision-making practice by espousing the need for more rational approaches to public policy-making, concentrating on what the environmental planning system *should* be designed to achieve, and devising new mechanisms supposedly capable of achieving the required ends. This group exhibits a diversity of views about desirable policy goals and appropriate management systems. There has, however, been a clear tendency for them to swarm locust-like from one 'failed' rational problem-solving method on to the next management panacea, shifting as they go both the assumed targets of environmental policy and the necessary tools and organizational structures required for implementation. Witness, for example, the flight from environmental impact assessment and participatory planning to the current alighting on anticipatory, or *ex ante* control.

This search for an improved quality of management is, of course, by no means confined to the environmental sector; it has permeated public sector planning since the 1960s and a parallel development of strategic/corporate planning mechanisms has occurred within industrial, commercial and financial organisations. Subsequent disillusionment with the performance of many of the introduced measures stems in no small part from unrealistic assessments of what they could ever achieve given the extant institutional framework, and of how bureaucracies would react to them (Lenz and Lyles, 1985).

Within the academic environmental literature, preventive management strategies have become associated with such policy objectives as 'ecologically sound development' (Simonis, 1984), 'ecological modernization' —of economic structures and technologies—(Janicke, 1985), sustainable utilisation, best practicable environmental option (BPEO) and least environmentally damaging development options. Indeed, the anticipatory notion can be regarded as central to attempts to give practical meaning and legitimacy to these objectives. They all, implicitly at least, accept that 'hard' ecological no-growth policies are non-starters economically, socially and politically; thus, mechanisms must be found to make development compatible with ecological/environmental principles, or more cynically to convince economic interests that environmental protection and damage minimisation can occur 'while on the other hand economic productivity together with industry's capacity for innovation are increased' (Janicke, 1985, p. 1). Clearly, existing strategies which are assumed to be of the post-damage generation repair, clean-up and abate type have failed to produce the required compatibility of objectives; moreover, more of the same medicine will obviously fail to appeal to business communities which blame environmental controls for unemployment, reduced productivity, declining economic growth rates and inflation (Comar, 1979). Thus, a *new* anticipatory approach appears to its advocates as the only way of ensuring that the structural changes needed for 'sound ecologically based' management of the economy occur.

This linking of the prevention notion with ecological/environmentalist goals in itself paves the way for it to become yet another ineffective 'failure'. Governmental statements on the subject quite clearly have other, much more pragmatic objectives in mind—reducing the economic and political costs of pollution and reducing the cost of controlling those impacts of economic activity which are, or are likely to be, regarded as nuisances by a significant segment of the electorate. Certainly there is little to suggest that they envisage any radical change of institutions, investment patterns or economic structures to make ecological security the keystone of public policy. Anticipatory control is thus not likely to produce the profound changes in political priorities and policy-making hoped for by its advocates. If there is a significant shift towards preventive mechanisms in written statements of environmental policy, the likelihood is that implementation will see the euphoria about their potential role disappear as quickly as it did in the NEPA case (Schnaiberg, 1980).

Anticipatory environmental management is not, of course, a new concept; after all, it underlies the entire land-use planning system, all pre-production vetting of manufacturing processes and products, and indeed the range of techniques designed to inform investment and conservation decisions. The uncomfortable truth is that the preventive tools employed in the past have been subject to all the well-rehearsed defects of reactive control. They inevitably have to operate within an institutional setting where policy goals are confused, shifting and frequently conflicting, where the implementation process does not, and cannot, operate along clear, consistent ends–means lines, and where they are prey to manipulation by interest groups within both the regulated community and the regulating authorities themselves. It is by no means obvious from the anticipatory literature what new management strategies, tools or administrative systems could be introduced; nor is it clear why any innovatory mechanisms (or revamped old ones) will prove any less obstinately 'irrational' than existing *ex ante* and *ex post* management tools.

As Majone pointed out some ten years ago, 'the search for a system that would resolve most of the political conflict over the environment . . . is bound to lead to disappointment' (1976, p. 592). To assume that the endorsement of a policy of anticipatory action will remove the need for bargaining and uneasy compromise is unrealistic. Even if the premise is accepted that economic development and environmental sustainability can be made *generally* compatible objectives, the crucial point is that some interest groups will still be losers; 'no policy change worthy of the name would have a universally neutral or beneficial effect' (Butlin, 1981, p. 4). Who these losers are, what resources they command, how they react in response to their loss, and what access they have to policy-makers (throughout the policy formulation and implementation system) are the critical questions which must be addressed before the efficacy and costs of policy instruments can be judged realistically.

The 'un-ideal' approach

Instead of this continual search for the 'ideal' policy strategy, it is worth reflecting on the limited freedom and power which any government has to make radical change. No single policy measure, or even a whole series enacted together, is likely to alter significantly the underlying and funda- mental structure of institutions. As Sharkansky (1970) has argued, all governments work within the prevailing political and economic system; the basic institutions—legal, governmental, social and economic—remain largely unaltered. Change is, therefore, always marginal and attempts to produce change have to operate within the constraints set by the system. At best, planners can 'nudge the process towards desired outcomes' (Majone, 1976).

Much more attention needs to be given to what has actually been achieved, at what cost and for whose benefit, by the whole range of pollution control mechanisms. Each control technique has a distinct set of consequences, which inevitably vary, both temporally and spatially, with the political, socio-economic and organisational context under which they are implemented. All can make, and have made, some contribution to pushing the system incrementally in a less environmentally damaging direction. The debate should not be over whether economic incentives are better, according to some notional criterion of public good, than direct regulation, or whether *ex ante* strategies are better than *ex post* measures. What is necessary is assessment of the relative performance (measured by a range of criteria such as efficiency, equity, acceptability and effectiveness) of all the tools under different institutional conditions, the aim being to establish whether there is enough consistency in the relationship between performance and conditions to be able to specify which sets of techniques are likely to be most appropriate to the tasks in hand.

It may, of course, be true, as Majone (1976) has argued, that 'the actual outcomes of environmental policies are affected more by the institutional arrangements emerging from the political process than by the technical characteristics of the instruments employed'. In which case, 'the significant choice is not among abstractly considered policy instruments but among institutionally determined ways of operating them' (p. 593). The view that, as far as environmental improvements are concerned, the specific approach taken to control has little significant effect on the results has recently been given some empirical bones by a multinational comparative study on air pollution control policies for stationary sources in selected EEC countries (Knoepfel and Weidner, 1983). This cannot however, be taken to mean that it is irrelevant which tool is employed; the fact that environmental outcomes may be broadly similar does not imply that ease of introduction, implementation costs, the administrative competence required, and the detailed distributional consequences need also be similar.

Given the range of objectives, conditions and constraints under which pollution control agencies have to operate, it seems intuitively plausible to suggest that each control mechanism has some role to play. Certainly it seems somewhat inconsistent for economists to dismiss measures of direct regulation because they 'will create further distortions in the allocation of resources', when economic models supporting price incentives only operate by ignoring the 'distortions' and 'imperfections' which already exist in the economic system. Likewise it can only be counter-productive to environmental interests for analysts to espouse the virtues of preventive environmental policy and then to have to define the objective as 'an "*ex ante*" elimination of repair measures for pollution damage and the minimisation of retrospective pollution control' (Janicke, 1985, p. 5). Such a definition basically takes us back to the physically based no-damage, no-risk goal. As with Pareto optimality (as originally defined), this is a worthy objective and would clearly benefit everyone if it could be achieved at no cost to anyone. But unless we abandon the idea of scarcity, on which both environmentalism and economics is based, then trade-offs between objectives are inevitable. No amount of sophistry will lend compatibility to objectives which are based on different ideologies and value systems.

It is always easier to talk in the abstract about 'higher order' policy objectives than it is to devise mechanisms capable of achieving them under less than conditions of theoretical purity in implementation and 'customer' response. Indeed, one of the basic problems is to translate what amounts to ethical ideas into goals the achievement of which can be tested in some way. How, for example, does an agency measure the allocative efficiency of its decisions, except in the tautological way of assuming that the closer they get to employing the mechanisms theoretically capable of producing social welfare maximisation, the more allocatively efficient they must be? There are similar difficulties in giving specificity to notions of sustainable development, while the objective of social justice (distributive equity, equality, fairness) is also problematic since the terms themselves are subject to markedly different meanings.

In practice, managers/policy-makers, operating at all stages within the policy-implementation process, work to a more concrete set of objectives, some influenced, of course, by the ethical notions contained in the 'higher order' ideas. Basically, managers have to translate an often vaguely defined concept into measurable terms; inevitably in the process they not only simplify but also interpret the concept, sometimes in ways which significantly weaken the ethical position originally taken. For example, as already mentioned, the anticipatory idea may thus be changed from its ecological/environmental base to minimising the *costs* of control. The same type of problem exists for another currently popular concept, BPEO. The notion behind this idea is clearly valid, namely since resource use produces a residual mass broadly equal to that initially extracted, it makes sense to arrange the remaining discharges (after all forms of recycling have been explored) into the global ecosphere in a manner which reduces overall pollution damage. However, pollution has no absolute meaning common to all people and total damage functions are uncalculable in any meaning-ful way; thus there are considerable difficulties in establishing the 'best' allocation of discharges between media. To operationalise the concept, managers would tend to translate it into minimising the control and disposal *costs* of achieving set standards for the area and environmental media over which they have jurisdiction. Even assuming that they achieve cost minimisation, this takes us a considerable way from the original intention of damage minimisation and, in addition, it maintains the bias towards discharge control rather than increasing the effective capacity of the environment to absorb and degrade wastes.

Figure 8.2, simplistic and generalised, lists the management goals reported by various water, pollution control and planning authorities in Britain and Australia, studied in a very unsystematic manner between 1974 and 1986. This listing is clearly time-dependent, and inevitably the priority attached to each goal can shift rapidly in response to exogenous changes in the political economy and somewhat more slowly with changes in authority personnel, their expertise and understanding. For example, although at the beginning of the period virtually all agencies talked about efficiency, it was rare for the term to have a meaning which even vaguely approximated to the economic notion. It meant operating at reasonably low cost, keeping to budget, and so forth. What is striking, particularly in the water authorities, is the speed with which economic ideas on efficiency (including an understanding of the dynamics of pricing) have permeated the corporate culture if not corporate action.

Given this list of multiple, often conflicting, goals, it becomes clear that there is no single pollution control device or method of operationalising it which can address them all, and certainly not one which can meet them all with equal effectiveness. It is worth pointing out that any change in the mechanism of intervention in itself tends to produce conflicts with

| Economic | 1. Allocative |
| | 2. Technical |

Financial	1. Expenditure reduction
	2. Increase revenue
	3. Revenue stability
	4. Balance budget
	5. Minimise price/rate increases

Physical	1. Reduce pollution discharges
	2. Improve stream quality
	3. Meet fixed quality standards
	4. Stop accidental pollution and illegal operations
	5. Protect fishing and recreation
	6. Reduce volume of discharges in summer to maintain the 'natural' river ecosystem
	7. Minimise environmental change

| Technical | 1. Improve monitoring |
| | 2. Reduce inspectors work load |

Socio-political	1. Equity (ensure 'fair' treatment)
	2. Minimise political intervention
	3. Minimise public flack

Figure 8.2 Management objectives

organisational goals. Agency resistance to change cannot just be explained by innate conservatism or manager self-interest. Not only are there transitional costs (often considerable) incurred by agencies in adopting different management tools—information collection, staff retraining or recruitment, departmental reorganisation, etc.—but also change almost inevitably increases the visibility of the authority and the amount of public flack it receives. Losers under the status quo are only imperfectly aware of

Economic incentives	Unit pricing — Damage-based
	— Penal
	— Equity/social redistributive

Economic incentives

Unit pricing — Damage-based
              — Penal
              — Equity/social redistributive
Access fees
Permit auctions
Tradeable permits
Bribes and subsidies

Direct regulation

Discharge standards/conditions
Location/building codes
Product specification
Use controls over polluting substances
Equipment design specification
Water system design (e.g. in house recycling)
Monitoring requirements

Persuasion/information

Habit change/lifestyle
Campaigns
Information schemes

Collective action

Central collection and treatment
Waste water reclamation for dual supply–
    recycling
Stream flow variation
Reoxygenation (naturally by changing channel
    character or artificially)
Land-use zoning
Design of urban run-off systems
River zoning
Investment in alternative technologies

Enabling measures

Jurisdictional change
Removal of established rights

Figure 8.3   Pollution control tools

(a)	Degree to which waste load is reduced.
(b)	Degree to which each management technique is effective, taken alone.
(c)	Time-span required for implementation.
(d)	Scope for implementation discretion, control avoidance and non-enforcement.
(e)	Administrative costs, administrative competence required and complexity of system.
(f)	Cost structures (total expenditure—time path—factor input combinations).
(g)	*Who* bears the damage reduction costs.
(h)	*Who* bears the administrative burden and costs.
(i)	*Who* bears continued pollution costs.
(j)	How do those affected in (g), (h) and (i) respond.
(k)	Political and public acceptability.

Figure 8.4 Variable consequences of management

their disadvantage and of the benefits they could derive under a different system; those whose relative position is affected by change are clearly much more aware of it.

Tools of intervention

There are basically four types of interventionist tool which governments can introduce, all of which may need to be accompanied by enabling measures to allow or facilitiate their use (Figure 8.3). Within each of the broad groups—economic incentives, direct regulation, persuasion/information, and collective (or community) action—there are numerous variants, all of which will vary somewhat in their effectiveness, acceptability and consequences (Figure 8.4).

It should perhaps be noted that all groups contain measures which promote *ex ante* reductions in residual generation and *ex post* reductions in subsequent discharges or the damage caused by them—at least they do conceptually. The existence of economic incentives should promote innovation in both 'cleaner' technologies and disposal methods (Pearce and Turner, 1984); moreover, the variants which rely on taxes/charges rather than subsidies should readjust relative product prices and thus act to shift patterns of demand in favour of products involving lower environmental damage costs.

Likewise, although many forms of direct regulation are essentially reactive in nature, there is considerable evidence to suggest that standard setting (particularly when accompanied by the threat of increased stringency) has stimulated innovative technological change (see Weidner, 1986, for example). Moreover, the existence of the more conciliatory forms of direct regulation, which necessarily involve persuasion and information as measures to alter polluter behaviour, may also help change business attitudes towards the environment. Such attitudes are not only vital to the acceptance of pollution control as a legitimate policy goal, but also to its incorporation into the set of factors considered when process, product and locational decisions are made, thus allowing preventive rather than reactive policies to come into play.

The popular capture theory of regulation, whereby the regulatory authorities come to act in the interests of the regulated, tends to simplify the situation and neglect the important role which the regulators play in promoting attitude and behavioural shifts. In reality, the relationship between the regulators and the regulated appears more often to be a two-way process: field officers accept that firms cannot be pushed too far but manufacturers absorb the notion that pollution reduction is a 'good thing' and that there are 'good reasons' why their freedom of action should be constrained. As Hawkins (1984, p. xiii) puts it much more eloquently, 'enforcement premised on moral notions is recognizable to people, and a perceived identity of values shared by the enforcer, the regulated, and their interested publics grants the enforcement of regulation a more secure footing in an environment of ambivalence'. This view has been formed by work on water pollution prevention in southern England and in several metropolitan areas of Australia. Vogal (1983), Hawkins (1984) and Weidner (1986) report somewhat similar findings from studies in Britain and Japan, but clearly these may not apply in other countries.

Collective action is the regulatory form most commonly associated with preventive environmental policy, although once again it has numerous variants which clear up residuals after generation—the most obvious of these is sewage treatment. It is difficult to imagine any situation, short of massive population reduction and a return to subsistence forms of living in small communities, when such *ex post* investments will not be necessary, which serves as a reminder that pollution is not just a product of economic growth, inappropriate technologies and market imperfections. Undoubtedly, there is much validity in the view that there has been a relative neglect of collective measures, which seek to anticipate and prevent environmental damage rather than treating pollution control as a fire-fighting exercise. Well before the current spate of literature on the subject, Bach (1972) was discussing the need to adopt measures to reduce residual generation and to increase the effective capacity of the environment to absorb waste products without creating damage. Similarly, numerous works on water pollution control argued that options such as stream flow variation and reoxygenation were omitted from the perceived package of damage abatement measures.

However, there are clear reasons, other than administrative myopia, bureaucratic conservatism and professional self-interest, why this bias in policy should have occurred and will probably continue to occur (O'Riordan, 1985). Apart from the obvious point that anticipatory action requires considerable sophistication in knowledge and understanding, not only of environmental system dynamics but also of likely technological innovations and production patterns, there is the very real problem that environmental groups (and the public) change the unacceptable damage goal-posts. In addition, there are often considerable difficulties in creating the organisations which have the appropriate jurisdictional and functional responsibilities to take some forms of preventive action. Further, there is the important question of the acceptability of anticipatory control. As Gladwin (1980) points out, 'research on conflict in general, for example, has shown that disputes tend to become more difficult to resolve the greater the extent to which the issues at stake are intangible (and) highly uncertain . . .' (p. 251). This clearly has implications for preventive policy as anticipatory action must involve high levels of uncertainty. Another feature which tends to reduce the feasibility of truly anticipatory measures is that they will inevitably be slow to produce any clear effects, whereas their costs to affected groups will be immediately apparent.

The evidence from experience

Some reference to implementation experience has been made in previous sections of the chapter. Here the intention is to note briefly some of the management implications which appear to arise from the use of three types of pollution control, tool-economic incentives, conciliatory forms of direct regulation and persuasion/information—in the water pollution case.

It has to be assumed that the relevant control objective is to reduce the waste load discharged either as much as is 'practicable' or to some politically bargained/administratively determined river quality standard. This assumption not only accords with practice, but also avoids the necessity to rehearse the well-known arguments why the damage function is not a calculable, discrete and exogenously determined entity which can be used to establish 'optimal' discharge levels. Concentration on the question of waste load reduction mechanisms clearly neglects all forms of collective response, except treatment plants. In Britain and Australia additional flow releases from impounding reservoirs have been authorised to increase the absorptive capacity of streams, but this has been a crisis response to specific pollution incidents and is not considered as a standard damage reduction option.

The first important point is that where pricing of some sort is employed it never can be used alone. This is not simply a product of the conservatism and lack of understanding by the regulators of the advantages and functions of the price mechanism. Nor is it solely due to 'manipulation' by the regulated, who oppose any moves to make them pay for the residual pollution they create, or to fears by the regulated and regulators alike that charges will increase industrial costs, reduce competitiveness and possibly increase levels of unemployment. Undoubtedly, protection of established economic interests and the need to 'buy' acceptance of pollution abatement are part of the explanation but there are legitimate behavioural, technical and administrative reasons why prices alone are not enough.

A number of studies have shown (primarily in the context of trade effluent charges) that a significant proportion of dischargers—probably between 25–30 per cent—do not understand even relatively simple pricing systems, in the sense that they do not perceive how significantly different levels of payment could arise if they altered the strength/volume composition of the effluent (Webb and Woodfield, 1979; Rees, 1985). Moreover, many of those firms which did understand the system did not have the knowledge about alternative treatment methods and costs, recycling opportunities or about the potential for product, process or input changes. They therefore failed to perceive ways in which they could respond to the charges. In these circumstances, the field officer's role in discretionary standard setting of giving information, persuading and advising the discharger to reduce the waste load, is also required under pricing systems. Rarely, then, is it valid to consider pricing as the least costly and self-administering form of control. In fact it will require all the monitoring and information services provided under discretionary standards and will incur the additional costs of billing.

Further, it is clear that no pricing arrangement can capture all the essence of the pollution problem; this applies equally to tradeable permits or permit auctions as much as to discharge fees. Not only would some polluting substances have to be omitted from any comprehensive price schedule or permit, but also standards do not simply attempt to influence the *quantity* and *quality* of discharge. Regulations may seek to affect the location of the waste storage and outlet points, control the timing and rate of output, and reduce the risk of accidental and highly polluting discharges. All these suggest that some form of consent conditions and monitoring would still be required both to minimise pollution damage and to utilise the natural absorptive and regenerative capacity of the watercourse (i.e. lowering the cost of dealing with a given biodegradable form of effluent).

Conceptually it would be possible to envisage an effluent fee structure incorporating a variant of peak-load pricing—to curb disposals occurring at times of day or periods in the year when the absorptive capacity of the stream was lowest, and to encourage the spread of discharges both spatially and temporally to avoid pollution surges. The practicality of such a structure is, however, another matter. Likewise in the case of tradeable permits there would be formidable problems in ensuring that discharge 'rights' were not exercised at points along the water course where the damage is greatest and over such short time spans that highly polluted conditions would result. Standards may also be required for highly dangerous substances where, at least above a certain concentration, discharges need to be avoided at all costs. It would be too risky to rely even on very high unit charges or permit 'weights' to produce the desired polluter response.

A number of writers have suggested that the fact that economic tools have simply been grafted on to existing standard setting and persuasion arrangements is regrettable, since this complicates an already confused regulatory framework. While recognising this as a legitimate concern— particularly in cases where the three tools have not been coordinated to give the polluter a consistent message—it is argued that a mixed system is essential not only to overcome resistance to the introduction of economic tools, but also to give the polluter the required information on which to base a response and to cover more fully the diverse dimensions of the pollution problem. Moreover, as Brown and Johnson (1984) have pointed out:

the benefit of having both a system of standards and charges is that the water quality regulations can each be adjusted through time to produce a result more harmonious with the desired water quality objectives. The objectives will change through time as a result of changing environmental and economic conditions.

A mixed system also 'hits' two, often quite distinct, departments within a corporation with the pollution control message. This is of relevance since, except in very small concerns, the person responsible for waste disposal is not usually in charge of paying the bills. Therefore, unless the payments were markedly out of line with inflation, were newly introduced or became a significant operating cost item, the financial staff would rarely challenge the waste engineer to rethink established practices.

An important implication of recent studies is that if the management objective is to improve stream quality quickly, or to hit particular dated targets for the reduction in the length of rivers of unacceptable river quality (Littlechild, 1986), then a unit charging system may be inappropriate (unless accompanied by standards and subsidies). This arises because technical and capital constraints within firms are significant response-inhibiting factors at least in the short to medium terms and because charges cannot give any guaranteed, finely tuned response (Storey and Elliott, 1977; Rothwell and Gardiner, 1983). It must also be pointed out that the response to charges may be particularly slow in situations where previous direct regulations have already encouraged producers to adopt the most obvious and least expensive abatement measures. Certainly this was the case for trade effluent discharges to sewers in England and Wales; the post-1974 rationalisation of charges and the substantial subsequent price increases did not appear to have a significant effect on discharge levels or quality. Amongst a variety of reasons given by firms for this was the suggestion that they had already done what they could in order to meet their discharge conditions. Inevitably, much more knowledge of the determinants of management response to pollution control incentives is essential before their effectiveness in meeting particular environmental quality objectives can be evaluated with any degree of certainty.

Further, in implementing any charging system or standard setting exercise for one part of the water-use and disposal cycle, an analysis of the linkages or interdependencies in the system can be crucial. This can perhaps be best illustrated by an example. Under the New South Wales Clean Waters Act, 1972, direct discharge standards for disposals to watercourses became in most cases much more stringent than those for the sewers. The result was a large increase in the trade effluent load received at local authority treatment works, which had not been foreseen in past investment planning. New capacity therefore became necessary at a time when expenditure on sewage treatment plants was already high to ensure that these too met the conditions of the Act. However, as is typically the case, trade effluent charges were based on historic accounting costs; they therefore increased markedly to cover the new debt charges. Ten years later, the trade effluent load had fallen substantially. In part the reasons for this were structural changes in industry and a downturn in the economy, but both water industry staff and manufacturers attribute a proportion of the fall to the higher charges. The result—excess development of treatment capacity. Problems of interdependency are easier to perceive and take account of with the sort of multi-functional regional water authorities which exist in England and Wales; they became much more intractable in fragmented jurisdictions (see Brown and Johnson, 1984).

It has commonly been asserted in the theoretical literature that charging schemes provide superior incentives for innovation in pollution abatement technologies (e.g. Kneese and Schultze, 1975; Russell, 1979; Downing and White, 1986). The difficulty is that it is necessary to assume that entrepreneurs are profit-maximisers, using discounted cash-flow techniques and with perfect information, in order to get this result. While there is some evidence that charges will promote innovation (e.g. Brown and Johnson,

1984), there is little which suggests that actually implemented pricing schemes are any better at doing this than discretionary standards. Certainly from an admittedly small sample of trade effluent discharges it was clear that the factors affecting a firm's decision to invest in innovation had little to do with charges. Most firms were 'innovation-takers', requiring proof that a system worked and detailed cost information (most often provided through the field inspectors) before they even considered changing accepted practice; in all cases the need for a change was cited as meeting discharge conditions. Further, in a number of industry groups, producers looked to one particular firm for research leadership and did not contemplate trying to innovate abatement technologies themselves.

Conclusion

Over the last few years the sometimes vitriolic condemnation of direct regulation has been leavened slightly by appraisals which have looked at how regulatory systems, which are based on cooperation between regulator and polluter, have worked in practice. While no one claims perfection for such systems, there is now growing recognition of their achievements in improving water quality while protecting economic interests. Use of pricing systems as a revenue-raising and redistributive device may also have a role to play. However, in a British context, not only should the advocates of pricing be wary of destroying the existing cooperative arrangements, but also of the dangers of introducing a 'commercial' approach to pollution control, given the difficulties in establishing the value of less polluted environments.

References

Bach, W., 1972, *Atmospheric Pollution, Problems in Geography Series*, McGraw Hill, New York.

Bacharach, S.B. and Lawler, E.J., 1981, *Bargaining: Power, Tactics and Outcomes*, Jossey-Bass, San Francisco.

Bardach, E., 1978, *The Implementation Game*, MIT Press, Cambridge, Mass.

_____ 1979, 'On Designing Implementable Programs', in Majone, G. and Quade, E. (eds), *Pitfalls of Analysis*, Wiley, London and New York.

Barrett, S. and Fudge, C. (eds), 1981, *Policy and Action*, Methuen, London.

Brown Jr., M.G. and Johnson, R.W., 1984, 'Pollution Control by Effluent Charges: It Works in the Federal Republic of Germany, Why Not in the US?', *Natural Resources Journal*, **24** (4).

Butlin, J.A., 1981, *Economics of Environmental and Natural Resources Policy*, Longman, London.

Comar, C.L., 1979, 'SO$_2$ Regulation Ignores Costs, Poor Science Base', in 'Has Environmental Regulation Gone Too Far?', *C & EN*, 23 April, pp. 42–6.

Dasgupta, P., 1982, *The Control of Resources*, Blackwell, Oxford.

Downing, P.B. and White, L.J., 1986, 'Innovation in Pollution Control', *Journal of Environmental Economics and Management*, **13** (1).

Dunsire, A., 1978, *Implementation in a Bureaucracy*, Martin Robertson, Oxford.

Gladwin, T.N., 1980, 'Patterns of Environmental conflict over industrial facilities in the United States 1970–78', *Natural Resources Journal*, **20** (2).

Hawkins, K., 1984, *Environment and Enforcement*, Clarendon Press, Oxford.

Janicke, M., 1985, 'Preventive Environmental Policy as Ecological Modernisation and Structural Policy', International Institute for Environment and Society, Discussion Paper 11UG dp 85–2, Berlin.

Jenkins, W.I., 1978, *Policy Analysis: A Political and Organisational Perspective*, Martin Robertson, London.

Kapp, K.W., 1970, 'Environmental Disruption and Social Costs: A Challenge to Economics', *Kyklos*, **23** (4).

——— 1972, 'Social Costs, Neo-classical Economics, Environmental Planning: A Reply', in Sachs, I. (ed.), *Political Economy of Environment: Problems of Method*, Mouton, Paris.

Kneese, A.V. and Schultze, C.L., 1975, *Pollution, Prices and Public Policy*, Brookings, Washington, DC.

Knoepfel, P. and Weidner, H., 1983, 'Air Quality Programs in Europe: Some Results of a Comparative Study', in Downing, P. (ed.), *International Comparisons in Implementing Pollution Laws*, Kluwer-Nijhoft, Amsterdam.

Lecomber, R., 1979, *The Economics of Natural Resources*, Macmillan, London.

Lenz, R.T. and Lyles, M.A., 1985, 'Paralysis by Analysis: Is Your Planning System Becoming Too Rational?, *Long Range Planning*, **18** (4).

Levitt, R., 1980, *Implementing Public Policy*, Croom Helm, London.

Littlechild, S.C., 1986, *Economic Regulation of Privatised Water Authorities*, report submitted to the Department of the Environment, 25 January, HMSO, London.

Majone, G., 1976, 'Choice Among Policy Instruments for Pollution Control', *Policy Analysis*, **2** (4).

Majone, G. and Wildavsky, A., 1979, 'Implementation as Evolution', in Pressman, J.L. and Wildavsky, A. (eds), *Implementation*, Chapter 9, pp. 177–94, University of California Press, Berkeley.

Mazmanian, D.A. and Sabatier P.A., 1981, *Effective Policy Implementation*, Lexington Books, D.C. Heath and Co., Lexington, Mass.

O'Riordan, T., 1985, 'Anticipatory Environmental Policy', International Institute for Environment and Society, Discussion Paper 85–1, Berlin.

Peacock, A. (ed.), 1984, *The Regulation Game: How British and West German Companies Bargain with Government*, Blackwell, Oxford.

Pearce, D.W. and Turner, R.K., 1984, 'The Economic Evaluation of Low and Non-Waste Technologies', *Resources and Conservation*, **11** (1).

Rees, J., 1985, *Natural Resources: Allocation, Economics and Policy*, Methuen, London.

Rothwell, R. and Gardiner, P., 1983, *The Impact of Environmental Regulations on*

Technological Change Processes in the UK Sugar Processing and Metal Plating Industries, SPRU, University of Sussex, Brighton.

Russell, C.S., 1979, 'What Can We Get from Effluent Charges?', *Policy Analysis*, Spring.

Schnaiberg, A., 1980, *The Environment: From Surplus to Scarcity*, Oxford University Press, New York.

Sharkansky, I., 1970, *The Routines of Politics*, Von Nostrand Reinhold, New York.

Simonis, U.E., 1984, 'Preventive Environmental Policy', International Institute for Environment and Society, Discussion Paper 11UG dp 84–12, Berlin.

Spulber, D.F., 1985, 'Effluent Regulation and Long-Run Optimality', *Journal of Environmental Economics and Management*, **12** (2).

Storey, D.J. and Elliott, D.J., 1977, 'An Effluent Charging Scheme for the River Tees?', *Chemistry and Industry*, 7 May.

Vogel, D., 1983, 'Cooperative Regulation: Environmental Protection in Great Britain', *The Public Interest*, **72** (1).

Webb, M.G. and Woodfield, R., 1979, 'Standards and Charges in the Control of Trade Effluent Discharges to Public Sewers', Discussion Paper 43, Institute of Social and Economic Research, Department of Economics, University of York.

Weidner, H., 1986, 'The Success and Limitations of Technocratic Environmental Policy', International Institute for Environment and Society, Discussion Paper 11UG dp 86–1, Berlin.

Chapter 9

Market Mechanisms of Pollution Control: 'Polluter Pays', Economic and Practical Aspects

John Pezzey*

I Introduction and summary

Introduction

For at least twenty years, many economists have suggested that firms discharging polluting effluents to the environment should somehow be made to pay a price for such discharges, related to the amount of environmental damage caused. The firms' decision about how much effluent to discharge would then be indirectly controlled by market forces created by a public pollution authority, rather than directly controlled by regulations laid down by the authority. The suggestion is made because, in theory, making all dischargers pay the same price for an extra unit of effluent discharged will achieve a cost-effective allocation of effluent control costs. That is, it will result in any target for the total effluent load from all firms being achieved at the lowest possible total of effluent control costs (ignoring any monetary transfers resulting from the price that dischargers pay for the effluent they still discharge), whereas regulations will generally result in higher total control costs for meeting the same overall effluent target.

The two main alternative *market mechanisms* of pollution control, which will result in all polluters paying the same price for an extra unit of polluting effluent, are levying a direct charge on each unit of such effluent

© Crown copyright 1988. Any views expressed in this chapter are solely those of the author. It is in no way intended to reflect a view of the Department of the Environment or any other government department. I am grateful to Robert Barrass, Robin Bidwell, Roger Bright, Michael Common, Philip Dale, Johnathan Fisher, David Fisk, John Knowles, Peter MacCormack, Peter McIntosh, Richard Mills, Christopher Nash, David Pearce, Adrian Sinfield, Kerry Turner, Derek Varley, Jan Vernon and Robin Wilson for their constructive comments and corrections at various stages during the writing of this chapter. Any faults that remain are mine alone. I am especially grateful to Peter MacCormack, David Pearce and Kerry Turner for their support and encouragement, and to personal computer word-processing for easing the writer's burden.

discharged (*pollution charges*), and allowing the right to discharge a given amount of effluent to be traded between dischargers (*tradable pollution consents*). Originally some economists proposed that such market mechanisms could completely replace regulatory controls on pollution (e.g. Zuckerman and Beckerman, 1972). However, as is discussed further below, it is nowadays generally recognised that controlling pollution by price alone may well not protect the environment adequately from abnormally high pollution loads. It is therefore generally assumed throughout this chapter that market mechnisms of pollution control would in practice incorporate or be accompanied by, some form of regulatory control over maximum pollution loads.

In the United Kingdom, public interest in market mechanisms goes back at least as far as the Third Report of the Royal Commission on Environmental Pollution (ACEP, 1972), and the ideas were further aired by McIntosh (1977) and by a parliamentary inquiry into the Polluter Pays Principle (House of Lords, 1983), all of which spoke favourably of at least some form of market mechanisms. Continuing interest is being shown by the Commission of the European Communities (EC, 1986). Yet, with the exception of charges for treating effluents discharged into sewers, no significant market mechanisms have so far been introduced into the United Kingdom system of pollution control in the intervening period. Market mechanisms have been more widely applied abroad, for example in the air emissions trading programme in the United States (Palmisano, 1985) and with water pollution charges in France, West Germany and The Netherlands (ERL, 1984, 1985), but they have not been without their critics (Liroff, 1986) and they have generally been used far less ambitiously than most economists would have hoped or predicted. In the author's opinion, progress has been slow not so much because of a failure to appreciate the theoretical cost-effectiveness of market mechanisms, although misperceptions certainly do exist that such mechanisms are simply intended to penalise polluters rather than to save resources, but more because there are genuine political and practical problems with such mechanisms. Many of these problems are highlighted by Rees's chapter in this volume.

This chapter pays particular attention to interpreting economic concepts in terms familiar to policy-makers and vice versa. It is not based on any new field studies, nor does it contain any new quantitative analysis of existing data. Instead it provides a framework for further quantitative study, which would ultimately be needed before the debate about market mechanisms can be resolved and more practical use made of them. It aims to be comprehensive rather than definitive, so that in some areas (such as the allocation of pollution subsidies and the hoarding of consents) it is made clear that further analysis would be fruitful. The examples used are mainly drawn from the author's experience in the UK water field, but most of the chapter is relevant to pollution control policy in any country and in any environmental medium.

Two general aspects of market mechanisms have had to be left out: first, there is no review of the *history* of the debate on market mechanisms, in the United Kingdom, EC or elsewhere. Second, and most important, the problem of *uncertainty* is generally ignored. In most of the chapter it is assumed that all costs and benefits are known now and in the future, but in practice there is often great uncertainy, particularly about the environmental effects of pollutants (Burrows, 1979). If the pollutant is nondegradable, the damage will be cumulative and irreversible as well as uncertain, making it much harder to analyse with conventional economic techniques, as Pearce (1976) has pointed out.

Concern over such uncertainty often gives rise to the precautionary principle of pollution control. This principle does not really recognise the concept, used throughout this chapter, of an 'optimal' or 'acceptable' target level of pollution, nor the aim to use a cost-effective allocation of controls to achieve this target. Instead, the precautionary principle generally aims to achieve 'maximum' reductions in pollution, using the 'best available technology'. Such concepts are not explored here, but provided the uncertainty is mainly over environmental damage rather than over effluent control options, market mechanisms may still play a useful role where there is uncertainty. If regional or national targets for effluent reduction can be agreed, it may be possible to show, after consideration of the practical and policy aspects of market mechanisms analysed in this chapter, that the use of market mechanisms can achieve these targets at significantly lower cost than by prescribing the use of best available technology.

Summary

This summary tries to describe the content of the chapter to the non-economist, and so uses as little economic jargon as possible. Any resulting lack of precision is resolved in the main text, where technical economic terms are used where appropriate. All the economic theory can be found in standard environmental economics texts (e.g. Baumol and Oates, 1975; Pearce, 1976; Burrows, 1979), so few theoretical references are given.

Section II looks at the basic concepts of optimal effluent and pollution, and at who pays pollution control costs and pollution damage costs, seen from the point of view of a single firm. It lists the numerous assumptions that for ease of analysis have had to be used in Sections II–IV, which are mainly that:

— firms are competitive and try to maximise their profits;
— firms have access to a finite local environment;
— firms discharge effluent at a constant rate which causes non-cumulative, reversible damage to the environment;
— the cost to a firm of reducing effluent by one more unit rises as more effluent is reduced;
— both pollution damage and pollution control costs can be monitored at negligible cost.

The common terms used in pollution economics are all carefully defined. The 'costs of pollution' are divided into effluent control costs (which falls as effluent rises) and environmental damages costs (which rise as effluent rises). *Pollution* is defined as occurring whenever effluent causes a perceived loss in environmental value, although other valid definitions are noted. The *optimal effluent load* is defined as the load which minimises the sum of control costs plus environmental damage costs, and *optimal pollution* is the environmental effect of this load. Finally, acceptable effluent is defined as meaning essentially the same as optimal pollution, both in the short and long run.

Section II then introduces the incentive pollution charge, which is a charge, levied per unit of effluent, at a rate which on its own will give an adequate economic incentive for dischargers to keep their effluent down to optimal levels, and with the charge revenue not returned to dischargers. It shows that, where there is considered to be a long-established pollution right—that, where a discharger has long had the consent of the control authority to discharge polluting effluent at a certain rate, free of any charge related to the effluent load, even if the control authority still technically has the legal right to take away its consent—then such incentive charging will be regarded as unacceptable by the dischargers. Section II then analyses the Polluter Pays Principle (PPP) in terms of optimal pollution and pollution rights. It argues that:

— the Standard interpretation of the Polluter Pays Principle (*Standard PPP*), generally applied by most Western countries, requires polluters to pay for controlling effluent down to the optimal (= acceptable) load, but not for the environmental damage caused by the optimal effluent load;
— Standard PPP therefore effectively grants polluters a *de facto* right to discharge the optimal level of effluent free of charge;
— therefore, wherever the Standard PPP holds, incentive charging would be unacceptable, because it would make dischargers pay in net terms for their optimal effluent discharges.

Section II finally examines whether there is any argument for eliminating pollution rights by applying an *Extended PPP*, defined so that polluters must pay damage costs as well as control costs. It suggests that an unwavering application of Standard PPP could result in somewhat arbitrary changes in pollution rights when new sources of pollution appear; but it concludes that any choice between Standard and Extended PPP, either generally or case by case, can be made only on political, not economic grounds.

Section III is not directly concerned with market mechanisms, although it looks at the effect on pollution control and damage costs of introducing a more cost-effective pollution control mechanism (such as a market mechanism) at industry level. It first shows that an increase in public demand for environmental services leads to a reduction in the optimal effluent load, and an associated increase in effluent control costs which under the Standard PPP are borne by the polluting industry. It then shows that the introduction of a cost-effective pollution control mechanism, which effectively makes overall effluent control cheaper, will generally mean that a further reduction in effluent load is socially justified. This effluent reduction will of course reduce environmental damage, but under the Standard PPP industry pays no damage costs anyway and so does not benefit from this. Industry will save money by achieving the existing level of effluent control more cheaply, but it will also have to pay extra control costs to achieve the further effluent reduction required. It is possible that these extra control costs could exceed the savings at the existing effluent level, in which case industry would have a financial motive to resist the introduction of the cost-effective control mechanism.

Section IV first shows that market mechanisms can theoretically achieve the most cost-effective control of an industry's effluents, provided that all effluents are uniformly dispersed throughout the environment. It shows how a market mechanism leads each firm to reduce its effluent down to a point where reducing it by one more unit will cost the same as for all other firms in that industry, so that it is the impossible to reduce the overall control costs for a given total effluent load by any redistribution of the total load between individual firms. It also shows how a market mechanism gives an incentive for inventing and introducing improved effluent control technologies.

The following market mechanisms are then examined in detail:

(a) *incentive pollution charges*: charging in proportion to the polluting effect of effluent discharges, with the revenue not being returned to polluters, and (it is assumed here) with backstop regulatory powers to control maximum discharge rates;
(b) *distributive pollution charges*: as for incentive charges, but with the charge revenue returned to polluters in the form of subsidies for new pollution control equipment;

(c) *granted tradable pollution consents*: converting existing consents to discharge effluent into property rights, which are granted to dischargers and may then be traded according to certain rules, but may be recalled in part by the issuing authority without compensation;

(d) *sold tradable pollution consents*: as for granted consents, except that the consents are initially sold or auctioned to dischargers rather than granted free of charge.

Other mechanisms such as subsidies, product charges and charges on potentially polluting inputs are mentioned in passing. Input charges are considered worth further study in cases where, owing to pollution being very diffuse or affecting several environmental media, monitoring costs are especially high.

It is shown that market mechanisms such as incentive charges and sold tradable consents, where the revenue from the market mechanism is not returned to dischargers, would make them pay for discharging effluent loads which are socially acceptable. If the Standard PPP applies, dischargers will at present consider themselves to have the *de facto* pollution right to discharge such loads free of charge, and so will be likely to resist the introduction of such charges. In contrast, distributive charges and granted tradable consents are both shown to be fully compatible with pollution rights derived from the Standard PPP. Distributive charging is shown to have the automatic effect of reducing total effluent load (so that it cannot be justified if no pollution reduction is called for), and to have certain disadvantages such as having to calculate the charge and subsidy rates and administer the subsidy scheme.

Section V examines what might be the practical advantages and disadvantages of the two market mechanisms—distributive charging and granted tradable consents—that are compatible with Standard PPP. It first of all notes that, in assessing market mechanisms, a thorough economic study of existing regulatory mechanisms would be needed, since a cost-effective and equitable regulatory system of sharing control costs between dischargers is theoretically possible. It then notes that many legal and institutional implications of market mechanisms would need to be assessed, such as whether market mechanisms would be run by existing or new control agencies.

It then looks at what happens when various assumptions made throughout Sections II–IV do not hold in practice. It shows how the existence of monopoly power or economics of scale in a polluting industry mean that market mechanisms do not necessarily reduce overall effluent control costs. It particularly shows how variations in the sensitivity of local environments to pollution—measured by *transfer coefficients*—need to be taken into account if market mechanisms are to achieve savings in control costs without allowing local environmental deterioration, but that this will require much expensive monitoring. It points out that in practice several pollutants may have to be handled by any control mechanism, and shows that tradable consents may be particularly difficult to handle where there are several pollutants or where local pollution increases are unacceptable.

Section V therefore shows that, before any overall conclusion could be reached about the desirability of introducing market mechanisms of pollution control, further practical study would be needed. Such study would both estimate the potential savings in overall pollution control costs from using market mechanisms of control, and make a realistic assessment of the administrative costs and political acceptability of such mechanisms. Section VI ends by highlighting the more important policy conclusions to be drawn from the chapter, and listing some of the practical questions that any further study would need to answer.

II Optimal pollution, pollution rights and the Polluter Pays Principle

Assumptions

Section II looks at who pays the costs associated with pollution, with any questions of changes in pollution costs through different mechanisms of pollution control being left to Sections III–IV. First, we must review the concept of optimal pollution, and in this section it mostly suffices to consider a single firm, with the analysis of a multi-firm industry being left till later. In order to make the analysis tractable, the following market conditions have to be assumed to hold throughout Sections II–IV, except where otherwise noted:

(a) The firm is in *perfect competition in its output market*, so that it has no control over the price it can get for its output. It also seeks to maximise its profits. On its own the firm cannot pass on any increases in pollution control costs to its customers by increasing its output price.
(b) The firm is in some sense environmentally isolated, in that it has sole access to a *finite local environment*. A small increase in the firm's effluent, if the assimilative capacity of the local environment is already used up, will cause a finite and increasing amount of extra damage to the environment. The total amount of environmental damage depends only on the firm's own effluent load, not on any other firm's effluents discharged to other environments.
(c) The firm faces *diminishing returns to scale*, both in its general cost structure and more importantly in its cost of effluent control. An

obvious cause of rising control costs would be where a single stream of effluent is cleaned up more and more thoroughly using ever more sophisticated technology. Having to assume diminishing returns to scale is quite restrictive, and we return to this problem later.

(d) The firm is assumed to discharge effluent at a *constant rate directly into the environment* (only in Sections IV and V do we briefly consider variable discharges and discharges into sewers).

(e) The polluting potential of the firm's effluent can be measured by a *single parameter* (e.g. biological oxygen demand, or the amount of a single contaminant or 'pollutant'), and the effluent causes reversible, *non-cumulative pollution damage*.

(f) The pollution damage is related solely to the *rate* of contaminant discharge (which is proportional to the effluent load) and not to the *concentration* of contaminants in the effluent.

(g) There are *negligible costs of monitoring* the effluent loads, its contaminant content or its detailed effects on the environment.

(h) There are *no externalities associated with effluent control* technologies, so that the marginal social cost of control is identical to the marginal private cost to the firm of control. This assumes, for example, that the firm would already be facing an optimal price for any *cross-media pollution effects*, whereby a liquid effluent might be converted to a solid sludge which itself imposes an environmental cost; or that effluent control does not cause social costs by *increasing employment* in local communities.

(i) The time-scale considered is the *long run*, so that the marginal cost of effluent control includes interest and depreciation charges on the cost of any new effluent treatment plant needed to reduce effluent by one unit. However, the important differences between short-run and long-run considerations are spelled out clearly at the start.

The extent to which these assumptions will hold in practice will vary from case to case, and by no means all of them are necessary to reach some of the conclusions that emerge below. However, no systematic analysis of either the accuracy or the need for the assumptions has been attempted here.

Given assumptions (a)–(i), a very useful way of analysing the economics of its effluent control is to use figures which plot marginal cost against effluent load (all except Figure 9.15 are of this form, and note that all 'curves' are shown as straight lines merely to make drawing easier). The horizontal axis measures effluent load, increasing from left to right, as measured by the mass of contaminant discharged in unit time. The vertical axis measures both the marginal cost to the firm of reducing effluent load and the marginal cost to the environment of increasing effluent load. Since the units of total cost are money/time, the units of marginal cost will be (money/time)/(mass/time) money/mass. The area under a graph will then represent total annual costs.

Cost of effluent control

Given these market conditions, curve C_1 in Figure 9.1 shows the long-run marginal private cost, assumed to be known at least by the firm, of decreasing effluent load below OH. OH is the load that maximises the firm's profits, which the firm would therefore discharge in the absence of any restrictions on effluent. By assumption C_1 is also the long-run marginal social cost of effluent control. The rise of C_1 from right to left reflects the diminishing returns to scale in pollution control. Area QRH represents the total cost to the firm in money/time units of discharging OQ rather than OH effluent load, or conversely the total benefit of discharging OH rather than OQ.

Note that, either in the long-run or short-run, the marginal cost curves in this chapter incorporate any changes in control technology that the firm may find economic for the particular level of effluent load and time-scale being considered. In the short-run the opportunities for economic changes in control technology are obviously more limited, giving rise to the steeper short-run marginal cost curve CO in Figure 9.1. Note also that the marginal cost is defined as the reduction in the firm's profits caused by the firm having to reduce effluent by one more unit. As Auld (1985) and others have pointed out, this definition includes more than just tangible extra spending on effluent control (which itself comprises both operating costs, and capital costs annuitised over the relevant time-scale). Effluent control might be achieved instead by a diversion of some of the firm's managerial effort away from producing output and into ensuring that existing control systems function properly, or simply by a planned reduction in the firm's output. Either of these will reduce the firm's profits and must therefore be counted as costs of effluent control.

There are of course many well-publicised cases where 'Pollution Prevention Pays', i.e. attention to pollution control is found to decrease associated raw material costs and increase profits. This presumes the existence of cost-reducing opportunities, which have nothing to do with pollution, which firms have somehow been ignoring. Such apparently irrational behaviour undoubtedly happens, but our chapter has to assume that firms have already exploited such opportunities to the full, so that effluent reduction will decrease rather than increase profits.

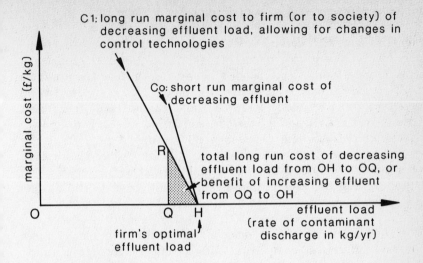

Figure 9.1   Effluent control costs

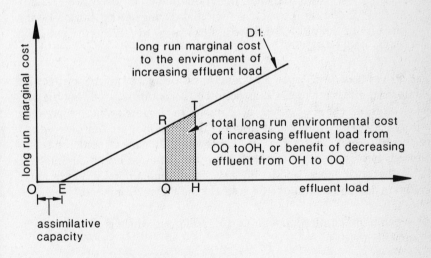

Figure 9.2   Effluent damage costs

Cost of environmental damage, and definitions of pollution

Turning to Figure 9.2, curve D_1 is the long-run marginal environmental damage by the effluent, also in units of money/mass (loss of environmental benefits in money/time units divided by increase in load in mass/time units). Note that damage is assumed to be non-cumulative and, in a world of perfect knowledge, to be known in both physical and value terms (we are conveniently ignoring whether damage is measured in terms of compensating or equivalent variations). But before we can refer to this as pollution damage, we have to define 'pollution', since there are a number of different, equally valid definitions in both everyday and technical use. For our present purposes it is most convenient to use the following definition:

(1) Pollution occurs if both man-made effluent to the environment causes physical effects, in comparison with a state of zero effluent, on amenities or on living or other resources, and human beings regard these effects as some kind of personal or social loss or damage. If physical effects occur and are known about, but nobody regards them as any sort of loss or damage, then pollution is not occurring. Strictly speaking, pollution is the environmental damage effect caused by the effluent, but it is also used, here as elsewhere, to refer to the polluting effluent load itself.

Thus a river which was once drinkable but is drinkable no longer because of industrial effluent is defined as polluted. As is further discussed below, such pollution can be either acceptable or unacceptable, depending entirely on whether the cost of stopping the effluent is greater or less than the benefit of making the river drinkable again. In general some pollution is socially necessary, since (assuming that the pollutant is non-cumulative) the cost to consumers of goods and services of eliminating the very last unit of effluent damage is bound to be greater than the environmental benefit of so doing.

A second, quite different definition of 'pollution' which is often explicitly or implicitly used is:

(2) Pollution occurs only when man-made effluent causes unacceptable environmental effects, such as hazards to human health or interference with legitimate uses of the environment.

With this definition, all 'pollution' should be eliminated; and conversely, if agreed environmental standards are complied with then no 'pollution' is occurring.

Yet a third definition of pollution is:

(3) Pollution occurs when man-made effluent contains potentially damaging contaminants, even if the actual contaminant load is so low that it causes no detectable environmental damage.

In this chapter, whenever the meaning of 'pollution' is in any doubt, it is always definition (1) that is implied and not definitions (2) or (3). Effluent and pollution are thus quite distinct concepts. Pollution is zero until effluent exceeds some finite assimilation capacity OE—the maximum effluent load that can be absorbed without causing perceived environmental damage.

Curve D_1 is usually very hard to determine in any practical sense, although some progress has been made in recent years (mainly by US economists, reviewed by Pearce and Markandya, 1987) in developing techniques such as hedonic pricing and contingent valuation, which estimate money values for environmental costs and benefits from behavioural or attitudinal surveys. Most of the arguments here remain true in theory even if D_1 is unknown, although as already noted uncertainty will have a profound effect on how readily they can be applied to policy-making.

Referring to Figure 9.2, area QRTH represents the increase in the total long-run rate of environmental damage caused by an increase in effluent load from OQ to OH, or conversely the environmental benefit due to a decrease from OH to OQ. As with pollution control costs, there may well be a difference between long-run and short-run costs of pollution damage, due to the gradual nature of the dispersal of and ecological adaptations to pollutants, and the changing human valuations of such ecological adaptations. However, unlike marginal control costs, one cannot in general say that marginal damage costs are likely to be higher in the short-run than in the long-run; this is a complex issue at the boundary of economics and ecology which is not explored further here.

Optimal and acceptable pollution

The *socially optimal effluent load* is defined as the effluent load that will minimise the sum of the total social cost of effluent control by the firm (assumed here to be identical to the private cost to the firm) and the total social cost of effluent damage to the environment.

In Figure 9.3, where the long-run marginal control cost curve C_1 and damage cost curve D_1 are superimposed, this represents the load that minimises the sum of the areas under the two curves. The optimal load is

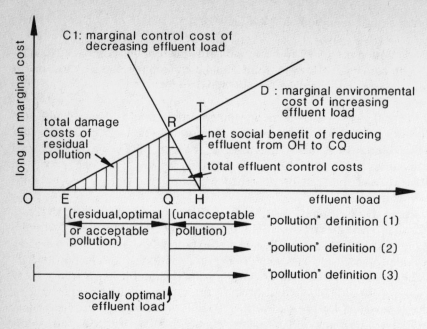

Figure 9.3   Socially optimal effluent load, and definitions of pollution

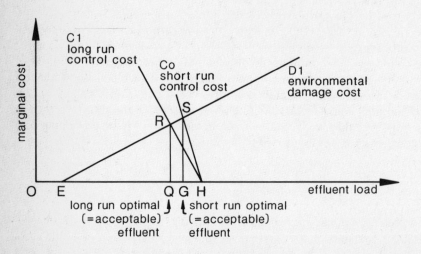

Figure 9.4   Long run and short run optimal effluent

therefore OQ, where the marginal control cost equals the marginal damage cost. In decreasing effluent load from the uncontrolled load OH to the optimum OQ, the benefit QRTH to the environment is greater than the cost to the firm QRH, giving a net social benefit of area RTH. The optimal effluent OQ can be subdivided into the assimilated effluent OE, and the polluting effluent load EQ, more commonly known as the 'residual pollution', which causes *optimal pollution* equal to cross-hatched area ERQ of environmental damage.

Figure 9.3 can also be used to illustrate the different definitions of pollution reviewed earlier. Under definition (1) (the one used in this chapter), pollution occurs when effluent exceeds OE, with effluent up to OQ being regarded as causing 'acceptable' pollution and beyond OQ as causing 'unacceptable' pollution. Under definition (2) pollution only occurs when effluent exceeds OQ, and under definition (3) pollution occurs for any effluent load at all.

Note that, as just illustrated, the concept of optimal pollution is rarely used in pollution control policy, which usually refers instead to acceptable pollution or an acceptable state of the environment (e.g. OECD, 1972). But acceptability implies, if only implicitly, an awareness that pollution has both environmental costs and commercial benefits, and that policy should be aimed at reaching a sensible balance between all these costs and benefits. It is therefore assumed here that optimal effluent means the same as acceptable effluent, and optimal pollution means the same as acceptable pollution, so that we can both use the normal tools of economic analysis and relate the results to policy. Using 'optimality' to mean the same as 'acceptability' departs from some common parlance, particularly with respect to short-run and long-run considerations. Consider Figure 9.4, where the long-run control cost curve C_1 meets the damage cost curve D_1 at an effluent level OQ, and the short-run curve C_0 meets D_1 at an effluent level OG. In common parlance one might say that OQ is the long-run 'optimum' which society is aiming for, but that in the short-run the costs of reaching it are too high and society must 'accept' the higher load OG. Here we simply regard OQ as the long-run optimal (= acceptable) effluent, and OG as the short-run optimal (= acceptable) effluent. In the very short-run, it is then possible to define optimal effluent as simply being whatever the actual effluent is now, even if it does not equal the declared environmental quality objective (thus we ignore problems of enforcement); for that objective may in fact be a long-run goal, and failure to achieve it now is a *de facto* acceptance that it is not optimal now.

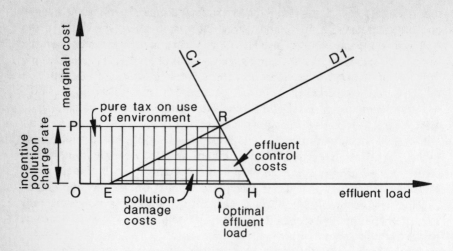

Figure 9.5   Pollution economics for an isolated firm

Pollution charges and pollution rights

Turning to Figure 9.5, how can OQ be achieved? The simplest way is by
setting and enforcing a regulation on the firm which requires a standard of
OQ. An alternative way, in theory at least, is by levying a charge of OP per
unit on the firm's effluent. This is known as an *incentive pollution charge*,
or *Pigovian tax*, to use the technical term. A profit-maximising firm will
then choose the effluent level OQ since then its marginal cost QR of
effluent control is equal to marginal cost of effluent increase, i.e. the
pollution charge OP. (If there are several firms discharging into different
local environments, then both optimal effluent OQ and pollution charge
OP may be different for each firm.)

Pollution charges will be explored further in Section IV, but the point to
note here is the striking difference between the regulatory and Pigovian tax
solutions as far as the firm's total (as opposed to marginal) finances are
concerned, namely the tax revenue OPRQ in Figure 9.5. If the firm is one
of the marginal ones in its industry, this extra tax burden on top of the cost
of effluent control QRH might well bankrupt it, when it could survive if it
only had to pay QRH alone. (The general reaction of the whole industry to
a Pigovian tax on its pollution will be to raise the price and reduce the
quantity of its output, reductions which may achieved by all firms reducing
output slightly, or by a few firms with higher than average costs ceasing
production altogether.) Bankruptcy leads to no pollution at all from the

firm, but no consumer benefits from its output either. Is this economically desirable?

A common-sense answer might be that it is economically correct for the polluter to pay all the pollution costs associated with its output, and for the price of its output to reflect these costs. But do 'pollution costs' include the cost of environmental damage caused by optimal (= acceptable) levels of effluent? There is no correct economic answer to this. The answer depends entirely on what are the firm's pollution rights, where we are talking not about *de jure* rights as understood by common or statute law (which are sometimes non-existent or far from clear), but about *de facto* or 'economic' rights, generally referred to as 'property rights' in the economic literature and defined here as someone having a *de facto* or 'economic' right to do something if it is accepted practice for them to do that something without paying for it. For example, we therefore regard motorists as having the economic right to drive on British (toll-free) motorways, but as not having the same right on French (toll) motorways.

We examine here three main possibilities (there are many others) for pollution rights, referring still to Figure 9.5:

(a) if the firm is considered to have the right to discharge *any effluent it likes*, then all the pollution control costs QRH needed to reach the social optimum OQ should be paid by the state;
(b) if the firm is considered to have the right to discharge the *optimal effluent OQ*, then the control costs QRH, but no extra charges on the residual pollution, should be paid by the polluting firm;
(c) if the firm is considered to have *no pollution rights* at all, it should pay both the control costs QRH and compensation for the pollution damage ERQ.

The optimal overall pollution control policy, which both conforms to established economic rights and minimises the combined costs of pollution control and pollution damage, is thus to choose a method which makes the firm pay a total amount appropriate to its pollution rights and at the same time a marginal amount equal to the marginal pollution damage caused. The resultant changes in the price of the industry's output should then be left to determine whether the firm survives in competition with other firms in the industry using different technologies and different environments. If the firm's profits (based on a higher output price) can withstand the charges imposed, this shows that its output is more valuable to consumers than the resources the firm pays for, so it is socially desirable for the firm to continue producing.

To see whether Pigovian taxes can achieve this doubly optimal result, notice that the full incentive charge of OP on the whole of the firm's effluent in Figure 9.5 means the firm pays an amount equal to area OPRE, as well as pollution damage costs ERQ and pollution control costs QRH. Even in case (c) above where the firm owns no pollution rights, the surplus OPRE cannot be justified on any environmental grounds. As noted by Marquand and Allen (1975), OPRE can only be paid out of some economic rent earned by the firm from its use of the environment. It must thus be regarded as a tax to raise revenue for general public expenditure (although of course taxing rents is frequently recommended by textbooks as a good way of raising revenue, because it does not distort resource prices or cause misallocation). Also, total tax revenue OPRQ is often many times greater than pollution control costs QRH. All this explains the fierce resistance met from industry in virtually all countries to any proposals for pure inventive charging on the full amount of effluent discharge, in spite of the overall reduction that such charging could achieve in the actual costs of effluent control (explored further in Section IV).

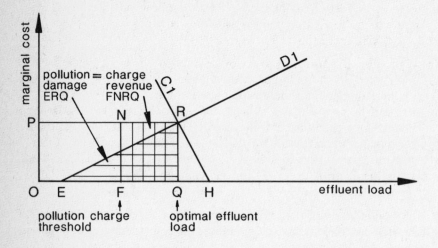

Figure 9.6   The pollution charge threshold

An obvious theoretical solution, to achieve the desired total charge (in the context of case (c)) while retaining the optimal marginal charge rate OP, is illustrated in Figure 9.6. All effluent below a threshold level OF is free of charge, so that total charge revenue FNRQ is equal to pollution damage ERQ. Other solutions would be reduced or tapering charge rates below the threshold. While there are obvious practical problems in calculating the threshold OF as well as the charge rate OP, the basic idea is appealing and has echoes in the current German system of pollution charge rates (ERL, 1985).

Pollution rights and the Standard and Extended Polluter Pays Principles

However, it is a central observation of this chapter that, in most industrialised countries, incentive charging (i.e. any charging at the incentive rate OP in Figure 9.5 where the charge revenue is not returned to polluters) is unlikely to be introduced because it is incompatible with the pollution rights derived from the standard interpretation of the Polluter Pays Principle (PPP). This statement requires some explanation, and we start with the original OECD definition of the PPP:

The PPP means that the polluter should bear the expenses of carrying out the [pollution prevention and control] measures decided by public authorities to ensure that the environment is in an acceptable state. [OECD, 1972]

Note that this makes no reference to whether polluters should perhaps also pay for the pollution damage that their effluents still cause when the environment has reached an acceptable state. However, a later OECD foreword comments:

If a country decides that, above and beyond the costs of controlling pollution, the polluters should compensate the polluted for the damage which would result from residual pollution, this measure is *not contrary* to the PPP, but the PPP *does not* make this additional measure *obligatory*. [Foreword in OECD, 1975, with emphasis added]

Public evidence submitted by the Department of the Environment to an inquiry into the PPP also supports this interpretation of the PPP (paragraph 2.1 of D.o.E., 1983).

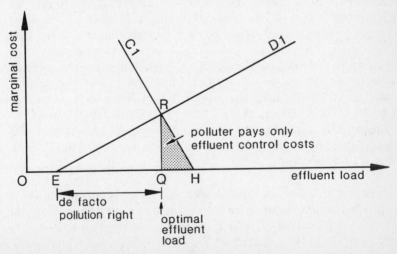

Figure 9.7   The Standard Pollution Pays Principle for a firm or industry

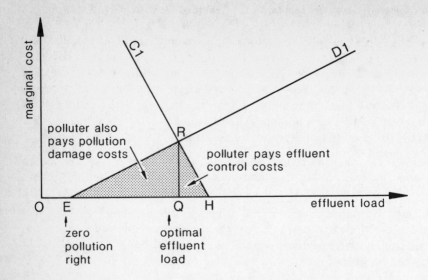

Figure 9.8   The Extended Pollution Pays Principle for a firm or industry

The first stage in interpreting the above definitions in terms of pollution rights and our diagrammatic analysis is to regard an 'acceptable' state of the environment as being identical to the 'optimal' state. Refer now to Figures 9.7 and 9.8, which could apply equally to an isolated firm or to a whole industry. If we define the effluent standards achieved by the pollution control authorities to be society's choice of what the optimum (= acceptable) effluent level should be, it is therefore clear that the PPP demands that the polluting firm should pay all the costs of controlling effluent down to the optimum level OQ (i.e. pollution control costs as defined by area QRH). However, the PPP only allows the control authorities to make the firm pay compensation for pollution damage caused by its optimal effluent (area ERQ). This distinction between the firm paying control costs and paying control plus damage costs is so crucial to the analysis of this chapter that two quite distinct versions of the PPP are defined and used henceforth:

(1) the *Standard PPP* requires that in net terms the polluters pay the cost of optimal effluent control, but not for the pollution damage done by the remaining optimal effluent (= residual pollution), i.e. polluters should pay QRH as in Figure 9.7;

(2) the *Extended PPP* requires that in net terms polluters pay the cost of

optimal effluent control and for the pollution damage done by the remaining optimal effluent, i.e. polluters should pay QRH plus ERQ as in Figure 9.8.

It is not suggested that this distinction can be applied rigidly in practice. It may not always be obvious what is the difference between a control cost, a prevention cost, a clean-up cost and a damage cost. Much will depend on where the boundary between the 'firm' and the 'environment' is drawn. Neither is there much reason to expect any country to adhere rigidly to either the Standard or the Extended PPP in all its pollution policies, nor to shift gradually from one version of PPP to another; both are allowed within the PPP as a whole. What can be said, as a very broad generalisation, is that at the moment most industrialised countries (including the United Kingdom), in most cases, apply the Standard PPP rather than the Extended PPP (the formal UK position is given in paragraph 3.3 of D.o.E., 1983). This is based on the observation that few means of charging for pollution damage exist; what charges are found are usually linked with schemes that return the charge revenue as subsidies to polluters for improved pollution control (ERL, 1985), rather than as compensation to those affected by environmental damage.

There are no good reasons for expecting the current position to change much; industry can generally be expected to oppose any general application of the Extended PPP such as incentive pollution charges (CIA, 1983). In order to clarify the analysis in the rest of this chapter, it therefore seems sensible to make a purely working assumption that control policies will apply the Standard PPP strictly. This is why Section V studies only those market mechanisms which Section IV has shown to be compatible with Standard PPP. It is not implied that Standard PPP is or will be applied with such absolute strictness by the United Kingdom or any other government. Note in passing that Standard PPP could be interpreted as including a requirement for polluters to pay the costs of pollution monitoring and enforcement incurred by public authorities, because these are control costs, rather than damage costs attributable to the amount of effluent discharged.

The above analysis of the PPP can readily be translated into the language of pollution rights (see possibilities (a) (b) and (c) reviewed earlier) by regarding anyone who is allowed in practice to do something without paying for it as having an economic right to do it. Standard PPP therefore corresponds to definition (b) (where polluters pay controls costs only), and Extended PPP to definition (c) (polluters pay both control and damage costs); definition (a) (polluters pay neither costs) is clearly ruled out by either version of PPP. We now see why Standard PPP and incentive charging are incompatible, since Standard PPP gives polluters the *de facto* right to discharge optimal effluent free of charge, whereas incentive charging makes them pay for pollution damage caused by the optimal effluent, and probably some economic rent as well. The PPP can thus be regarded as an international agreement on pollution rights. However, its origin, and certainly its basis for incorporation into the 1975 EC Recommendation (EC, 1975), lay in the desire to prevent any shifts in pollution control costs, due to differing economic pollution rights in different countries, from causing major disruption to established patterns of international trade.

Choice between the Standard and Extended Polluter Pays Principles

Could a clear policy choice on pollution rights, between Standard and Extended PPP, be made by appeal to 'fairness' or 'equity', instead of on pragmatic political grounds? The answer is yes only if there is a consensus on the meaning of 'equity'; in practice, one person's equity is usually someone else's iniquity! One view of equity in pollution policy is that all polluters should pay equal rates for environmental services, no matter how much the cost of these services may vary; a quite different view is that equity requires polluters to pay the exact cost of the service. For example, the 'Mogden formula', used in England and Wales to calculate the charges that firms pay for treatment of any effluents they discharge to sewer, charges the same rates for all dischargers in one region. Given the large variations in sewage treatment costs from one treatment works to another in the same region, this means that dischargers to low-cost treatment works pay more than it costs to treat their effluent. Such dischargers therefore cross-subsidise dischargers to high-cost treatment works. Whether this is considered equitable or not depends entirely on one's point of view.

Nevertheless, one might argue that unwaveringly strict application of Standard instead of Extended PPP, so that polluters are invariably allowed the economic right to discharge optimal pollution free of charge, could result in somewhat arbitrary changes in pollution rights when new sources of pollution appear. For example, consider Figure 9.9, which shows these changes in two distinct circumstances:

(1) The replacement of our isolated firm (firm A, say, with marginal control costs C_A as before) by a different firm B with control costs C_B: if firm B happened to have a higher unconstrained level of effluent (OK instead of OH) and more steeply rising marginal costs of pollution control than A (as shown by slopes C_B and C_A), it would have a right under Standard PPP to discharge more effluent than A (OJ instead of OQ) and might even have to spend less on pollution

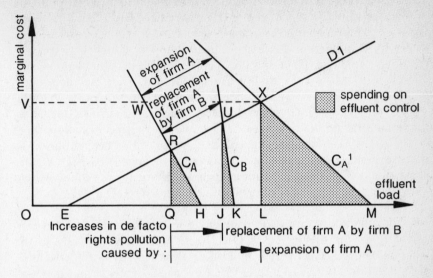

Figure 9.9 Changes in de facto pollution rights and control spending under the Standard PPP

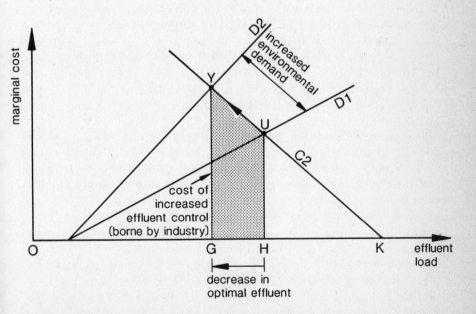

Figure 9.10 Standard PPP: effect of increased demand for environmental services

control costs (JUK instead of QRH), although its residual pollution damage would be much greater (EUJ instead of ERQ).

(2) The expansion of firm A's output to a level where control costs are C_{A^1}: let us suppose firm A's expansion happens by doubling its present inputs of labour, plant and raw materials, with no change in production method, so that output is exactly doubled. Then the control cost curve C_{A^1} is found by doubling C_A horizontally (i.e. OM = 2OH, VX = 2VW, etc.). (In general, unless industrial growth is achieved by the introduction of new, cleaner technology or results in economies of scale, it is likely that growth will shift the control cost curve outwards, as explained in Appendix 9.1, Lemmas 2 and 3). Under a pure Standard PPP, this would automatically shift the firm's economic right to discharge marginally optimal effluent out from OQ to OL.

In both the above cases, no compensation would be paid to environmental users for the increases QRUJ and QRXL respectively in the pollution damage which they would suffer. This accords with the Kaldor–Hicks criterion used as the basis for cost–benefit analysis, and it is well known that the decision to use such a criterion is ultimately a matter of polticial, not economic, judgement. Two observations follow. The first is that in most industrialised countries a firm is not simply allowed to set up or expand where it likes, but has to get the approval of some public authority or authorities both for constructing a plant and for discharging an effluent. The constraints in effect aim to ensure that the firm's expansion is of net social benefit, so that it does at least fulfil the Kaldor–Hicks criterion (and note that an element of Extended PPP might creep in here by asking the firm to contribute to some worthy local project). However, there may well be expansions that will result in a net social cost, but are hard to refuse because they fall within standard planning and pollution control guidelines.

The second observation is that there may well be external costs of effluent control, which cannot be ignored. If the Extended PPP were applied and pollution damages were paid, then the firm might go bankrupt and the public would lose more from increased unemployment than it would gain from an improved environment. The answer to this in theory is to use at least as many policy mechanisms as there are policy objectives, and not to try to use environmental policy to address both unemployment and environmental problems. In theory, correct pollution charges should be imposed (gradually and with due warning, to prevent excessive adjustment costs) and any resulting unemployment threat should be tackled with, say, direct regional employment subsidies or housing reforms, to assist any long-term transfer of workers to less polluting industries or other regions. However, few governments would consider altering overall labour or housing market policies just to allow environmental policy to be more rational, so this ideal solution may well not be available.

The rest of this chapter starts from the hypothetical position that the Standard PPP is assumed to determine the pollution rights underlying pollution control policies. We explore whether market mechanisms of pollution control could be introduced, particularly when optimal pollution is being lowered because of greater demand for a clean environment, to make pollution control more cost-effective without changing pollution rights.

III The incidence of costs and benefits when optimal effluent load changes

Assumptions and context

The same assumptions generally have to be made in Sections III and IV as were spelled out at the start of Section II, except that the single firm of Section II is replaced here by an industry of many small firms competing with each other in the output market. The firms are assumed to have common access to the same finite environment as the single firm, with the additional assumption now that the environment is well mixed. The time-scale is still the long term. The change to an industry is so that we can analyse the different regulatory or market mechanisms of allocating overall effluent control costs between firms in an industry. Refer now to Figure 9.10. The industry has overall marginal costs of effluent control given by curve C_2. C_2 is derived from the total costs of effluent control actually imposed by the existing control mechanism, not from the minimum possible control costs for the industry. We shortly examine the effect of introducing a more cost-effective mechanism (i.e. one which reduces the total effluent control costs).

Given that the environment is well mixed, environmental damage can still be related to just the total effluent from the industry, so the marginal damage cost curve is still D_1 and does not depend on which particular firms are discharging effluent where. As mentioned earlier, it is not at all easy to put a value on environmental damage in practice, and the estimation of curves D_1 and C_2 (or relevant parts of them) in order to calculate the optimal (= acceptable) effluent level OH rarely gets beyond the academic stage, except perhaps in the United States (Pearce and Markandya, 1987). The level OH—which may or may not be the declared environmental quality standard—is usually determined by a pragmatic political process, and D_1 and C_2 are merely *post hoc* rationalisations of this process. Nevertheless they remain useful constructs for analysing both cost-effectiveness ('can total costs of achieving the quality standard be reduced?') and equity ('who pays these costs?'), as will now be shown.

We start from an achieved, and by definition optimal, effluent load of OH, with total costs HUK being paid by the industry to keep effluent down to OH rather than OK. Now suppose that the damage curve on Figure 9.10 shifts up from D_1 to D_2 owing to 'increased environmental demand' i.e. an increased demand for environmental services or benefits such as clean air and water to breathe and drink, beautiful landscapes to look at and plentiful and interesting wildlife to study. There are many theoretically possible causes of this increased demand, listed at (i)–(v) below. It is plausible that all five causes have applied at various times, or often simultaenously, in Britain since the industrial revolution. Note that (i)–(iv) are changes in value relationships, and (v) is a change in scientific relationships:

Possible causes of increased environmental demand
   (i)   a general rise in incomes from economic growth, combined with a positive income elasticity for environmental services;
  (ii)   a shift in basic tastes away from industrial and towards environmental services;
 (iii)   new economic research (e.g. by direct survey of consumer preferences, as in the United States) shows that environmental damage is more highly valued than previously realised (see Chapters 6 and 10 in this volume);
  (iv)   a serious pollution incident that suddenly changes political valuations (as opposed to (i)–(iii), which work through the political process more gradually);
   (v)   new scientific research shows that objective damage to the environment is greater than previously realised, or that cumulative pollution has reduced the assimilative capacity of the environment.

The shift from D_1 to D_2 in Figure 9.10 causes optimal effluent to be reduced from OH to OG, with an increase GYUH in pollution control costs which is entirely borne by the industry. The value of optimal pollution damage changes from EUH to EYG, not necessarily a decrease.

Costs and benefits of a move to cost-effective pollution control

Now suppose a new pollution control mechanism is introduced in response to the increased environmental demand, in order to keep the increase in pollution control costs to a minimum. To do this the new mechanism must be more cost-effective than the old one, that is it must achieve a given reduction in pollution at lower total cost. ('Economic efficiency' is generally avoided as a term in this chapter, both because it is less understood by non-economists, and because we are often looking at the cost-effectiveness of achieving standards which may themselves not be economically optimal). The new mechanism could be market-based, or just a more flexible and much better informed regulatory mechanism. Its effect is usually to reduce the industry's marginal cost curve from C_2 to C_3 in Figure 9.11 (but this may not always occur—see the counter-example in Lemma 4 of Appendix 9.1), and the optimum point from Y to W. This would clearly reduce the total social costs of pollution from area EYK to EWK, releasing WYK of potential benefits to be shared between industrial and environmental interests.

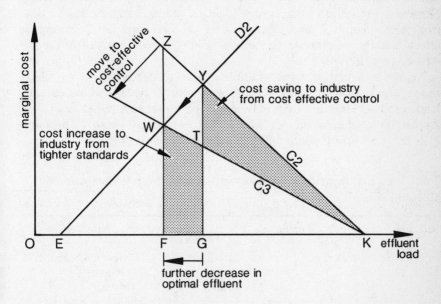

Figure 9.11 Standard PPP: effect of more cost-effective effluent control

However, note the effect that such a step might have on the industry's pollution costs, given that under Standard PPP it pays control costs but no damage costs. As the optimum effluent load is reduced further from OG to OF, pollution control costs change from GYK to FWK, which is not necessarily a decrease: whether an increase or a decrease depends entirely on the shape and position of the actual damage and control cost curves D_2, C_2 and C_3 in any particular case. It is possible that the industry's cost savings (TYK) from more cost-effective control of the existing effluent OG are outweighed by its cost increases (FWTG) from having to meet the tighter standard OF. Of course, pollution damage is reduced by FWYG as well, but this is of no direct benefit to industry under Standard PPP.

We therefore have the noteworthy result that under Standard PPP, any move to a more cost-effective pollution control mechanism which would warrant a decrease in optimal effluent is not necessarily in industry's commercial interest. Therefore the industry may well resist a newfangled, more cost-effective control mechanism—better the devil it knows than the devil it doesn't—unless it can be shown beyond doubt that the net effect is in the industry's favour. One may try to avoid this paradox by simply threatening a reduced effluent standard OF in the future, and hoping that the industry will then agree to a more cost-effective control mechanism in order to save itself WZK (see Figure 9.11) in control costs. However, the industry may instead cling to an existing, inefficient control mechanism (C_2) and lobby against the standard OF, claiming in effect that the environmental benefit (FWYG) does not justify the increased cost (FZYG).

Figures 9.10 and 9.11 can readily be used to derive Table 9.1 which shows who pays increased costs and who benefits when optimal effluent load is reduced, on the assumption that C_3 lies everywhere below C_2 (see Appendix 9.1, Lemma 4, for why it may not always do so). The table includes results for Extended PPP as well as Standard PPP.

Table 9.1   Likely incidence of costs and benefits from reducing optimal effluent load

Affected	Basis of pollution rights	Reason for reducing optimal effluent	
		Increased environmental demand	More cost-effective effluent control
Industry	Standard PPP	Cost ($-$)	Uncertain ($+/-$)
	Extended PPP	Cost ($-$)	Benefit ($+$)
Environmental users	Standard PPP	Uncertain ($+/-$)	Benefit ($+$)
	Extended PPP	No effect (0)	No effect (0)

In conclusion, the analysis above shows that introducing more cost-effective effluent control mechanisms into a country which generally applies the Standard PPP may result in losers as well as gainers, and the losers are more likely to be discharging firms than environmental users.

More cost-effective pollution control, especially using untried market mechanisms, may therefore be hard to introduce, for if the losers have political influence, a strong political will is needed to counter this. Nothing daunted, we now go on in Section IV to analyse the cost-effectiveness and equity aspects of all such mechanisms, and in Section V to examine the practicalities of those which conform to the Standard PPP. These practicalities are very important and could provide an alternative explanation of why market mechanisms are little used; further study is therefore needed.

IV   Economic analysis of market mechanisms of pollution control

Cost-effectiveness of market mechanisms

The assumptions listed at the start of Section II still apply in most of this section, except that as in Section III we are considering an industry rather than a single firm. A particularly important assumption that carries over from Section III is that all firms' effluents are uniformly dispersed into the same, finite environment, so that one extra unit of effluent causes the same pollution damage wherever and by whomever it is discharged. In the water pollution context, the 'industry' would normally include all plants discharging effluent into the same body of water and would therefore include sewage treatment plants.

The market mechanisms of pollution control that we define and analyse in this section are as follows:

(a) incentive pollution charges;
(b) distributive pollution charges;
(c) granted tradable pollution consents;
(d) sold tradable pollution consents.

It is worth emphasising here yet again that it is always assumed that charges would not be used alone, but together with some backstop regulatory control over maximum discharge rates. We also make mention of:

(e) pure subsidies for pollution control;
(f) product (= output) charges;
(g) input charges;
(h) cost-sharing within a regulatory system;
(i) combinations of the above mechanisms.

The analysis in this section is essentially theoretical, but with an eye to policy implications. As in Section II, it is assumed that the overall aim of pollution control policy is to minimise the total social costs of pollution control and pollution damage. Within this overall aim, all the above mechanisms are aimed at cost-effectiveness: achieving any given level of overall control with the lowest possible total cost of control resources, whether by better allocation of existing technologies or by invention of new ones. The primary purpose of our study is therefore to see if a significant proportion of the substantial resources devoted to effluent control can be saved. Whether those savings are used to benefit industrial consumers or environmental users is a matter for political choice, determined among other things by the interpretation of the Polluter Pays Principle, as shown in Section II.

The theoretical way in which market mechanisms reduce overall effluent control costs is essentially the same for all such mechanisms. Each firm in an industry is persuaded by market incentives to operate at an effluent load such that the marginal cost of effluent control is the same for all firms. (Recall that this marginal cost is the reduction in the firm's profits caused by reducing effluent load by one unit on a long-term basis). This then ensures that total control costs are at a minimum, since reallocating one unit of pollution control resources from any one firm to another cannot achieve any further reduction in total effluent (see Appendix 9.1, Lemma 1). Moving to this equality of marginal cost might be seen as more equitable, and also as giving more freedom, than simply setting discharge standards that may impose widely varying marginal costs; but it will probably seem inequitable to those dischargers who lose a favoured position in the readjustment! The size of the savings from using cost-effective controls, instead of more expensive regulatory controls such as uniform emission standards, will depend on how much the marginal cost curve for effluent control varies from firm to firm. If all firms are identical, then there will be no saving. If marginal costs vary a great deal, then the savings will be large and the cost-effective levels of effluent will vary greatly from firm to firm.

Market mechanisms make firms' marginal costs of effluent control equal by somehow creating a uniform price for effluent, that is to offer each firm the same money in return for a unit decrease in effluent. Each firm (assuming they are all cost-minimising) will then choose an effluent load at which its own marginal cost of effluent control equals this same money amount, and the industry's marginal cost curve will be the horizontal sum of the firms' curves (see Appendix 9.1, Lemma 2). Note that the cost-minimising assumption is often challenged by industrialists as 'not the way real industry behaves' with regard to pollution control costs. Research into this would be useful, but in the meantime one can only observe that cost-minimising behaviour increases a firm's profits and chances of survival, and thus presume that in the longer term it will be such cost-minimising firms that survive.

Another, less immediate, way in which market mechanisms can make pollution control more cost-effective is by encouraging the economic use of innovation to find and develop new technologies with lower control costs (Downing and White, 1986). A very simplified treatment is in Figure 9.12, where some market mechanism has created an industry-wide equivalent price OV for a unit change in effluent load. If an individual firm with existing marginal control costs K'U' can develop a technology with lower costs K'W' (including annualised development costs), then the firm has an incentive to adopt the new technology and reduce its effluent from OH' to OF', thus benefiting the environment. The firm saves F'W'U'H' in charges (or can sell a consent for F'H' of effluent for the same amount) and makes a net saving of K'W'U'. In contrast, a regulatory mechanism gives no incentive to reduce effluent below the initial level OH'. This incentive to innovate is one of the big economic advantages of market mechanisms.

An important practical question is whether or not the existing mechanisms of regulatory control are already fully cost-effective. Here we assume they are not, either because they do not equalise marginal control costs, and/or because they do not give an incentive to innovate. The total costs resulting from market mechanisms will then be lower than the existing costs, and this will generally lead to a new marginal cost curve C_3 below the existing one C_2 (see Appendix 9.1, Lemma 4), as shown in Figure 9.11, and also in Figure 9.13 to which we now turn. Note that curves C_3 and C_2 touch the horizontal axis at the same point K, the total effluent load that the industry would discharge in the absence of any regulatory or market constraint. The underlying plan might be to use an exogenous increase in

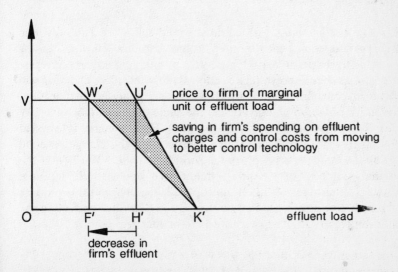

Figure 9.12   Control technology innovation incentive

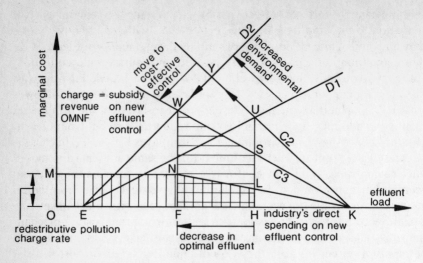

Figure 9.13   Redistributive charging mechanism

demand for a cleaner environment, shifting D_1 to D_2, to trigger off a move to the cost-effective control curve C_3 and a move from U to W rather than to Y.

Pollution charging

An *incentive pollution charge*, which most would call a tax if the revenue from dischargers does not correspond to some cost imposed on others by the effluent, achieves point W on Figure 9.13 by charging effluent at a rate FW. It has already been shown (see Section II) why incentive charging will probably be unacceptable to dischargers, so it is not analysed further here.

A *distributive pollution charge* creates the same marginal incentive FW to reduce effluent load as follows (OECD, 1980). First, a charge is levied at a rate FN much less than the incentive charge; then the charge revenue OMNF is used to pay for a proportional subsidy (at rate NW/FW) on the long-run marginal cost of keeping effluent load down to the optimal effluent level OF in Figure 9.13. If appropriate, the charge rate could be lower or zero below a threshold effluent such as OE without affecting the marginal incentive at OF. The two criteria to be met are:

— for cost-effectiveness, that FN + NW = FW;
— for compatibility with Standard PPP, that subsidies (= NWSL, depending on the precise subsidy scheme) are equal to charge revenue

(= OMNF, depending on the precise charging schedule). Note that distributive charging has not always been accepted as being compatible with the PPP because of the presence of subsidies, and in some sense it conforms more to a collective Polluters Pay Principle. However, distributive charging is explicitly allowed for in paragraph 4 (b) of the Annex to the EC Recommendation (EC, 1975), and is now generally accepted as PPP-compatible.

In practice it is hard to subsidise long-run marginal costs in the way that economic logic would perhaps dictate, which would be to subsidise both operating and capital costs of both new and existing effluent control plant (further analysis here would be interesting). Defining what are the existing costs of effluent control is very hard, so subsidies are hardly ever given for existing plant. Defining what part of new capital spending is a pollution control cost and what part is ordinary productive investment is not much easier, particularly with 'clean technologies'. However, various continental schemes have set up workable rules for this (ERL, 1985). It is also clearly desirable where possible not to leave operating costs out of a subsidy scheme, to avoid distortions in favour of capital-intensive pollution controls. A final distortion might be the tendency for subsidy schemes to overlook very small dischargers to avoid excessive administrative costs.

Three disadvantages of distributive charging are immediately obvious. The first is that calculating the charge and subsidy rates, needed to achieve the effluent level OF and the balancing of revenue and expenditure, requires detailed data on pollution control costs. These will be expensive to collect, although the same problem would occur in any attempt to make regulatory control more cost-effective. If the rates are incorrect, they may fail to provide adequate protection against damagingly high effluent loads. One suggested solution, that of changing the rates periodically until the desired target is achieved ('iterating'), is unattractive; it would cause high adjustment costs by making expensive capital investment suddenly redundant, and also would discourage investment and innovation by creating a general climate of uncertainty.

The practical solution to adjustment costs is to introduce a charging scheme gradually and/or with advance warning. To avoid very high pollution loads doing irreversible damage, the way now accepted everywhere where charging schemes are used is to bolster charging by retaining regulation on maximum loads, for example set at the pre-existing effluent level OH in Figure 9.12. The French certainly seem to think that setting sensible charge and subsidy rates is no great problem, given their new scheme for SO_2 charging on top of existing water pollution charging schemes; but whether their rates actually achieve optimal effluent levels is hard to determine.

The second disadvantage is that the subsidies will have to be administered. Even if the rule is simple, e.g. a fixed percentage subsidy for the capital cost of any pollution control investment, one will still have to decide on what portion of the costs of a multi-purpose industrial investment is attributable to pollution control.

The third and quite different disadvantage is that in practice redistribution is politically infeasible if there is no target of reducing pollution. Distributive charging takes money out of an industry, and only gives it back as subsidies for new effluent controls. So unless regulatory controls are relaxed at the same time (which is generally ruled out for fear of allowing local environmental deterioration), distributive charging effectively makes an industry spend less on output and more on effluent control. If there is no recognised need to reduce pollution, industry will therefore rightly object to distributive charging.

Tradable pollution consents

A scheme of *tradable pollution consents* (better known in the US air pollution context as 'tradable emission permits') works by setting up a competitive market to allow discharging firms to trade in 'unit consents'. A firm owning, say, 10 unit consents would be permitted to discharge, probably for a limited time period only, effluent at a rate of 10 units, and would be free to buy or sell unit consents. To achieve the new optimal effluent load OF in Figure 9.14, all the control authority has to do is fix the total number of consents at OF. Cost-minimising trading by firms in the industry should then establish a market-clearing price of FW for a unit consent, and cost-effectiveness is achieved. An important practical difference between tradable consents and pollution charging is that consents usually work on maximum (consented) discharges, whereas charging usually works on average (actual) discharges. Where discharges are highly variable over time this can obviously make a big difference. A related problem for tradable consents is that if, as frequently occurs, actual discharges are below consented amounts, then controls on consents (whether by buying them up, or reducing their size) may have little immediate effect on actual discharges.

A practical way of gradually achieving the optimal effluent load OF, consistent with Standard PPP and without excessive adjustment costs, might be as follows. The control authority could declare consents for the original effluent OH to be owned by existing dischargers and freely tradable (they would thus be granted tradable pollution consents), but could also announce that all consents will be suddenly scaled down by a factor OF/OH in X years' time. Period X would be chosen to allow enough

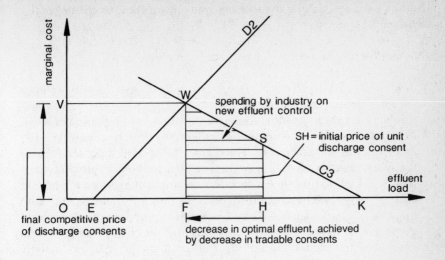

Figure 9.14   Granted tradable discharge consents

time for consent trading and shifts in pollution control investment to take place without excessive transition costs.

However, industry may resist the introduction of tradable consents precisely because of the sort of subsequent reduction in effluent totals described above. One way to overcome this resistance might be for the central authority to buy up some or all of the reduction in consents required. However, this costs the taxpayer money. It also effectively grants industry rights for effluent loads which have now become unacceptable, so it would not conform with any kind of PPP. Conversely, any attempt to introduce sold or auctioned tradable consents would force polluters to pay an amount OVWF. This would be equivalent to applying the Extend PPP and is therefore likely to be as unacceptable as pure incentive charging. Another way, compatible with the Standard PPP, would be to make existing consents tradable (within limits) without announcing any intention to cut back on total effluent; this would simply give industry a cost-saving opportunity. How much industry would use this opportunity, and how they would then react if consents were later scaled down, is another matter!

An immediate disadvantage of tradable consents is that unrestricted trades between dischargers will almost certainly lead to some local increases in discharges, even within a substantial reduction in overall discharges. This would be no problem if the environment is homogeneous, as assumed in this section, but usually it is not and local increases may be unacceptable.

Subsidies, product charges, input charges, and combinations of charging and tradable consents

Other market mechanisms which will not be analysed here are:

(a) *pure subsidies* for pollution control, omitted because they do not even conform to Standard PPP;
(b) *product charges* on goods whose manufacture uses a polluting process, or *input charges* on the amount of potentially polluting material used as an input to manufacturing. The classic examples of input charges are the Norwegian and Swedish charges related to the sulphur content of fuels (ERL, 1985). In theory, product and input charges do not lead to cost-effective pollution control, because they offer no incentive to improve effluent control technology. But if in practice pollution is very expensive to monitor because it is very diffuse or appears in several environmental media, then product or input charges may be the only practicable market mechanisms available. Most agricultural pollution is very diffuse, so for example taxing nitrate discharge from farmland is not practicable, whereas a tax on nitrate fertiliser clearly is. Also, many industrial pollution problems can affect several media, with control of sulphur dioxide emissions, disposal of sewage sludge and disposal of chlorinated hydrocarbons as classic examples. There may then conceivably be a case for taxing an elemental input, such as sulphur or a toxic heavy metal, which tends to damage the environment in whatever form it is discharged, rather than trying to monitor and tax all the various gaseous, liquid and solid wastes containing the element. Input taxes are therefore an interesting area for further study.

We are left with distributive charging (as opposed to incentive charging) and granted tradable consents (as opposed to sold or auctioned consents) as the two surviving market mechanisms which are both cost-effective in theory and compatible with the Standard PPP. In Section V, where we go on to consider the practical problems of using them, we continue to treat them as pure, distinct mechanisms, but it is important to note that there is no theoretical reason why a combination of the two could not be used in practice. Consents could be sold at a price proportional to the consented pollution amount; this is equivalent to a pollution charge. Consents could then be made tradable, with the revenue from consent sales refunded as subsidies for pollution control.

V   Practical aspects of using distributive charging and granted tradable consents as mechanisms of pollution control

This section examines what might be the practical advantages and disadvantages of using distributive charging, or tradable consents (understood throughout this section to be granted rather than auctioned or sold consents), to control pollution. It is not based on any new field research other than the recent ERL reports on European charging and subsidy systems (ERL, 1984, 1985). Most of the examples used are drawn from the author's knowledge of UK water pollution control, but nearly all the points made are intended to be relevant to pollution control in any medium (unless they specifically refer to sewage treatment), and in any country.

In the light of the daunting list of unanswered practical questions that have been drawn up in this chapter, it could be concluded that genuine market mechanisms which charge the proper marginal price for pollution are inherently impractical. However, in the author's opinion one cannot reach such a conclusion without considerable further study. Existing regulatory systems of pollution control may well be imposing a substantial and unnecessary economic burden on polluting industries, and market mechanisms might be able to reduce that burden by a margin that far outweighs any extra administrative costs they incur. Many of the problems listed below apply equally to regulatory and to market controls. Quite a few countries have overcome the practical and presentational problems and are now using market mechanisms of pollution control, although this does not necessarily mean they are achieving a least-cost or even lower-cost solution. It would therefore seem unwise to write off market mechanisms as impractical in any country without first conducting a detailed practical study.

One study which was done in the United Kingdom, in response to the recommendation in the Third Report of the Royal Commission on Environmental Pollution (RCEP, 1972), and which together with a critical review by Lawrence (1980) provides many of the illustrations below, is the 'Rowley Report' (Rowley et al., 1979). This studied various hypothetical combinations of pollution charging and regulations for controlling direct discharges of industrial effluent to the tidal River Tees in north-east England. It used a one-dimensional model of water quality in the Tees Estuary, and information gathered on industrial dischargers' treatment costs, to calculate the least-cost allocation of new treatment plant which would reduce pollution enough to allow the passage of migratory fish. It also calculated the rates of incentive charges on three critical pollutants that would theoretically bring about this least-cost solution, and the overall cost savings of this solution in comparison to alternatives such as uniform cutbacks in discharges.

Regulatory, legal and administrative considerations

Before concentrating on how well the economic theory behind market mechanisms might work in practice, many other important practical considerations need to be discussed first. The first consideration is that any further work in this area would have to start with a thorough economic study of existing regulatory systems of pollution control. If one cannot show that the current system is seriously wasting pollution control resources, there is not much justification for trying novel alternatives!

This is particularly important where regulatory control is applied in a pragmatic way taking economic factors into account, as is generally the case in the United Kingdom. For in theory, with enough information and cooperation, a regulatory system of water pollution control can be just as cost-effective and as fair as a market mechanism, by using a cost-sharing system. Under this, polluters provide a central authority with full information on their pollution control costs, the central authority calculates the least-cost pollution control system (which might involve only a few polluters reducing their effluent), and polluters are willing to share out the costs of the least-cost system amongst themselves. Consents can then be set which will achieve the cost-effective solution directly.

A second, very general practical consideration is how far market mechanisms are compatible with a country's existing laws, institutions and administrative procedures. Market mechanisms may be so unprecedented in a country's legal system that this alone will constitute a serious obstacle. This is especially true where there is no legal concept of pollution rights, let alone tradable pollution rights, or no legal enshrinement of the Polluter Pays Principle. In any case, market mechanisms would probably require new legislation, which would be an obstacle in itself.

And what institution(s) would administer the financial aspects (charges, subsidies, trades, etc.) of any market mechanism of water pollution control, and the legalistic aspects (consents, monitoring, enforcement) that earlier discussion has shown will still be required to back up a market mechanism? How much would such administration cost? Would such institutions be local or national, and within or separate from government? Financial and legal control of a market mechanism both require similar expert knowledge of technologies to control effluents and the environmental damage that effluents cause, and both require a similar, expensive system of monitoring effluents and environmental quality. It is also possible that a charging mechanism would make enforcement of existing regulations easier, as high charge rates for excess pollution would be easier to administer than legal prosecutions. There would thus seem to be a good case for making the same body or bodies responsible for both financial and legal control. This would also enable the body to recoup its costs for administering both regulatory and market mechanisms, from a levy on the charge revenue or a commission on the consent trades that it arranges.

However, in practice much depends on the existing legal, historical and geographical situation. This is particularly true for water pollution, since economies of scale and economies from joint operation occur in many but not all of parts of the water industry, leading to a variety of public water institutions and no universally best solution:

— in England and Wales the water industry is fully integrated in the form of Water Authorities covering each river basin (the privatisation of these Authorities would obviously affect the way in which any market mechanism could be administered);
— in Scotland the agencies for water pollution control are separate from the rest of the water industry;
— in France sewage treatment is carried out by the communes, the Agences Financières des Bassins adminster the distributive pollution charging scheme, but power to control discharges rests with the Service d'Industries et des Mines (ERL, 1985);
— in Germany sewage treatment is carried out by local authorities, and the states (*Länder*) control both sewage discharges and the system of pollution charges for all discharges (ERL, 1985).

The basic aim, whatever institutions and mechanisms of pollution control are chosen, should be that dischargers face rational economic choices as to how much effluent to treat itself, how much to discharge to the environment, and (if the discharge is liquid) how much to discharge to sewer. However, this aim must be balanced against the administrative cost of achieving it. It is obvious that the transition to a market mechanism system would incur large, if temporary, administrative and legal costs. (In contrast, it is worth noting here that an earlier report by ERL (1979) indicated that permanent monitoring and administration costs may not be significantly higher for market mechanisms than for regulatory control, but this would obviously need checking in each case.) The transition cost is one good reason why market mechanisms are unlikely to be taken seriously unless there is the clear need for further large reductions in pollution, and a reasonable chance that such reductions could be implemented more cheaply by market mechanisms than by existing regulatory controls.

Effect of environmental medium and location

It is now necessary to analyse the consequences for market mechanisms when the simplifying assumptions about competition, perfect information, and uniform dispersion of pollutants characteristic of conventional economic break down in practice. The intention is to provide an agenda for any future field research in this area. Most of the problems found are examples of the standard Second Best problem which pervades much economic policy-making, but must not be allowed to paralyse it (Lipsey and Lancaster, 1956). In a nutshell, the Second Best problem is that if there are several market imperfections that need to be removed or corrected in order to maximise economic welfare (given an initial distribution of income and wealth), then removing or correcting just one of these imperfections does not necessarily increase welfare and thus is not necesarily the second best solution (the first best being to remove all the imperfections). A good example was the trade-off between pollution and unemployment; reducing excessive pollution is not necessarily a good idea if there is also excessive unemployment.

The following points are discussed:

(a) general differences between air and water as pollution media, and between different geographical locations;
(b) problems of monitoring both the type and quantity of pollutants discharged, and also their relative effects on the environment;
(c) general problems of industrial structure, principally economies of scale and imperfect competition, which mean that, even if there were no problems of monitoring pollutants, theoretical results from Section IV might not hold;

and for ease of reference we draw together:

(d) five miscellaneous problems of distributive charging;
(e) five miscellaneous problems of tradable consents.

Although most of the examples in this chapter are drawn from water pollution, market mechanisms can be used in other environmental media. The obvious application in air pollution might be to the acid rain problem, to find the cheapest way to reduce sulphur dioxide emissions by whatever percentage is deemed politically necessary. The main differences between air and water pollution (we do not consider solid waste here) are the relative difficulty of measuring total gaseous emissions compared with liquid discharges from a plant, and conversely the relative simplicity with air pollution of not having the existence of central sewage treatment works to take into account.

Location is a vital factor in pollution control. Liquids may be discharged into lakes, rivers, estuaries or the sea, and gases discharged from low chimneys or high chimneys, in urban or rural areas, and in differing local climates. Given such diverse local environments, one then has to consider how widely any practicable market mechanism would eventually have to be introduced as part of a nationwide scheme: just for one or two local environments of a particular type on an *ad hoc* basis, or for the whole environmental medium (air or water)? Would both tradable consents and pollution charges be tried out in separate pilot schemes, or would a prior choice have to be made between the two mechanisms?

Problems of monitoring: (1) transfer coefficients

In the analysis in Section III it was assumed that the environment is well mixed, so that one extra kilogram per day of effluent load does the same damage to the environment wherever it is discharged. It practice this is usually true only on a small scale or not at all. For example, estuaries are generally more well mixed than rivers, so this means that tradable discharge consents are more likely to be acceptble there. And in estuaries the assimilative capacity due to vigorous tidal scouring is generally much greater at the mouth than higher upstream. The one-dimensional model of water quality in the Tees, used in the Rowley Report's modelling, showed this vividly. It estimated that a unit of pollutant discharged in one stretch of the estuary did about fifteen times as much damage to biochemical oxygen demand in the critical stretch as a unit of pollutant discharged in a lower stretch of the estuary. And this ratio of discharge in one stretch to pollution damage done to a given target stretch of the estuary, known as the *transfer coefficient*, was different for each of the other thirty-nine stretches into which the Tees is divided by the model!

The theoretical solution for distributive charging is therefore to have an environmental quality model, identify the critical location, and vary local charging and subsidy rates so that the marginal price of effluent is proportional to the transfer coefficient to that location. But the critical location and the ratios of transfer coefficients could well change as charges are imposed and pollution is reduced, and the detailed monitoring and modelling work that this requires will obviously be costly. However, a cost-effective regulatory system would have to face up to similar problems, and the pragmatic solution would probably be a combination of charging and regulation.

As already mentioned, a general problem with tradable consents is that unrestricted cost-saving trades between dischargers will almost certainly lead to local increases in pollution, even though total pollution may decline. (In heavily used rivers, consent trades may also cause damaging changes in rates of flow.) In many locations any such increase in pollution would be quite unacceptable, for example in a stretch of a river just upstream of an abstraction point for drinking water. The only way in which tradable consents could work here would be if there were a clear target to reduce overall pollution. Firms would then be required to deposit effluent reduction credits with the pollution control authority. They would be free to sell or buy credits, as well as acquire them by cutting back their own effluent, but would not be allowed to increase their own effluent.

Even when some local increases in pollution are unacceptable, there would probably have to be restrictions on trades to prevent local environmental quality standards being breached. And to control the overall pollution level, trades would have to be subject to scaling by transfer coefficients (the analogy for pollution charges would be local variations in charge rates). These scaling factors are called *offset ratios* in US emission trading schemes. A margin for error would have to be built into the scaling to allow for scientific uncertainty, as in the following example:

— suppose a unit of pollutant is thought to be somewhere between two and four times as damaging if discharged at A rather than at B;
— then the offset ratio would perhaps be 1:2 for consents being sold from A to B, but 4:1 for consents being sold from B to A;
— this means that if A owns a consent for 20 units, if he sells it to B then B is entitled to discharge $20 \times 2 = 40$ more units; but if B sells a consent for 40 units to A, A is only entitled to discharge $40/4 = 10$ more units.

As well as offset ratios, there would also probably have to be absolute limits to trades in consents to maintain minimum environmental standards in every locality.

Problems of monitoring: (2) numbers of pollutants

Given that in practice there will usually be several pollutants contributing to a water quality problem, there are obvious administrative limits on how many pollutants could be monitored, in how many places and how frequently. The Rowley Report identified nine principal pollutants of the Tees: BOD, suspended solids and the seven toxic pollutants, ammonia, phenols, zinc, copper, lead, chromium and cyanide. Ideally all of these need to be monitored and charged for, but think of the cost of monitoring and administering 360 different charge rates (9 pollutants $\times$ 40 stretches of estuary), even if all these rates have been successfully calculated! Clearly a decision will have to be taken with any market solution about which pollutants will be practical to control by the market mechanism.

As an example, the Rowley Report reckoned that, in addition to biochemical oxygen demand, only three toxics—ammonia, copper and cyanide—really affected water quality in the River Tees. This left the problem of how to measure their toxicity to fish. One way that still involved measuring all three toxics was to add their fractional toxicities together. A cheaper way, to cover many toxic pollutants together, could well be to use biological monitoring tests. One such test, used in European charging schemes, measures the rate at which daphnia (water fleas) are killed by being in the effluent sample (ERL, 1985).

Economies of scale and imperfect competition

A serious problem with market mechanisms, which rely on financial incentives at the margin, might in practice be economies of scale in pollution treatment technology (i.e. non-convexity of total treatment costs). One can easily imagine situations where there are increasing returns to scale available to one firm from applying the same control technology to more and more effluent, for example in centralised sewage treatment, or from investing in cleaner technologies. The Rowley Report found that as quality standards for the River Tees were tightened and more effluent removal was required, it became economic to add major improvements in sewage treatment works to the optimum solution. But owing to the economies of large-scale sewage treatment, the marginal costs of such improvements were lower than those of the smaller treatment options that were optimally required of industrial dischargers to achieve less effluent removal in total. This is contrary to the assumption of rising marginal costs of effluent treatment that was made throughout Figures 9.1–9.14.

When marginal costs fall as well as rise, it is no longer possible to use a uniform marginal price of effluent to make all dischargers choose effluent treatment options that minimise the total cost of control, as is further explained in Appendix 9.2. The trouble is made worse by often not knowing whether marginal costs are falling or rising in the current situation, and there is no easy solution. On the Tees it was known that there were economies of scale in sewage treatment, so the Rowley Report suggested that optimal treatment for sewage should first be decided by the pollution control authorities (who in England run the treatment plants) as a separate planning exercise, and there would be no charges on sewage effluent. This is not a perfect solution either, since there might also be economies of scale in treating some industries' effluents at source.

A particular second best problem for water pollution may be that effluent treatment charges for discharges to sewer are not based on the same economic logic as the market mechanisms to control discharges direct to the environment. In the United Kingdom, effluent treatment charges are not set at marginal treatment cost for reasons of 'equity'. In France and The Netherlands, effluent treatment charges are calculated at exactly the same rates as pollution charges on direct discharges to the environment

(ERL, 1985). Distortions from the economic optimum are likely to arise in either situation.

A general problem that applies especially to tradable consents is the problem of imperfect competition in the market for discharge consents. If a single large discharger could influence the price of consents, then the market outcome would not be cost-effective. The Rowley Report commented that this could be a problem on Teesside as one large chemical firm (ICI) is so dominant there, and likewise in the United Kingdom the Central Electricity Generating Board would dominate any market for sulphur dioxide consents. In the extreme case a powerful firm might buy up all the consents and establish a monopoly, with all the problems that causes. Likewise with pollution charges, a firm which has monopoly power over its output market will be more able to pass on the charge to its customers than a competitive firm. There is also a general worry that markets in consents will be 'thin', i.e. that trades in discharge consents will be so infrequent that a proper competitive price will not be established anyway.

Even if competitive consent markets can be set up, a problem that has already emerged in the US emissions trading programme is hoarding. Firms may get credits for emission reductions and hoard them against possible future tightening of emission targets by the authority. Sometimes, particularly where there is an initial gap between consented and actual pollution, these reductions may be on paper rather than in actual emissions. Hoarding can be tackled either by buying up the hoarded consents, thus breaking the PPP, or by forcing consents closer to actual emissions before starting the trading scheme, which may provoke protests from polluters. However, similar hoarding problems may occur under a regulatory system, particularly since regulation gives no financial incentive against hoarding. Further work on the economics of consent hoarding would perhaps be interesting.

Finally, pollution control techniques do not form a continuous spectrum, but come in discontinuous steps (except perhaps in the very long term). This was a problem identified by the theoretical modelling in the Rowley Report: in some cases, the need to keep a large unit of treatment plant economic in order to achieve the environmental quality objective for the river, meant that charges had to be kept high and the objective was in fact significantly over-achieved. Such discontinuity problems make the market solution harder to manage, but they also cause difficulties with regulatory consents.

Five problems with distributive charging

For ease of reference, this subsection and the next collect together problems specific to distributive charging and to tradable consents as pollution control mechanisms. The first three practical problems with distributive charging are:

(a) getting the data needed to set cost-effective charge and subsidy rates; the advantage of tradable consents is that the market should set its own price for consents, thus avoiding the data collection;
(b) having to administer subsidy schemes; against this might be set a reduction in the administrative costs of enforcing regulations;
(c) the more fundamental 'problem', that distributive charging will only be acceptable where there is a recognised need to reduce pollution.

The fourth problem is allowing for industrial growth and decay. Often there is a target to maintain overall effluent at a constant level, despite the fact that in principle optimal effluent levels should in fact change in reponse to such growth or decay. Constant effluent should be achievable automatically under tradable consents. New firms wishing to start discharging are free to buy up consents, force up the price of consents and thus induce existing firms to reduce their effluents, so that the industry's total effluent remains constant; and vice versa if firms are leaving the area. With distributive charging there is such no obvious mechanism, and care will have to be taken not to let pollution increase too much by being too lax on charges rates for new consents, nor to stifle industrial change by being too strict. Also, growth and decay can cause problems for the financing of a distributive scheme: as effluent is reduced, either rates will have to be adjusted so that a falling charge revenue remains adequate to finance subsidy expenditure, or some subsidies will have to be paid in advance of charge revenue. Again, workable solutions appear to have been found on the continent, but no one really knows how cost-effective they are.

A fifth problem which may be encountered is how to recycle the charge revenue directly into a specific fund for subsidies for pollution control investments. Some countries such as the United Kingdom do not normally allow such 'hypothecation' of charge revenue, but presumably given sufficient political will a solution could be found.

Five problems with tradable consents

The five problems have all been discussed previously:

(a) the first, and probably the most serious, problem is the way in which unacceptable local increases in pollution may occur as a result of free trading in consents;
(b) the second problem, more of a consideration perhaps, derives from the distinction between maximum and average pollution. If pollution damage is determined more by average than by maximum effluent load, charging will probably be more effective than traded consents at controlling pollution; and vice versa;
(c)–(d) the third and fourth problems are those of imperfect competition: markets in consents may be taken over by a monopolist, or may be too 'thin' ever to allow competitive trading;
(e) the fifth problem is that firms may hoard unwanted consents as a hedge against future cutbacks.

The above points would need to be explored much more thoroughly, both theoretically and empirically, before any firm choice could be made between distributive charging and tradable consents as market mechanisms of pollution control. The choice would vary with the pollution being considered (one mechanism might be more appropriate to air, and the other to water) and a pragmatic combination of distributive charging, tradable consents and/or regulations might well emerge as the best all-round control mechanism.

VI Conclusions

Large parts of this chapter have been used to set out clearly the main concepts involved in the use of market mechanisms for optimal pollution control, and not to look specifically for conclusions. However, several general conclusions can now be drawn.

It is already well known that if the costs of effluent control vary between different firms in an industry, and if current regulatory control mechanisms cannot take proper account of these cost variations, then market mechanisms of control could potentially save a significant proportion of the industry's current costs of effluent control. This conclusion holds even if it is uncertain what environmental damage is being caused by the effluent. However, this chapter has shown that:

(1) some market mechanisms would effectively take away the existing *de facto* pollution rights that dischargers may consider are implicitly

conferred by regulatory controls on pollution; such mechanisms would therefore encounter strong resistance from dischargers;

(2) where (as will generally be the standard case) the Polluter Pays Principle (PPP) is interpreted to mean that polluters are required to pay effluent control costs but not effluent damage costs, in some cases industry might find that its savings from a cheaper system of overall effluent control were outweighed by the extra cost of the further lowering of effluent loads that cheaper control would make socially desirable;

(3) there would be significant administrative and legal transition costs from introducing market mechanisms;

(4) the administrative costs of operating a market mechanism to give proper economic incentives for pollution control, particularly the costs of monitoring effluent loads and pollution damage, are likely to be high.

Therefore, attempts to introduce market mechanisms are only likely to succeed where all the following general conditions hold:

(1) the costs they impose on polluters are consistent with current or likely future pollution rights as derived from a country's interpretation of the PPP;

(2) any permanent extra monitoring and administration costs of running the market mechanism have been shown to be significantly smaller than the permanent savings they will achieve in effluent control costs; this will be most likely where the relevant environmental medium is relatively well mixed and there are relatively large variations in control costs between polluters;

(3) they are introduced as part of major reorganisation of pollution control arrangements, or where there is already a clear need to reduce pollution for some specific pollutant or location, so that the temporary legal and administrative costs of introducing market mechanisms will be felt to be justified.

The following conclusions can be drawn about specific market mechanisms:

(1) the costs imposed on polluters by incentive pollution charges, or by sold or auctioned tradable consents, cannot be justified by the above standard interpretation of the PPP (Standard PPP), so these mechanisms are unlikely to be introduced;

(2) distributive charges are generally compatible with the Standard PPP, but they would have to be backed up by regulatory control over maximum pollution levels. They could only be justified under the PPP if there were a clear intention to reduce overall effluent load;

(3) granted tradable consents are also compatible with the Standard PPP, but they cannot be operated freely where it is completely unacceptable to allow even small increases in local discharges, and would be hard to administer for several pollutants. They therefore will be most appropriate to controlling a few pollutants in a well-mixed environment — perhaps to achieve target reductions for national emissions of sulphur dioxide to the high atmosphere, or for discharges of toxic metals to the sea?

(4) input charges may be worth considering where monitoring costs are high because pollution is very diffuse or can affect several environmental media;

(5) the correct choice between distributive charging and granted tradable consents, or a combination with any other control mechanisms, is complex and depends on many practical considerations.

Before a firm decision could be reached, either to introduce or to dismiss any market mechanism of pollution control, there would have to be detailed practical research to estimate the costs of the monitoring and administration needed to operate the mechanism, compared to the savings that might be achieved in control costs for specific pollutants and locations. Many other questions would need to be answered, such as:

(1) would market distortions, due to economies of scale in pollution control technologies or imperfect competition between polluters, reduce or eliminate the savings in control costs achieved by the market mechanism?

(2) could one make a choice between distributive charging and granted tradable consents, without actually trying them out? Or would one or more demonstration schemes be necessary?

(3) what new legislation would the market mechanism need?

(4) which would be the best agency or agencies to administer the financial and/or legal aspects of any market mechanism?

This chapter provides a framework for such detailed research.

Appendix 9.1

Lemma 1: If cost-minimising firms all face a market mechanism which creates the same marginal price for reducing effluent, then the resulting total effluent load will be achieved at minimum total cost.

Proof: The following proof for two firms is easily generalised to many firms.

Let E_A and E_B measure the reductions in the effluents of firms A and B below their unconstrained values (this is to avoid total and marginal costs being negative). Let $C_A(E)$ and $C_B(E)$ be the firms' total costs of effluent reduction. We assume these are well behaved in the normal way:

$$C_A(0) = 0, \; C_A'(E) > 0 \text{ and } C_A''(E) > 0 \text{ for } E > 0,$$

similarly for B.

The total cost of any total effluent load $E_T = E_A + E_B$ is then

$$C_T(E_T) = C_A(E_A) + C_B(E_T - E_A)$$

and this is minimised with respect to E_A when

$$C_T' = 0 = C_A' - C_B'$$

i.e. when the firms' marginal costs of effluent control C_A' and C_B' are equal.

Lemma 2: The marginal cost curve of effluent reduction for an industry of competitive, cost-minimising firms which all face the same marginal effluent price is the horizontal summation of each firm's marginal cost curve. An analogous result applies to a cost-minimising firm comprising a number of plants, since to minimise its costs of production the firm will want each plant to face the same notional marginal effluent price.

Proof: Merely by observing that each firm determines its cost-minimising effluent load by reading horizontally, say on Figure 9.5, at the ruling price OP until it hits its marginal cost curve at effluent load OQ. Total effluent load at price OP is then the sum of these individual effluents in the direction of the effluent axis, i.e. horizontally.

Lemma 3: If an industry grows by the number of firms increasing (rather than by technology changing), its marginal cost curve will generally shift outwards. This is exactly true where the firms are all competitive and face the same marginal effluent price. An analogous result applies to a firm growing by increasing the number of plants it operates. Proof follows from Lemma 2.

Lemma 4: The marginal cost curve for effluent reduction in an industry which is not controlled by a single effluent price will generally lie above the curve for an industry that is.

Proof: From Lemma 1, the total cost curve for control by a single effluent price (created by a market mechanism such as charging) is the minimum possible, so the total cost curve for any other control mechanism will lie everywhere above it. This does not mean that this higher cost curve must be everywhere steeper (i.e. with a greater marginal cost) than the minimum total cost curve, but for most mechanisms determined by a consistent rule one would expect this to be so, as illustrated in Figure 9.15.

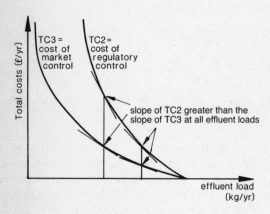

Figure 9.15 Total market control and regulatory control costs

However, Figure 9.16 illustrates a counter-example in which, for certain levels of total effluent, a market mechanism leads to a higher marginal cost of effluent reduction than a simple regulatory mechanism such as uniform cutbacks. Suppose there are just two firms, A and B, with marginal cost curves C_A and C_B respectively, and an unrestrained total effluent of OP = OH + OK. If a market mechanism sets an effluent price of OS, then firm A will be at U and B at V where GU = IV = OS, total effluent has been reduced by GH + IK, and overall marginal cost at this point is of course OS. To get the same total reduction in effluent by uniform cutbacks, A

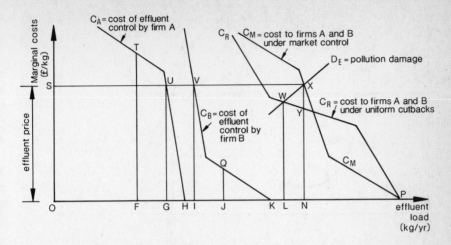

Figure 9.16   Marginal market control and regulatory control costs

must cut back by FH and B by JK such that FH = JK and FH + JK = GH + IK. The overall marginal cost of yet further marginal cutbacks is now (FT + JQ)/2, which as drawn is less than OS. Of course the total cost under market mechanisms, the sum of areas GUH and IVK, is less than the total cost with uniform cutbacks, areas FTH plus JQK.

The overall marginal costs for the industry comprising Firm A and Firm B are shown on the right-hand side of Figure 9.16. C_A is the curve for the regulatory solution of uniform cutbacks; C_M is the curve for the market mechanism solution, being from Lemma 2 the horizontal sum of C_A and C_B. For total effluent ON = OG + OI = OF + OJ, C_M at X (NX = OS) is above C_A at Y (NY = (FT + JQ)/2). If it so happened that the marginal environmental damage cost curve D_E passed through X on C_M (thus justifying the effluent price OS to reach X), and point W on C_A, then the optimal effluents under market mechanisms (or any cost-effective system of pollution control) and uniform cutbacks would be ON and OL respectively, i.e. greater under market mechanisms.

Appendix 9.2

The theoretical complexity caused by the existence of increasing instead of decreasing returns to scale in the costs of effluent control is illustrated in Figures 9.17 and 9.18. In Figure 9.17, where the marginal environmental damage curve is at its old position D_1, the 'switchback' marginal cost curve

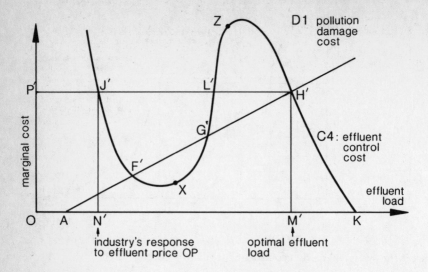

Figure 9.17   Problems of economies of scale: original environmental demand

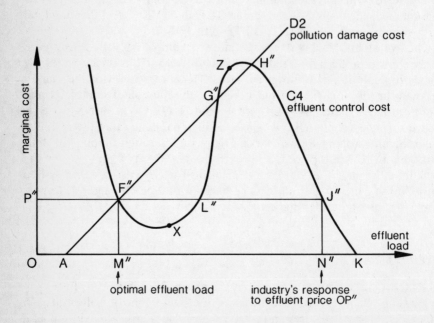

Figure 9.18   Problems of economies of scale: increased environmental demand

C_4 (assumed to reflect cost-effective effluent control) intersects D_1 at F', G' and H'. F' and H' are both stable local optima, but the global optimum is at H' because area G'ZH', which is the social cost of reducing effluent from H' to G', is greater than area F'XG', the social benefit of reducing effluent further from G' to F'. However, using a simple incentive charge of OP' could not achieve optimum effluent OM', even if the whole industry acted as if it were one firm. From the industry's point of view, with a charge rate of OP' its best choice is effluent level ON', because the charge saved N'J'H'M' is greater than the cost of treatment N'J'XZH'M'. The net result is that a locally optimal charge on effluent leads to a global excess of expenditure on effluent treatment.

The converse holds in Figure 9.18, where environmental demand has increased from D_1 to D_2 but costs remain as C_4. The global optimum effluent is now OM" (because the social cost G"ZH" is now less than the social benefit F"XG"); but a locally optimal incentive charge OP" would, even if the industry acted as one firm, lead to effluent ON" (because the extra charge M"F"J"N" is less than the cost savings M"F"XZJ"N"). The net result is then that the locally optimal charge leads to a globally inadequate amount of effluent treatment.

The general conclusion is that when, because of economies of scale, marginal costs fall as well as rise, it is no longer possible to use a uniform marginal price of effluent to make all dischargers choose effluent treatment options that minimise the total cost of control.

References

Auld, D.A.L., 1985 'Equity and Equivalence Aspects of Effluent and Output Taxes', *International Journal of Environmental Studies,* **24** (1).

Baumol, W.J. and Oates, W.E., 1975, *The Theory of Environmental Policy*, Prentice-Hall, Englewood Cliffs, New Jersey.

Burrows, P., 1979, *The Economic Theory of Pollution Control*, Martin Robertson, Oxford.

CIA., 1983, *Chemical Industries Association Memorandum*, in House of Lords, 1983.

DoE, 1983, *Department of the Environment Memorandum* in House of Lords, 1983.

Downing, P.B. and White, L.J., 1986, 'Innovation in Pollution Control', *Journal of Environmental Economics and Management*, **13** (1).

EC, 1975, *Council Recommendation Regarding Cost Allocation and Action by Public Authorities on Environmental Matters*, Official Journal of the EC, No. L 194/1–4.

EC, 1986, *Fourth Environment Action Programme 1987–1991* (Section 2.5), Commission of the European Communities, Brussels.

ERL, 1979, *The Administrative Costs of Water Pollution Control with Special Reference to Charging Systems*, Report for the Commission of the European Communities, ERL, 106 Gloucester Place, London W1.

ERL, 1984, *Pollution Control Subsidies for Industry in Europe*, Report for the Department of the Environment, ERL, 106 Gloucester Place, London W1.

ERL, 1985, *Charging Systems for Pollution Control in Some EC Member States*, Report for the Department of the Environment, ERL, 106 Gloucester Place, London W1.

House of Lords, 1983, *The Polluter Pays Principle*, Select Committee on the European Communities, Session 1982–83, 10th Report, HMSO, London.

Lawrence, J., 1980, *The Rowley Report on Effluent Discharges to the River Tees: A Reaction*, ICI Brixham Laboratory Policy Briefing, Brixham, Devon.

Lipsey, R.G. and Lancaster, K., 1956, 'The General Theory of the Second-Best', *Review of Economic Studies*, **24** (1).

Liroff, R.A., 1986, *Reforming Air Pollution Regulation: The Toil and Trouble of EPA's Bubble*, Conservation Foundation, Washington, D.C.

McIntosh, P.T., 1977, 'Charging for Direct Discharges, or Paying for Dirtying the Water', Water Research Centre, Seminar on the Economics of Charging Structures for the Waters Services, Oxford University, 5–6 July.

Marquand, J. and Allen, D.R., 1975, 'A Note on some Aspects of the "Polluter-Pays" Principle and its Implementations', in OECD, 1975.

OECD, 1972, *Annex to Recommendation on Guiding Principles Concerning International Economic Aspects of Environmental Policies*, OECD, Paris.

OECD, 1975, *The Polluter Pays Principle: Definition, Analysis, Implementation*, OECD, Paris (out of print).

OECD, 1980, *Pollution Charges in Practice*, OECD, Paris, p.13.

Palmisano, J., 1985, 'Emissions Trading Reforms: Successes and Failures', Air Pollution Control Association Annual Meeting, Detroit.

Pearce, D.W., 1976, *Environmental Economics*, Longman, London.

Pearce, D.W. and Markandya, A., 1987 *The Benefits of Environmental Policy*, Report for OECD Environment Directorate and EC Directorate, General XI, University College London.

RCEP, 1972, *Pollution in Some British Estuaries and Coastal Waters*, Third Report, Royal Commission on Environmental Pollution, Cmnd. 5054, HMSO, London, p. 72.

Rowley, C., Beavis, B., Walker, M. *et al.*, 1979, A Study of Effluent Discharges to the River Tees, DoE/DTp Research Report 31, (Rowley Report), HMSO, London.

Zuckerman, S. and Beckerman, W., 1972, *Minority Report* in RCEP (1972).

Chapter 10

Valuation of Wildlife: A Case Study on the Upper Teesdale Site of Special Scientific Interest and Comparison of Methods in Environmental Economics

K.G. Willis and J.F. Benson*

Introduction

The cost and value of wildlife resources (plants and animals), and by implication the land upon which they are based, to a large extent depend upon which community of reference is adopted to base the assessment and valuation. Under the Wildlife and Countryside Act 1981 (WCA 1981), the frame of reference is the farming (and forestry) community: wildlife is conserved by forgoing increased agricultural output. In agreeing to forgo the right to intensify agricultural production and accept and continue current agricultural practices which maintain wildlife habitats, compensation is paid by conservationists (e.g. the Nature Conservancy Council (NCC)) for the net profit on the agricultural development forgone.

Historically, the problem of gains and losses associated with land development, arising out of state intervention, has been handled in two main ways (Parker, 1965). The first method (which was also used by town planning, 1909–39), and that adopted by the WCA 1981, can be termed a 'continuing' solution: it attempts to deal with gains and losses from development (or forgone development) as they arise. Compensation is payable (annually or as a lump sum) under the WCA 1981 for (temporary or permanent) loss of property rights. Compensation value will vary depending upon alternative opportunities available at the time. The second approach (and that incorporated in the 1947 Town and Country Planning Act) involves what may be termed a 'once and for all' solution: the vesting of development rights in land in the state. Since the landowner no longer

* This study was funded by a grant from the Economic and Social Research Council (Reference D00232178). Lesley Mitchell and Caroline Saunders have provided able research assistance. The views expressed are those of the authors and do not necessarily reflect those of any official body such as the Nature Conservancy Council who generously supplied information on management agreements.

owns the right to develop, compensation for a development opportunity forgone is irrelevant. The General Development Order (1975), however, permits agricultural intensification and development without planning permission; so farmers' rights to change agricultural land-use must be purchased in the interests of conservation.

The financial compensation perspective in the WCA 1981 is heavily dependent upon another frame of reference: the European Economic Community (EEC) and its Common Agricultural Policy (CAP) support for agriculture. If CAP support for agriculture was reduced, the financial value of agricultural output forgone by conservation would decrease and so would the financial compensation payable. This has led some (notably Bowers and Chesire, 1983) to argue that the relevant frame of reference for wildlife conservation is the real resource cost of agricultural output forgone: the cost of replacing the lost output on the world market. Moreover, it might be argued that financial compensaiton and the social valuation (at world prices) of output forgone, merely represent opportunity costs (to different communities of reference) of wildlife conservation: they do not measure benefits conferred by wildlife itself.

The benefits of wildlife may be measured by a travel cost (TC) method as revealed evidence of willingness to pay (WTP). This essentially used visits to wildlife sites for recreation, education or other purposes, to develop an econometric model to estimate net economic benefits. Alternatively, benefits can be measured by a contingent valuation (CV) method. CV techniques try to assess people's expressed preferences: by asking people directly how much they value wildlife rather than by inference as under the TC method. CV can be used, unlike TC methods, to estimate the value placed on wildlife sites by non-visitors, e.g. by way of 'expected' consumer surplus, preservation, bequest and option values. Again, the community of references for these measures of benefits is distinctly different from those of financial compensation and its social valuation. TC is concerned with actual visitors, CV with non-use values, as well as actual use by those with environmental preferences (general public, scientific community, and interest groups).

This chapter compares the magnitude of the costs and benefits estimated by different techniques and communities of reference for an internationally important Site of Special Scientific Interest (SSSI) and National Nature Reserve (NNR) in north-east England, namely Upper Teesdale. This research is continuing and the chapter includes some preliminary results and speculation.

Upper Teesdale

This upland grassland and moorland, including valley meadowland, is a complex area. The site overall is a unique mosaic of habitats, including neutral grasslands, heather moorland and rarer floristic assemblages. A large number of rare plants occur on parts of the site and there is also geological interest (sugar limestone). The fame of the area can be traced back to the seventeenth century, but it was the proposal for and the eventual building of Cow Green Reservoir during the late 1960s (Bines *et al.*, 1984) which stimulated intensive programmes of research (Clapham, 1978), a major growth of public interest (and visits), and a variety of new conservation management initiatives, all of which continue today.

The key zone in the area is the NNR on Widdybank and Cronkley Fells which is farmed, used as grouse moor and sheep-walk, as well as accommodating a nature trail, the Pennine Way, and two scenic waterfall attractions for visitors, Cauldron Snout below the Cow Green Dam, and High Force at the eastern tip of the reserve. A car park and footpaths, incorporating a nature trail, provide access. A second feature of interest is the hay meadow land in the valley, particulary between High Force and Langdon Beck; this is often visible from the public road but there is no direct access. Much hay meadow and fell land outside the NNR is also designated SSSI. The pattern of designation and status is complex. The total area is some 9,200 ha, of which 3,500 ha is NNR land and 5,700 ha additional SSSI land.

The value of conserving wildlife at Upper Teesdale is analysed in terms of the four techniques outlined:

(1) financial compensation, for agricultural output forgone;
(2) social value of agricultural output forgone;
(3) WTP and consumer surplus on visits to wildlife site by TC method;
(4) WTP for preservation, bequest and option values over and above expected consumer surplus, by CVM.

Financial value of conservation

One way of judging whether a project is worthwhile (avoiding the limitations of the Pareto criterion) is the compensation principle. WTP for environmental gains under the WCA 1981 permits 'required compensation' for losers (farmers); and, moreover, this is actually paid (thus avoiding the limitations of the Kaldor compensation 'possibility', though not associated ethical questions of distribution between the two interest groups—see Layard and Walters, 1978). Thus a Pareto superior situation may be established. The major problem with the financial value of conservation is specifying the magnitude of WTP, i.e. how much compensation should actually be paid.

Two methodologies using 'market' information have been used to assign financial values to enviromental effects:

(1) the revealed preference or surrogate market approach;
(2) the alternative cost approach.

The *revealed preference* or *surrogate market* approach uses situations where consumers have a choice between incurring expenditure or forgoing the environmental benefit in question. This approach has been used to value environmental commodities such as green belts (Willis and Whitby, 1985), air pollution (Ridker and Henning, 1967), noise (Walters, 1975), and occupational risks (Marin and Psacharopoulos, 1982), through hedonic models (analysing house prices or wage rates as appropriate). Hedonic models can also be used to determine option price and to value environmental risks and safety such as potential earthquake or hazardous waste damage (Smith, 1985). Charging for some environmental improvements and public goods by taxing resulting changes in property values as a consequence of them has been historically a more important method than is currently the case (Parker, 1965). But with wildlife, people do not normally explicitly move house nor do property prices vary with, nor reflect proximity to NNRs or SSSIs. So a market approach is not a feasible financial valuation vehicle for wildlife conservation issues, except where the output of conservation is harvested (e.g. shooting rights to grizzly bears, bighorn sheep etc.—Schulze, d'Arge and Brookshire, 1981; Brookshire, Eubanks and Randall, 1983) and a licence fee can be charged. Rarely is a specific entry fee to a given wildlife site charged (zoos excepted). (A revealed preference valuation, through non-paying visitors, via the TC method is discussed later.) Occasionally a public appeal may raise funds to purchase and secure a site, thereby revealing consumers' choice; but this shades into the alternative cost approach since the purchase seeks to remove the threat to wildlife.

The *alternative cost* approach determines what expenditure is necessary to remove the (agricultural) threat to wildlife at specific sites. Under the WCA 1981, financial compensation is payable to landowners and/or occupiers, where, to preserve wildlife, agricultural output cannot be expanded. Compensation is based on the difference between the proposed improvement in agriculture and the existing pattern regarded as compatible with wildlife habitats. The net annual profit forgone, i.e. the annual value of financial compensation payable, is

$$(c + d) - (a + b) - k$$

where c = extra revenue from agricultural improvement
d = variable and operating costs saved on existing agricultural pattern
a = extra variable and operating costs incurred in the improvement
b = revenue forgone from existing agricultural pattern
k = additional capital expenditure to effect the agricultural improvement (annuitised)

But the financial cost of conservation is the compensation payable for lost agricultural output, plus administrative costs and legal fees incurred in the process, as well as labour (wardens, etc.) and material costs (fencing, etc.) in maintaining the habitats:

$$FC = [(c + d) - (a + b) - k] + l + m + w$$

where FC = annual cost of conservation
l = legal and administration costs (annuitised)
m = material costs in maintaining the habitat (annuitised)
w = warden and labour costs.

Conservation rarely recognises these additional costs, although they may exceed the amount of compensation paid to farmers in some cases.

In general the wildlife conservation interest of the fells is compatible with the landowners' interests in grouse management; restrictions on stocking rates and times for grazing are imposed on tenants. Although payments are made on this land, they do not reflect any output forgone (NCC do not in general wish to impose constraints on existing land management practices), but rather acknowledge the status of the land and secure access for research, conservation studies and management (by NCC). These agreements with landowners are long term (e.g. twenty-one years) and current payments are around £1.30 ha/yr or an annual total of around £4,500 year^{-1} for the whole area.

The main incentive for agricultural improvement is by tenants on inbye land (particularly hay meadow) by drainage, fertilisation and reseeding in order to improve the quantity and quality of animals reared, and management agreements (existing and under negotiation) are based on restrictions on these activities. Widdybank Fell in the NNR comprises 124 ha of improvable land, and management agreements have also been concluded (by 1986) on some 108 ha of hay meadow land (mainly in the SSSI) out of 522 ha of hay meadow. Agricultural intensification would allow increases

Table 10.1   Financial and social costs* of wildlife conservation at Upper Teesdale

Area of land on which cost calculations are based	233 ha
Financial compensation (under WCA 1981) to farmers for not intensifying (mean)	£145/ha/yr
Additional costs of conservation: legal, administrative, warden, material, etc., costs (estimates)	£57/ha/yr
Social opportunity or resource cost of agricultural output foregone	£80/ha/yr
Public Exchequer savings if land is not developed (excluding EEC flows)	£24/ha/yr
Net cost to UK from EEC expenditure changes	£17/ha/yr
Net resource cost (SOC £80/ha and EEC expenditure changes £17/ha)	£97/ha/yr
Total financial cost of conserving whole site (9,200 ha)[†]	£143,412/yr
Social opportunity or resource cost of conserving whole site[‡]	£99,484/yr

*   Figures are rounded to nearest £.
†   Actual Upper Teesdale site is 9,200 ha, but under WCA 1981 compensation would only be payable (proposed) on 646 ha of improvable land currently subject to threat. Because proportion of land types varies over the whole site compared with area on which agreements have already been concluded, the mean financial payment/ha will be £165/year (plus additional legal, administrative, etc. costs).
‡   Because of variations in protection rates for different agricultural commodities, the average social opportunity cost for the 646 ha is £97(ha/yr).

in hay yield and/or stocking rates (of suckler calves and fat lambs) of around 50 per cent, with associated hill livestock allowances (HLA) of approximately £67 per cow and £8 per ewe. Compensation payments on this land range from £114 to £181/ha/yr (Table 10.1).

Extrapolating these payments in respective proportions to the whole area indicates a potential total annual cost of conservation of around £143,412/yr. This includes a considerable cost in 'conservation management' made through wardening services, providing and controlling access and detailed land-management activities not controlled by general agreements (see Table 10.1).

Social opportunity cost of agricultural output

In theory the market (financial) price should reflect social opportunity cost. In practice, due to a variety of factors, principally government intervention

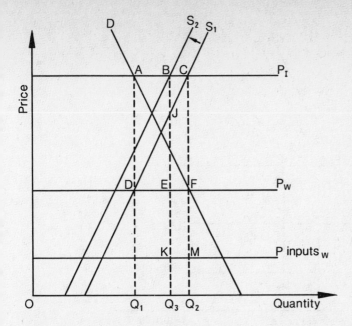

Figure 10.1 The social benefit/opportunity cost of agricultural output including costs and benefits to the public Exchequer for commodities where the UK is a net importer

in agriculture, engendering protective tariffs and subsidies, these are not equated. The resource cost of the agricultural output forgone may be determined in a 'naïve' way by simply revaluing the output at world prices. However, this will tend to overestimate the benefit of the output, as no account has been taken of the alternative uses of inputs.

The resource cost can be determined more correctly by revaluing output at world prices and deducting the world price of inputs which have alternative uses. This is illustrated in Figure 10.1, which outlines the supply and demand of a commodity subject to price support. The world market price is given by P_w and the domestic minimum price (equivalent to the intervention price) is given by P_i. The intervention price is assumed, in this case, to be above the domestic equilibrium where demand equates supply; therefore the country is a net exporter. In the absence of restrictions (management agreements) on the SSSI, the supply is S_1. Therefore at the intervention price P_i, OQ_2 is produced and OQ_1 is consumed. The excess supply, OQ_2-OQ_1, is removed from the domestic market and either stored and/or exported on to the world market with the aid of a subsidy, represented by ACFD. If restrictions are then placed upon the

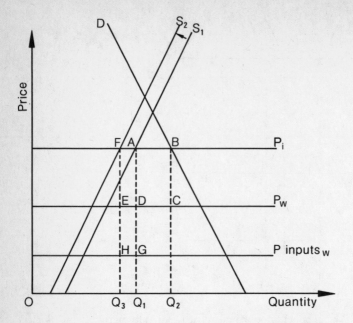

Figure 10.2   The social benefit/opportunity cost of agricultural output including costs and benefits to the public Exchequer for commodities where the UK is a net exporter

SSSI, the supply curve shifts upwards to S_2 and production falls to OQ_3. The public Exchequer cost falls to ABED, a net gain to the Exchequer of BCFE. However, some of the gain to the Exchequer has been lost due to a fall of BJC in producer surplus, although this is extremely difficult to measure in practice. The cost of reducing supply or the opportunity cost of the output is the world value Q_3EFQ_2 (world price × quantity) minus the cost of inputs at world market prices, i.e., the area KMFE.

If the intervention price was below the domestic equilibrium price (that is, where domestic demand equates supply), then the country would be a net importer and the social benefit/cost would differ from the above. This is illustrated in Figure 10.2 where P_i is assumed to be the same as the threshold price at which imports are allowed into the domestic market. In the absence of restrictions on the output from Upper Teesdale, the domestic supply is OQ_1, demand OQ_2, and imports Q_1Q_2. The government then receives the area ABCD in revenue from import levies. Imposing restrictions on Upper Teesdale shifts the supply curve to S_2, as in Figure 10.1, and domestic supply falls to OQ_3. Imports have increased to

Q_3Q_2 and government revenue has as a consequence increased by FADE. However, the social benefit/cost of the output is the world valuation of the output lost minus inputs.

Changes of government revenue or public Exchequer subsidy savings if the land is not developed are merely transfer payments which now revert to the Exchequer (or consumers/producers in the case of import tariffs) and, while relevant in a financial appraisal, should be ignored in a cost-benefit analysis (except from a distributional viewpoint) since they do not affect social efficiency values.

However, restricting output would also affect net budgetary flows between the United Kingdom and the EEC, and hence the social value of benefit forgone from a UK viewpoint (given UK legal obligations to the EEC). Reduced FEOGA spending in the United Kingdom reduces UK contributions to CAP funds (Fennell, 1979, describes the complex budgetary flows involved); but under the Fontainebleau agreement (Commission of the European Communities, 1985), the United Kingdom receives a net rebate on the remaining budgetary flow (see Thomson, 1986). There is a net cost to the United Kingdom of reductions in FEOGA spending in the United Kingdom. Such net budgetary flows were estimated by commodities and aggregated to the Upper Teesdale SSSI.

Producer Subsidary Equivalents (PSEs) were suggested by Josling (1973) as a method of measuring the social value of agricultural outputs:

$$PSE = \frac{V_m + D - V_w}{V_m}$$

where V_m = output at domestic market prices
V_w = output at world prices
D = direct subsidies

The method was adopted by Black and Bowers (1981, 1984) in their analysis of protection of UK agriculture, and the results used to assess the social benefits of extra agricultural output from land drainage schemes (Bowers, 1983), as well as the resource cost of wildlife conservation (Turner, Dent and Hey, 1983).

The PSE method, however, concentrates on the value of outputs and direct subsidies, and ignores inputs, which may result in a biased estimate of the resource valuation of outputs. The operational application of the method has also attracted criticism. Black and Bowers (1981, 1984) tried to overcome the problem of obtaining a world price by using the domestic price minus the variable import levy, adjusted by MCAs (Monetary Compensation Amounts) (see Ritson, 1980, for an explanation of the workings of the CAP). However, the variable import levy for each commodity, set by the EEC (and based upon the difference between the lowest c.i.f. (cost, insurance and freight) offer (import) price of that commodity at Rotterdam and the threshold price (or support price in the Community)) is tied to the lowest quality commodity/offer price. Thus this methodology probably underestimates the world price. A more accurate estimation of the world price might be to take the domestic market price minus the export refund, which is the difference between the intervention price and the best possible offer price for EEC exports, given that the EEC is in surplus for most commodities; although the accuracy and suitability of such a method will vary considerably according to the individual commodities chosen. However, all of this represents a complicated method which is open to considerable data problems and errors when the world price is available in some detail for many commodities. Policy and price changes since 1977–9 render Black and Bowers's estimates of the social value of agricultural output somewhat historical; and by also including export refunds as a direct subsidy, an element of double counting is introduced, rendering a slightly larger estimate of producer surplus than would otherwise occur.

The social value of forgone agricultural development was determined in this study by using Corden's (1966) theory of effective protection, which also includes the effect of protection on inputs on the final level of protection on outputs. Protection is measured in terms of the value added element in production:

$$\text{EPR} = \frac{VA_m - VW_w}{VA_w}$$

where   EPR   = effective protection rate
$\quad\quad$ VA_w = value added at world market prices
$\quad\quad$ VA_w = $P_j(1 - A_{ij})$
$\quad\quad$ VA_m = value added at domestic market prices
$\quad\quad$ VA_m = $P_j[(1 + T_j) - A_{ij}(1 + T_i)]$
$\quad\quad$ P_j = nominal price of commodity j in free trade
$\quad\quad$ A_{ij} = share of input i in the cost of j at free trade
$\quad\quad$ T = nominal tariff rate

The inclusion of inputs is important in valuing the social cost of agricultural output as it implies that the inputs have alternative uses and therefore a social opportunity cost. There are problems in defining inputs to be included in the social valuation of the output of each commodity, since management agreements under the WCA 1981 only detail forgone outputs and forgone inputs and do not always ascribe particular inputs to specific agricultural commodities.

EPRS were determined by comparing the UK price with the world price in terms of value added over a number of years (1981–5) to average out fluctuations in harvests and prices. Non-traded commodities were converted into traded commodity equivalents (e.g. hay was converted into a barley equivalent, since barley is a livestock feed subsititute for hay, at its appropriate energy rate—see Nix, 1985). The EPR on barley, for example, varied over 1981/2–1984/5 from 15.2 per cent, 5.2 per cent, 0.3 per cent, to 22.4 per cent respectively. The EPR for all the output for the whole of the improvable land at Upper Teesdale was 76.4 per cent, 114.1 per cent, 102.5 per cent and 108.0 per cent over the years 1981/2–1984/5. An average of these four years was taken against which to compare the domestic value added from the farm plans and management agreements. Details of the approach adopted and the calculations made can be found in Saunders, Willis and Benson (1987) and Saunders, Benson and Willis (1987).

The implication of this EPR for the social value of agricultural output at Upper Teesdale is outlined in Table 10.1. While the financial cost of conservation is £145 to £165/ha/yr, the social resource cost (unadjusted for any net changes in British payments or contributions from CAP) is £80/ha/yr: the social value of lost agricultural output is approximately only half of the financial UK market cost. However, the net social cost of conservation (£97/ha/yr) is the value of the lost agricultural output (£80/ha/yr) plus any losses to the UK from EEC expenditure changes as a result of restricting output. Thus the net resource cost of wildlife conservation at Upper Teesdale is approximately 60 per cent of the financial cost payable under the WCA 1981.

Willingness to pay for wildlife benefits: travel cost and consumer surplus

In the absence of market prices for wildlife-related experiences, willingness to pay may be estimated from user behaviour (revealed preference). The travel cost (TC) method has been widely applied to estimate benefits and consumer surplus (CS) from non-priced outdoor recreation. From its (TC) early application (Trice and Wood, 1985; Clawson, 1959; Clawson and Knetsch, 1966), the basic model has been much criticised for its gross assumptions and omissions, e.g. failure to take into account multi-purpose trips, the existence of substitute sites, the value of travel time, and so on. Subsequent elaborations of the basic model,

$$V_i/N_i = f(\text{TC}_i)$$

where V_i = total number of trips by residents of zone i per unit of time to the site

N_i = population of the ith zone

TC_i = average round trip travel cost from zone i to the site which related visit rates to travel costs, sought to deal with these problems. Thus the proposed theoretical model for Upper Teesdale site visitors was

$$V_{ij}/N_i = f(TC_{ij}, T_{ij}, P_j, D_i, Q_j, TC_{ik}, T_{ik}, Q_k)$$

where TC_{ij} = travel cost between origin i and area j
T_{ij} = travel time from origin i to area j
P_j = (any) entry fee for the use of area j
D_i = characteristics of individuals at origin i
Q_j = quality characteristics of wildlife experiences available at area j
TC_{ik} = vector of travel costs from origin i to substitute sites $(k \neq j)$
T_{ik} = vector of travel times from origin i to substitute sites $(k \neq j)$
Q_k = vector of quality characteristics of experiences available at substitute sites $(k \neq j)$

The TC method utilises cross-sectional observations on the cost of access to the (wildlife) site and the frequency of visits in order to estimate the demand for access to the site. A survey of visitors to Upper Teesdale was undertaken to estimate the parameters of the model and consumer surplus. This covered 463 wildlife visitors out of an estimated 66,844 visitors (mean annual number 1980–5) (Durham County Council, NOC counts and estimates).

However, it quickly became clear that not only did ecology experts think that no substitute sites existed for Upper Teesdale, but wildlife visitors also considered this to be the case. The qualitative characteristics of Upper Teesdale are quite unique in England: a similar assemblage of plants is only found at Ben Lawers in Perthshire, Scotland, and The Burren in south-west Ireland. Thus demand for wildlife at Upper Teesdale can be estimated by a single equation: it was felt unnecessary to incorporate attributes of and visits to other sites as advocated by Cesario and Knetsch (1976), nor was it necessary to use multi-equation models, which have also been suggested as a technique to try to account for substitutability among sites (Burt and Brewer, 1971; Samples and Bishop, 1985) and thus avoid missing variable bias.

Upper Teesdale is a remote site so that those living farther from the site not only have higher money costs per trip, but also expend more time getting there. Travel time, intuitively, has some opportunity cost either in terms of wages or some alternative leisure activity forgone. To avoid bias from an omitted relevant variable in the estimating equation, time was included. But since TC_{ij} and T_{ij} were highly correlated, time costs were monetarised (at £3 per hour) and added to travel costs (this time price was 43 per cent of respondents' average hourly earnings and within the 25 per cent–50 per cent of wages range suggested by Cesario, 1976, and is the current rate advocated by the Department of Transport, 1987).

The best data fits were derived from models of the form

$$\ln (V_i/N_i) = \propto + \ln (TC_{ij} + T_{ij})$$

Adding socio-economic characteristics of the zones (from survey or 1981 Census data), e.g. income, car ownership, percentage in higher socio-economic groups or particular social classes, did not improve goodness of fit and these variables were not found to be significant in explaining visit rates. R^2 in all the models was $> +0.847$; and TC or (TC + T) was significant at a 95 or 99 per cent level.

The consumers' surplus (CS) was calculated for each of seventeen zones, based upon two different travel cost rates: petrol costs alone and another (RAC) rate covering petrol, maintenance and depreciation costs, and for two different sets of visitors: wildlife and all visitors to the site. The percentage of wildlife visitors was determined by two independent means: first, from NCC figures on the sales of nature trail leaflets at the site (averaged over 1980–5, per car, and per car occupancy rate) which suggested wildlife visitors were 14.3 per cent of all visitors; second, from our survey which covered all visitors using the nature trail. Comparing nature trail visitors who had studied wild plants, geology or birds, to all other visitors (fishermen, picnic, walkers, etc.) recorded at the site on the survey days, suggested that 12.6 per cent of all (66,844) visitors to the site were wildlife visitors. These independent estimates are quite close, and their average was used, namely 13.5 per cent.

CS, aggregated for all zones, is shown in Table 10.2 for wildlife visitors and all visitors to the Upper Teesdale site. The spatial distribution of total visitors was assumed to be the same as that for wildlife visitors for the purposes of estimating the demand curve. Since trips are often multi-purpose, the visitor survey also sought to estimate by a contingent valuation question the percentage enjoyment of the whole trip which could be attributed to the Upper Teesdale site: Table 10.2 takes this percentage enjoyment into account (which varied between zones) and shows the net consumer surplus attributable to the Upper Teesdale site.

The net benefits (consumers' surplus) from wildlife trips to Upper Teesdale are quite low in total and in per hectare terms. Accepting full travel plus time costs as the relevant model, this produces net benefits of only £34/ha/yr. These benefits are only a fraction of the financial cost of conserving the area (£165/ha/yr). Benefits comparable to these financial costs only occur if CS is aggregated across all visitors; but non-wildlife

Table 10.2 Consumer surplus estimates from travel cost method (£ per yr)

	Travel cost only		Travel plus time cost	
	Low rate	High rate	Low rate	High rate
Wildlife visitors only	3,978	11,761	13,571	21,730
Per ha of improvable land	6	18	21	34
All visitors to site	29,967	92,282	100,969	162,165
Per ha of improvable land	46	143	156	251

visitors would still visit the area (to fish, see Cauldron Snout, picnic, etc.) if the wildlife character of the area was reduced to the level of the surrounding non-NNR and SSSI land. However, net visitor benefits (CS) attributable to wildlife visits (£34/ha/yr) are still only one-third of the net resource cost (opportunity cost of agricultural output forgone) of wildlife conservation (£97/ha/yr). However, these estimates are minima and do not take account of the large number of educational and specialist groups which visit the area each year. Data on the latter visits have yet to be examined and analysed but, with annual visits at more than 5,000 individuals, could result in a significant increase in consumer surplus for the site.

Willingness to pay for wildlife benefits: option value and contingent valuation

Contingent valuation (CV) has been widely applied (see Schulze, d'Arge and Brookshire, 1981; and more recently by Walsh, Loomis and Gillman, 1984; and Walsh, Sanders and Loomis, 1984). CV techniques assess people's expressed preferences by direct questions to individuals on how they value (non-marketed) commodities, rather than by inference as with TC. While TC focuses on those who make trips to the site, CV can cover both these and non-users (people who are not currently using the resource may still value the option to use it in the future or the knowledge that the resource exists). It thus broadens the population of subjects to include those with option and existence values. Maximum WTP, contingent upon changes in the availability of the enhanced flora of Upper Teesdale, is assumed to correspond to the point of indifference between income and the floral stock level of UT for each individual.

A sample of seventy-one members of the British Ecological Society and 127 members of the Institute of Biology participated in a mail survey, which represented a 43 per cent reponse rate. Respondents were asked to make a series of budget allocation decisions based on the total annual benefits received for wildlife in Britain, and benefits from wildlife at UT, by writing down the maximum amount they would be willing to pay. Once this budget allocation was completed, respondents were then asked to allocate the amount ascribed to UT among four categories of value: recreation use, option, existence and bequest demands.

Thus recreation-users allocated a portion of their total WTP for UT to (1) *consumer surplus* (CS) from actual use; and (2) a payment of a kind of insurance premium to retain the *option* of possible future visits, in addition to CS. Visitors and non-visitors allocated the remaining WTP for UT to (3) *existence value*—the satisfaction of knowing that UT as a habitat exists; and (4) *bequest value*—the satisfaction from knowing that this habitat will be protected for future generations. The average total WTP for UT was £15.83/yr per 'expert'. This comprised a use payment of £2.46; an option value of £3.10; an existence value of £4.69; and a bequest value of £5.58. The principal reservation about CV (or stated preference techniques) is whether valuing public goods through direct monetary expressed preference price models will yield biased results. Strategic, information, instrument, starting-point, as well as traditional sampling bias are all thought to influence results.

Strategic bias is difficult to estimate, but a number of studies have found that it either failed to affect the outcome (Bohm, 1972) or did not appear to be a major problem (Schulze, d'Arge and Brookshire, 1981). Laboratory and field experiments have indicated that free riding is sometimes weak and that incentive mechanisms can be designed to determine optimal quantities of public goods with reasonable success, provided excludability is possible and perceived individual effectiveness is not nil (Smith, 1980). In addition, strategic behaviour can be neutralised by sound survey design and analysis (Raiffa, 1982). Thus CV can, under certain circumstances, provide reasonably accurate, rational and consistent results as far as strategic bias is concerned.

The significance of information and starting-point bias was assessed in a pilot CV questionnaire. One group had an open-ended questionnaire with no ecological information; another an open-ended questionnaire with detailed ecological information on the sites to be assessed and substitute site possibilities; and the final group had information but also had a closed questionnaire with structured monetary scales which had random starting-points ranging from 10p to £2 per week. In a regression analysis of the first two groups, for each of four sites, WTP was always positively influenced by information (incorporated as a dummy variable), but was never statistically significant. Presumably an individual's bid will be affected by accurate information only if his perceptions concerning the site in relation to substitutes vary from reality. If, on the contrary, the individual's perceptions are correct, then no information bias will exist. Information about the sites relative to others seems, in this case, to have resulted in a slightly upward-biased bid. But knowledge of alternatives could, a priori, bias the individual's bid behaviour in either direction depending upon his initial preferences (Thayer, 1981), so that the net aggregate effect might be negligible and difficult to detect. Whether the respondent should be made aware of the quality and quantity of proposed alternatives is a philosophical issue: many other market decisions on expenditure are made on the basis of very incomplete information, as are current preferences for wildlife. This parallels a debate on the value of life and safety as to the basis upon which decisions should be made (see Mooney, 1977, p. 126–9).

Starting-point bias is much more important as evidenced by a number of studies (Boyle, Bishop and Welsh, 1985). Our pilot study indicated that an increase in the starting-point on the questionnaire resulted in a statistically significant increase in WTP for wildlife as a whole and more for the individual sites. Starting-point bias seems to be an artefact of hypothetical markets: respondents tend to fixate on the starting bid as being indicative of a 'reasonable response': it is possible to influence a respondent's bid over a substantial range by the choice of the initial starting-point (Boyle, Biship and Welsh, 1985). For this reason an open-ended approach was adopted in the main questionnaire, with no suggested starting-point. It can be argued that iterative bidding is not cost-effective: it produces bias in a hypothetical market in that people bid money that they would not bid if the money were real. Starting-point bias may not be such a problem in a simulated market application, i.e. where participants have a real opportunity to buy a permit to participate in the activity e.g. hunting or boating (launch permit). Where this occurs, open-ended CV approaches have been criticised for providing significantly lower estimates of average consumer surplus (CS) than close-ended formats and travel costs methods (TCM) (Seller, Stoll and Chavas, 1985). But a simulated market is not a feasible analytical technique in some wildlife conservation valuations, which must instead rely on a hypothetical market. Where this occurs, to avoid starting-point bias, an open-ended CV format is perhaps inevitable.

It could be hypothesised that WTP_{ij} by individual i for UT (site j) could be written

$$WTP_{ij} = f(Q, S, T, R)$$

where Q = quantity of wildlife protected
        S = socio-economic variables

T = taste and preference variables
R = relevant information on wildlife sites

Alternative functional forms of the model were tried with logarithmic (but with income as quadratic) transformations of dependent variables providing the best fit of the relationships of interest.

However, an econometric analysis of this model for total WTP did not produce statistically significant results. Individual consumer surplus (one element of total WTP) was positively related to preference for upland habitats, actual visits to UT and income; but the R^2 was low at 0.08. Option value too was positively related to visits to UT (at a 90 per cent level) and to income, but negatively related to distance from UT and preferences for upland habitats. Although the R^2 was 0.13, this is still a low level of explanation for cross-sectional individual data. However, 62 per cent of the variation in bequest value was explained by variables included in the function with bequest value being positively related to visits to UT (significant at a 97 per cent level) and income, and negatively related to distance and preference for upland habitats. The persistent, and sometimes statistically significant, negative relationship between preference for uplands in general and WTP for UT in the various models was unexpected. It may be linked to information bias as explained earlier: those who did not prefer uplands so highly subsequently placed a higher monetary valuation than others because of information about UT provided later in the questionnaire.

The econometric model of option value (OV) predicts that a 10-mile increase in distance reduces OV by 15p. However, because of the logarithmic relationship, an additional 10 miles only reduces OV by a further 4p. Five visits to UT increases OV by 45p, but an additional five visits only increases OV by another 19p. Visits to UT were much more important in determining OV than existence value (EV) or bequest value (BV). Distance was much more important in determining OV and BV than EV. These seem logical relationships.

Option value (OV) may be interpreted as the amount an individual would be willing to pay to retain the option of the use of a particular good while his future demand is uncertain. The OV reported for UT is high, exceeding 'expected' consumer surplus (CS). Most American studies report an OV of about 50 per cent of CS. The high OV in relation to CS may have occurred because the 'experts' sampled:

(1) were extremely risk-averse: many ecologists are unwilling to accept environmental trade-offs;
(2) have very low probabilities of future demand, hence are willing to pay more in terms of OV than CS;

(3) misunderstood the question in the survey: other values were transferred to and incorporated in OVs. For example, quasi-option value
(measuring people's aversion to an irreversible change—see Hodge,
1984) may have been incorporated. Quasi-OV is a supply-side problem
and should be reflected in EVs and BVs.

Supply-side option value (SSOV) complicates the analysis (Freeman,
1985). If existence and bequest values are really SSOVs, then 'experts' are
clearly more concerned with maintaining the option of future supply than
with the uncertainty about their own demand for visits to the site (or OV
per se).

The average total WTP for UT by each 'expert' sampled was £15.83/yr
(OV + EV + BV = £13.37). The total membership of the expert groups in
the North East Region (excluding student members) is approximately
1,200 (200 BES + 1000 IoB), which allows the average WTP to be grossed
up to £18,996 (£16,044 for OV + EV + BV), or £29 (£25)/ha/yr of
improvable land at UT. These figures are of course speculative; the usual
problems of non-respondents exist, and the preliminary analysis shows
some unusual and/or insignificant relationships between WTP and explanatory variables. The members of the groups are highly specialised and
atypical of the general population. The BES has a total membership of
approximately 4,300 of which 2,600 live in the British Isles. At least 90 per
cent hold a Bachelor's degree and more than 45 per cent hold a Ph.D. The
total membership of the IoB is over 16,000 (mainly British Isles) and, as a
professional body, the majority of the members are qualified to Bachelor's
degree standard; further socio-economic data are not available. Further
work is in progress to examine total WTP by other groups (e.g. Wildlife
Conservation Trust members) and the general public. The present figures
show, however, that the total WTP for UT by each household (general
public) living within 100km of the site (1.49 million) would have to be 6p/yr
to cover the financial cost (when added to experts' WTP).

Conclusion

The opportunity costs and the benefits of wildlife conservation at Upper
Teesdale (UT) differ according to the technique of valuation adopted. This
is hardly surprising given that the techniques really evaluate different
frames or communities of reference and property rights structures. There is
a general presumption that any movement from the current property rights
distribution should require that any losers be compensated. This points to
the system of financial compensation, currently operated, as being the
correct one. But compensation to farmers, payable under this property

Table 10.3 Summary and comparison of results from each valuation technique

	£/ha/yr (646 ha improvable land only)
Financial cost	222
Social cost	154
Consumer surplus (TCM)	
Wildlife visitors	6–34 (range)
All recreational use	46–251 (range)
Option, existence and bequest values	
(CV) ('expert' groups only)	25

rights position, far exceeds the resource costs, to society as a whole, of forgone agricultural intensification.

The benefits from wildlife conservation at UT were measured by a travel cost (TC) method, and secondly by contingent valuation (CV) methods to estimate consumer surplus (CS), option (OV), existence (EV and bequest (BV) values. The results are summarised in Table 10.3. The benefits are probably under estimated. The sample of TC visitors only represented about two-thirds of all wildlife visitors: it did not include organised specialist groups who may have travelled longer distances than the casual wildlife visitors sampled. Thus total TC net benefits to wildlife visitors might range from £12 to £68/ha/yr. But if this was the case, benefits would still not exceed the resource cost of the lost agricultural output, and they would only cover one-third to one-half of the total social costs (lost agricultural output plus warden and other conservation resource costs).

However, OV, EV, and BV are additional benefits to CS. For 'experts' option, existence and bequest values exceeded consumer surplus, although 'theoretically' they should perhaps be lower (Freeman, 1984). Accepting the TC estimate of CS, and 'experts' demand-and-supply-side option values, the OV of general public non-users for UT would only have to be 6p per household per year for those living within 100 km of the site for the benefits to offset the financial costs of £222/ha/yr. Early indications suggest average OV may exceed this figure.

References

Black, C.J. and Bowers, J.K., 1981, 'The Level of Protection of U.K. Agriculture', School of Economics, Discussion Paper No. 99, University of Leeds.

1984, 'The Level of Protection of U.K. Agriculture', *Oxford Bulletin of Economics and Statistics*, **46** (4).

Bines, T.J., Doody, J.P., Findlay, I.H. and Hudson, M.J., 1984, 'A Retrospective Review of the Environmental Impact on Upper Teesdale of the Cow Green Reservoir', in Roberts, R.D. and Roberts, T.M. (eds), *Planning and Ecology*, Chapman and Hall, London.

Bohm, P., 1972, 'Estimating Demand for Public Goods: An Experiment', *European Economic Review*, **3**.

Bowers, J.K., 1983, 'Cost Benefit Analysis of Wetland Drainage', *Environment and Planning*, A, **15** (2).

Bowers, J.K. and Chesire, P., 1983, *Agriculture, the Countryside and Land Use: An Economic Critique*, Methuen, London.

Boyle, K.J., Bishop, R.C. and Welsh, M.P., 1985, 'Starting Point Bias in Contingent Valuation Bidding Games', *Land Economics*, **61** (2).

Brookshire, D.S., Eubanks, L.S. and Randall, A., 1983, 'Estimating Option Prices and Existence Values for Wildlife Resources', *Land Economics*, **59** (1).

Burt, O.R. and Brewer, D., 1971, 'Estimation of Net Social Benefits from Outdoor Recreation', *Econometrics*, **39** (4).

Cesario, F.J., 1976, 'Value of Time in Recreation Benefit Studies', *Land Economics*, **52** (1).

Cesario, F.J. and Knetsch, J.L., 1976, 'A Recreation Site Demand and Benefit Estimation Model', *Regional Studies*, **10** (2).

Clapham, A.R. (ed.), 1978, *Upper Teesdale: The Area and Its Natural History*, London, Collins.

Clawson, M., 1959, *Methods of Measuring the Demand for and Value of Outdoor Recreation*, Reprint No. 10., Resources for the Future Inc., Washington DC.

Clawson, M. and Knetsch, J.L., 1966, *Economics of Outdoor Recreation*, Resources for the Future, Johns Hopkins University Press, Baltimore.

Commission of the European Communities, 1985, *The Agricultural Situation in the Community: 1984 Report*, Office for the Official Publications of the European Communities, Brussels.

Corden, W.M., 1966, 'The Structure of a Tariff System and the Effective Protection Rate', *Journal of Political Economy*, **74** (3).

Department of Transport, 1987, *Values of Journey Time Savings and Accident Prevention*, Department of Transport, London.

Fennell, R., 1979, *The Common Agricultural Policy of the European Community*, Granada, London.

Freeman, A.M., 1984, 'The Sign and Size of Option Value', *Land Economics*, **60** (1).

_____ 1985, 'Supply Uncertainty, Option Price and Option Value', *Land Economics*, **61** (2).

Hodge, I., 1984, 'Uncertainty, Irreversibility and the Loss of Agricultural Land', *Journal of Agricultural Economics*, **35** (2).

Josling, T., 1973, *Agricultural Production: Domestic Policy and International Trade*,

International Agricultural Adjustment Supporting Study No. 9., Food and Agricultural Organisation (FAO), Rome.

Layard, P.R.G. and Walters, A.A., 1978, *Micro Economic Theory*, McGraw-Hill, New York.

Marin, A., and Psacharopoulos, G., 1982, 'The Reward for Risk in the Labour Market: Evidence from the U.K. and a Reconciliation with Other Studies', *Journal of Political Economy*, **90**.

Mooney, G.H., 1977, *The Valuation of Human Life*, Macmillan, London.

Nix, J., 1985, *Farm Management Pocketbook*, Department of Agricultural Economics, Wye College, Ashford.

Parker, H.R., 1965, 'The History of Compensation and Betterment Since 1900', in Hall, P. (ed.) *Land Values*, Sweet and Maxwell, London.

Raiffa, H., 1982, *The Art and Science of Negotiation*, Harvard University Press, Cambridge, Mass.

Ridker, R.G. and Henning, J.A., 1967, 'Determinants of Residential Property Values with Special Reference to Air Pollution', *Review of Economics and Statistics*, **49**.

Ritson, C., 1980, *The European Community's Common Agricultural Policy: Present Problems and Future Prospects*, series of lectures delivered at the Agricultural Bank of Greece, Agricultural Bank of Greece, Athens.

Samples, K.C. and Bishop, R.C., 1985, 'Estimating the Value of Variations in Anglers' Success Rates: An Application of the Multiple Site Travel Cost Method', *Journal of Marine Resource Economics*, **2** (1).

Saunders, C.M., Benson, J.F. and Willis, K.G., 1987, 'The Social Costs and Benefits of Agricultural Intensification at Three Sites of Special Scientific Interest', Departmental Working Paper No. 3, Department of Town and Country Planning, University of Newcastle.

Saunders, C.M., Willis, K.G. and Benson, J.F., 1987, 'The Resource Cost of Agricultural Intensification or Wildlife Conservation: A Theoretical Analysis of the Social Benefit/Cost of Agricultural Output from Marginal Areas of Land', Departmental Working Paper No. 1, Department of Town and Country Planning, University of Newcastle.

Schulze, W.D., d'Arge, R.C. and Brookshire, D.S., 1981, 'Valuing Environmental Commodities: Some Recent Experiments', *Land Economics*, **57** (2).

Seller, C., Stoll, J.R. and Chavas, J.P., 1985, 'Validation of Empirical Measures of Welfare Change: A Comparison of Non-Market Techniques', *Land Economics*, **61** (2).

Smith, V.K., 1985, 'Supply Uncertainty, Option Price and Indirect Benefit Estimation', *Land Economics*, **61** (3).

Smith, V.L., 1980, 'Experiments with a Decentralised Mechanism for Public Good Decisions', *American Economic Review*, **70**.

Thayer, M.A., 1981, 'Contingent Valuation Techniques for Assessing Environmental Impacts: Further Evidence', *Journal of Environmental Economics and Management*, **8** (1).

Thomson, K.J., 1986, 'The EC Budget and the Fontainebleau Agreement', Internal Working Paper, Department of Agricultural Economics, University of Aberdeen.

Trice, A.H. and Wood, S.E., 1958, 'Measurement of Recreation Benefits', *Land Economics*, **34** (2).

Turner, K., Dent, D. and Hey, R.D., 1983, 'Valuation of the Environmental Impact of Wetland Flood Protection and Drainage Schemes', *Environment and Planning*, A, **15** (4).

Walsh, R.G., Loomis, J.B. and Gillman, R.A., 1984, 'Valuing Option, Existence and Bequest Demands for Wilderness', *Land Economics*, **60** (1).

Walsh, R.G., Sanders, L.D. and Loomis, J.B., 1984, *Wild and Scenic River Economics: Recreation Use and Preservation Values*, American Wilderness Alliance, Denver, Col.

Walters, A.A., 1975, *Noise and Prices*, Clarendon Press, Oxford.

Willis, K.G. and Whitby, M.C., 1985, 'The Value of Green Belt Land', *Journal of Rural Studies*, **1** (2).

Chapter 11

Cost-Benefit Analysis in Theory and Practice: Agricultural Land Drainage Projects

John Bowers*

Introduction

This chapter is a study of the practice of cost–benefit analysis (CBA) in the UK land drainage industry. It is based on examination of CBA's of ten land drainage schemes prepared by or for statutory drainage bodies, Water Authorities (WAs) and Internal Drainage Boards (IABs) (reports and supporting documentation for all the schemes are available from the author on request). All of the schemes are agricultural ones where a threat to the quality of the natural environment (particularly wetlands) was perceived. The study is a historical one not only in the obvious sense but also because, following the 1985 Government Green Paper on land drainage (MAFF, 1985), the guidelines for CBA and the financial and political climate in which grant applications are made and decisions taken have altered. Since the theme of this chapter is the manipulations of CBA by interested parties, these changes in time will offer the opportunity for further study.

We are concerned with investment projects where the primary objective is that of facilitating agricultural improvement by the removal of presumed hydrological constraint and where grant aid from Ministry of Agriculture Fisheries and Food (MAFF) is anticipated.

The definition is framed with care and the reasons for its various qualifications will hopefully become apparent. The unifying feature of

* The invaluable help and assistance of the following bodies is gratefully acknowledged: The Royal Society for the Protection of Birds, The Nature Conservancy Council, The Yorkshire Wildlife Trust Ltd., The Council for the Protection of Rural England, The Norfolk Naturalists' Trust Ltd., The Somerset Trust for Nature Conservation, The Devon Trust for Nature Conservation, The Lincolnshire and Humberside Trust for Nature Conservation, and the Leicestershire Naturalists' Trust. This chapter is a modified version of a study grant-aided by the Nature Conservancy Council. Acknowledgement must also be made of the help and advice received from Professor Claude Henry of the École Polytechnique and of my colleague, Cyril Black, at Leeds University. None of these individuals and bodies is in any way responsible for what is said here.

these projects is that a cost–benefit analysis is normally required as a condition for the payment of grant aid. This is essentially a Treasury requirement applicable to a wide range of public investment projects and not merely to land drainage. In consequence, whilst the restriction of MAFF as the grant-giving agency confines the argument strictly to England and Wales, much of what is said applies also to Scotland and Northern Ireland where the institutional arrangements are different. With Water Authority projects that fall within the definition, the investment would normally at some stage be included in published capital works programmes.

The notion of 'removing hydrological constraints' is intended to cover a variety of activities, namely: lowering water tables via pumping and deepening ditches and dykes; protection against fluvial and tidal flooding via bank-raising, river-widening and deepening, hydraulic barriers and barrages; and methods of speeding the evacuation of flood water via pumps, improved land drains, dykes and channels, with or without increases in the capacity of the river system. That is, it covers all activities encompassed by the terms 'land drainage' and 'flood protection' falling within the ambit of IDBs and Water Authorities. All of these activities can qualify for grant aid. Differentiation is made below where it is necessary or helpful.

The essential point about all of these activities is that they do not of themselves yield any agricultural benefit. What they do is to increase the return to the farm or landowner from investment in agricultural improvement. It is this fact that causes many of the problems for benefit assessment which are discussed below. Because of it benefit measurement must be based on a forecast of investment behaviour and a forecast must be implicitly or explicitly based on a theory of the determinants of investment behaviour. It also means that the direct capital costs of most projects fall short of the capital expenditure necessary to achieve the benefits.

The land drainage investment problem has two basic dimensions: the set of rules and conventions which are used in the CBA to value cost and benefits; and the institutional and adminstrative framework within which the appraisals are carried out. These two aspects are intricately intertwined. While the principles of CBA derive from economic theory, together with a set of practical solutions to theoretical problems enshrined in what could be considered case law, and mediated through the Treasury in its guidelines on the conduct of CBA (HM Treasury, 1983), there is still plenty of freedom left for interpretation by practitioners. How they interpret guidelines depends on who they are and their motivations, in essence on the institutional framework in which the appraisal is conducted. Before discussing and criticising existing CBA practices we consider the framework of decision-making.

The institutional framework

CBA is an aid to decision-making. The paradigm is the decision-maker faced with a number of competing projects between which a priori he has no preferences. His objective is to choose the combination of projects which, given the resources at his disposal, maximises the benefits to society. CBA aids him to do this by supplying an accounting framework in which social costs and benefits of competing projects may be displayed, a set of rules for aggregating and comparing these costs and benefits, and some criteria for selecting projects based on these aggregates. The effective use of the system requires that the analyst or compiler of CBA understands its purpose and the concept of social welfare that underlies it; it probably helps also if the decision-maker understands the system. How far does decision-making in land drainge and flood protection match up to this paradigm?

The decision-making in land drainage is a structural hierarchy. At the top, the total volume of expenditure is controlled by Parliamentary vote. Within that, ultimate power to allocate budgeted expenditure between projects lies with MAFF but is subject to the rules for public project selection and expenditure control laid down by the Treasury. Apart from the need for CBA already mentioned, projects costing more than £1.5 million require Treasury as well as MAFF approval. All projects submitted are subject to technical scrutiny by MAFF regional engineers before going to the Administrative Division for final decision.

Below that level it is necessary to distinguish IDBs from WAs. IDBs have access to MAFF directly. WA projects, all main river capital schemes for which grant aid is sought and non-main river schemes for which WA has responsibility—schemes for areas where there is no IDB—come through the local and then the Regional Land Drainage Committees (LDCs). LDCs are responsible for determining the Capital Works Programmes of the Drainage Divisions of WAs and therefore for allotting priorities among potential projects, rejecting them, or passing them on to MAFF. Project specification and CBA is the responsibility of WA staff and is, in preliminary stages at least, usually carried out by divisional engineers. Consultants are employed only on the larger projects and often only when the project is at an advanced stage. In IDBs, appraisal is almost invariably the responsibility of the Board's consulting engineer. Having described the system from the top, let us appraise it from the bottom.

None of the conditions of the paradigm applies to IDBs. They typically have only one project to which they are firmly committed. As the Tavistock study showed (Friend and Laffin, 1983) IDBs tend to be dominated by the agricultural lobby and often by local farmers who regard them as a private fief. IDBs are thus promoters rather than assessors of projects within their purview. It seems likely that in any case they often do not understand the purposes of CBA and it is clear that the consulting engineers who are conducting the analyses frequently do not understand it at all.

With WAs the situation is not fundamentally different. At the divisional level there are probably few capital projects in prospect at any one time and the major ones at least will be strongly supported by divisional staff. One reason is that projects are often technically linked so that major projects not only keep the drainage teams in work over their construction period, but open the way to subsequent projects and subsequent work, e.g. Severn–Trent Water Authority's Soar Valley Improvement Scheme. A similar situation prevails on the Somerset Levels and Moors with the Parrett Barrier, although the interlocking with other schemes is more complex.

If the divisional engineers and the staff who actually carry out CBA cannot be expected to be uncommitted to the projects that they are appraising, no offset is to be expected from the LDCs. From their composition, typically with a dominance of agricultural and land drainage interests, one might expect these bodies to be strongly pro-drainage in general and anything but indifferent in choices between agricultural schemes and urban flood protection. It is clear that LDCs, particularly local LDCs, sometimes go much further than this and conceive their functions as that of the promotion of agricultural drainage.

It might be thought that a pre-disposition in favour of agricultural drainage would not prevent LDCs from judging objectively the merits of alternative agricultural schemes coming within their purview. But LDCs are no doubt as aware as divisional engineers of interrelationships between current schemes and the volume of future schemes. Given this, a commitment to land drainage in general is sufficient to bias decisions on individual schemes. LDCs are not choosing between a range of self-contained options: they are implementing and controlling a number of long-term programmes whose ultimate objectives are the elimination of drainage problems as constraints on agricultural activities.

Thus we might expect that the information that is reaching the Ministry in the form of applications for grant aid is likely to be considerably biased. Is MAFF likely to subject it to something akin to objective scrutiny, as envisaged in our paradigm? The answer there must be a resounding negative. MAFF's 'departmental view' is that its function is to ensure the maximum growth of agricultural output and of agricultural productivity within the limits of the resources at its disposal (Bowers, 1985), and in addition, of course, to get the largest share of resources for that purpose. Land drainage is seen as a strategic instrument in securing those ends. At the time of the passing of the 1973 Water Act, the Ministry fought a long and ultimately successful campaign in conjunction with the agricultural lobby to keep the control of land drainage with itself, thus preventing the WAs from being connected with water (Richardson, Jordan and Kimber, 1978a, 1978b). This separation of land drainage from other activities of WAs eliminates a possible check on bias. Land drainage is not competing with sewage and water supply works for grant aid, since it is financed by a separate Ministry and it is not even in competition for the water rate.

Thus it is not to be expected that MAFF will operate any effective check on economic analysis of drainage benefits. In fact there have certainly been cases where they have advised drainage bodies on how they might improve their benefit–cost ratios. Furthermore, apart from problems of allocating expenditure within budget, MAFF has an interest in increasing its budget. For that purpose a good flow of projects with high benefit–cost ratios seeking grant aid plainly strengthens its bargaining position.

We are left with the conclusion that the only effective check on investment in land drainage above the level which is socially desirable must lie with the residual and reserve powers of the Treasury. That check is ineffective for two reasons. First, it may be circumvented by the simple expedient of dividing an integrated project into phases and treating each phase as a separate project for purposes of CBA and grant aid. One example here is the scheme for lowering the water table on Halvergate Marshes by increasing the capacity of the pumps and deepening drainage dykes. This was initially presented as three separate schemes each with its own CBA. No one scheme exceeded the Treasury expenditure limit although the complete set did. Such a procedure can be justified as being in accordance with engineering practice for the phasing of work and the exigencies of capital budgeting. This expedient can only be used if each phase can be made to show a satisfactory benefit–cost ratio on its own. It was not used for the Soar Valley improvement scheme because there are several phases which on their own cannot be made to look viable by any expedient.

Second, even where projects are referred to it, the Treasury usually does not challenge the CBA. Its view is that in the details, as opposed to the basic methodology, it does not have the expertise to evaluate CBA. It therefore issues general guidelines to the ministries and relies upon them to translate and interpret these guidelines for the field of public investment under their charge and to supply the expertise to examine the CBAs which accompany the consequential applications for grant aid. Once the Ministry has satisfied itself that the CBA has been properly conducted and that the scheme is viable, then that is the end of the matter. This system breaks down with land drainage because of the unique nature of MAFF with its close identification with the interests of its agricultural clientele.

Cost–benefit practices

The attitude of the land drainage industry towards CBA, one that extends from the site engineer through IDBs and LDCs up to and including MAFF itself, is that it is a hurdle to be crossed if it is to be allowed and financed to do what it wishes. That the drainage projects are desirable is treated as self-evident; CBA is merely a tiresome ritual that is forced upon it. Since there is no understanding of the purpose of the technique it is scarcely surprising that the rules are manipulated to get the desired result—a benefit–cost ratio above unity at the test rate of discount. CBA may be so manipulated because the guidelines given are not, and probably from their nature cannot be, sufficiently precise to ensure a proper appraisal by those who neither know nor care what it aims to do. The large number of degrees of freedom that exist to the analyst, if he may be so called, can be indicated by listing the expedients that I have discovered being used to improve the benefit–cost ratio. Here I exclude those issues, where it may be argued that the MAFF guidelines (MAFF, 1974, 1978) themselves are specifically at fault. Those defects common to almost all schemes are discussed subsequently. The scheme-specific expedients with indications of the schemes on which they are used are as follows:

    (i)   scheme life extended (Yare Barrier, phases 2 and 3; Seaton Marshes);

   (ii)   rates of 'take-up' of opportunities for agricultural improvement increased (Yare Barrier, phase 2; Soar Valley);

  (iii)   proportion of potential benefit area to experience agricultural improvement increased (Yare Barrier, phase 2);

  (iv)   potential benefit area extended (Yare Barrier, phase 2);

   (v)   assumption made that in the absence of the scheme, farming will cease (Halvergate; North Duffield Carrs);

  (vi)   post-scheme flood damage ignored (Amberley; Soar Valley; Yare Barrier, phases 1 and 2; Halvergate; North Duffield Carrs);

 (vii)   post-scheme cropping pattern altered to give greater weight to high-value crops (Yare Barrier, phase 2; Soar Valley);

(viii)   farm fixed capital requirements ignored or set unrealistically low (Amberley; Soar Valley; Halvergate);

  (ix)   current yields set at levels inconsistent with current cropping patterns, given assumption of efficient farming otherwise made (Soar Valley);

   (x)   excessive credence given to admittedly irrational fears of flooding (Yare Barrier, phases 1 and 2; Soar Valley).

In addition to these agricultural expedients we have some non-agricultural ones:

(xi) separable or otherwise unrelated urban flood protection schemes integrated into the programme (Soar Valley; Yare Barrier, phases 2 and 3);

(xii) residual value of drainage works and equipment 're-estimated' downwards without justification (Yare Barrier, phase 2);

(xiii) running and maintenance costs of pumps ignored (N. Duffield Carrs; Halvergate);

(xiv) notional savings of planned improvement schemes rendered redundant by scheme being appraised treated as benefits (Yare Barrier, phase 2);

(xv) labour costs 'shadow priced' at less than current wage rates (Soar Valley);

(xvi) arbitrary valuation of dubious environmental benefits included (Yare Barrier, phase 3).

While it is possible to argue that some of these expedients are in breach of the letter and certainly the apparent spirit of the MAFF guidelines, many are not obviously so. Given motivation, the ability of drainage bodies to get away with such stratagems is not difficult to explain. First, project objectives are not properly specified. Typically, the method of achieving the proper objective—reducing flood risk, lowering water table—is taken as the scheme objective. The procedure is then to search for benefits which satisfy the cost–benefit requirements of a scheme which is almost guaranteed to be a success in its own terms; the engineering problems are not normally very complex. The search for benefits has no obvious limits because there is no economic model relating the solution —lowering the water table, reducing flood risk—to the problem—bringing about an increase in agricultural output from the land. It is implicitly assumed that the hydrological constraint is the cause of the continuation of unimproved farming, although how this constraint operates is not analysed and probably often not understood. In a number of cases it is clear that the persistence of traditional farming patterns is not determined by hydrological factors at all and it is then impossible to properly justify a scheme.

Hydrological conditions are one of the factors determining the rate of return on investment by the farmer in agricultural improvement. Flooding leads to crop loss or damage and, if the water is saline, may also affect subsequent yields. Water-table levels affect yields, adversely for cereals and root crops as well as for certain grass leys. A reduction in flood risk or a lowering of water tables will therefore raise the expected revenues from changes in cropping patterns; they may also reduce the costs of investment, e.g. by increasing the expected life of field drains. Thus, provided that they do not equally raise revenues from existing cropping patterns (and they normally will not do so since, in the presence of high flood risk and/or high water tables, the agricultural enterprises will be those least sensitive to hydrological problems: summer grazing, livestock enterprises generally, spring-sown crops), hydrological improvements will normally increase the return on investments in agricultural improvements.

With knowledge of the opportunity cost of capital to the farmer it is possible for a given set of farm-gate prices and costs to determine the level of flood risk or the water-table level which will make it worth his while to invest in improvement. This opportunity cost will vary with the financial circumstances of the farmer, his title to the land, his existing farming pattern, the extent and nature of his holding in the potential area, etc. As the flood risk/water table is lowered therefore, increasing numbers of farms, or an increasing proportion of the affected land, will become suitable for improvement. Thus the proportion of a flood plain which will be improved by protection works depends on the level of protection chosen.

The level of protection will also determine the rate of take-up as well as the extent. Raising flood protection above the critical level at which conversion becomes worthwhile raises the rate of return above the opportunity cost of capital. The other obstacles to conversion can be overcome by this route. The ability of a farmer to borrow depends upon the expected return on the investment, and (negatively) on the riskiness of that investment. Similarly the price of land depends on the rate of return from improvement. A high level of protection thus facilitates land transfers if the structure of holdings is a constraint on improvement. For a given set of non-hydrological constraints on improvement, the rate of take-up will be positively related to the difference between the level of flood protection chosen and the critical level.

Thus the level of flood risk (scheme design standard) extent and rate of 'take-up' are jointly determined for specified non-hydrological constraints on farm improvements and for given sets of prices and costs. With these data the minimum necessary level of flood protection to persuade farmers to improve their land may be determined. Above this critical level, increases in the rate and extent of take-up may be altered by adjusting design standard. The optimum degree of flood protection is determined then from knowledge of the engineering costs of raising flood protection. The optimum level is that at which the incremental or marginal costs of raising that level is equal to the increment to the present value of benefits (arising from a more rapid and more extensive 'take-up') resulting therefrom.

When conversion to higher yielding enterprises is made, a benefit is experienced in every year when there is not a flood. Thus for a flood return period of, say, 1 year in 10 there will be a benefit of 9 years out of 10. Once take-up has occurred any further reduction in flood risk will only result in damage avoidance, that is to say, a benefit will be experienced only in years when there otherwise would have been a flood. Thus if flood risk is reduced further to 1 year in 11, the benefit is only the savings from the flood which would otherwise have occurred, i.e. the difference between 1/10 and 1/11 of the annual output. Thus benefits from damage avoidance of existing crops are small relative to those from agricultural conversion. At current capital costs, damage avoidance schemes are normally not economic. If flood risk is lowered below the critical conversion level to overcome non-hydrological constraints on agricultural improvement (e.g. fragmentation of agricultural holdings, or poor borrowing capacities of farmers), then it will normally be the case that once these constraints are overcome, flood risk could be raised again without reversion to previous farming patterns. The extra flood protection then achieves only damage avoidance —typically, as noted, of small value. Thus, provided that there are other ways of overcoming these non-hydrological difficulties, the least-cost solution is likely to be to design structures for the critical level of protection and to use other means to overcome the other obstacles. This is in accord with a good working principle that efficiency requires choosing the solution appropriate to the problem and not relying on indirect, more roundabout, and hence less certain, remedies. In my view the optimal design standard is normally that which is just sufficient to remove the hydrological constraint. The job of drainage authorities is to remove these constraints on agricultural improvements, not to ensure that agricultural development occurs.

The optimum design standard, so defined, is still an economic variable dependent on the level and structure of agricultural prices and farm capital costs. When the movement of prices and costs is such as to make arable farming more profitable, the optimal level of flood protection falls. The working assumption of drainage bodies is the reverse of this, that rising value of arable crops justifies increases in the design standards of drainage and flood protection works.

This long digression on design standards has been necessary to point up the deficiencies of current practice. Since no attempt is made to model the process of agricultural decision-making, the design standards are arbitrarily chosen and the key variable for determining benefits, the 'take-up' rate, is left floating also.

The design standards are to MAFF specification for different grades of agricultural land or enterprise types (Water Space Amenity Commission, 1980). Their derivation is from agricultural science and they are related to the characteristics of water tables necessary for maximum plant growth. To insist upon them for structural design is equivalent to insisting that all roads should be to motorway standards because then they pose no constraint on vehicle performance! In fact these standards must be nonsense since they are unrelated to either relative valuations of crops, profitability of farm-level investments, or the cost of drainage works, and are constant over time despite variations in economic conditions. Strictly adhered to, they could lead to the rejection of all hydrological improvement on CBA criteria when more modest improvements than those considered might be socially worthwhile, although, given our view of the manipulation of CBA, this is unlikely to occur in practice.

In practice, design standards are often above what can be justified. Two examples should suffice. The Soar Scheme was originally designed for a flood return period of 1 in 5 (Bowers and Black, 1983). This appears to be quite close to the optimum standards; at MAFF's instigation the standard was doubled to 1 in 10. The most glaring case is the Yare Barrier. Structure design was for a return period of 1 in 100. From the consultant's own figures, the optimum return period appeared to lie between 1 in 5 and 1 in 8. Existing levels of protection over most of the benefit area were in excess of that level so that flood risk was not a deterrent to agricultural conversion. Indeed, the construction of the Barrier could not have been expected to have much effect on the rate of conversion. By the time of the reappraisal of the project in 1983, the rate of conversion *without the Barrier* had taken place at a faster rate than the consultants had forecast to happen *with the Barrier*, thus proving the point. None the less, the consultants continued to believe that the Barrier would accelerate and extend conversion.

The extent of take-up is normally treated as coterminous with the range of suitable soils within the potential benefit area. Given the extent, take-up rates are typically forecast either by the imposition of some mathematical curve (straight line, hysteresis loop) or derived from a survey of farmers. Phase 1 of the Yare Barrier assumed take-up to follow a straight line from the date of barrier operation for the first twenty years. Phase 2 rested on a telephone survey of farmers with some follow-up interviews of those expressing enthusiasm. This yielded a much more irregular take-up profile but one concentrated in early years and offering therefore a higher present value of benefits. In neither case, and indeed in no case of which I am aware, was there any attempt to relate take-up to flood-risk levels. Attitude and intention surveys of this sort may be expected to result in over-statements of take-up because of 'free-rider' effects. It is unlikely that those conducting the surveys will attempt to minimise 'free-riders'. Attitude and intention surveys are becoming the norm in major schemes and are recommended in Penning-Rowsell and Chatterton (1977).

Farm-level surveys are not always confined to attitudes and intentions: they are also used to determine present and future cropping patterns, yields and investment costs. In this sense they are necessary as they also generate the data from which rates of return and hence probabilities of investment can be determined for various hydrological techniques. But the data needs to be used to model the system and to obtain an understanding of its dynamics. Without this not only will scheme design and aspects of take-up appear arbitrary and hence legitimately open to manipulation to get the desired answer; other parameters are also not validated. Thus, for the Soar Valley we were able to show (Bowers and Black, 1983) that the assumptions of yields and gross margins used were incompatible with the existing enterprise pattern; and that in consequence the benefits from improvement must be smaller than was being assumed. Without proper modelling almost all the data are essentially arbitrary.

Practice and guidance

How far is the general approach to the problem of land drainage and flood protection that we have just criticised and the various expedients for raising benefit–cost ratios listed earlier sanctified by MAFF guidance?

The first question is easily answered. The methodological errors we have discussed are directly recommended by MAFF. Paragraph 11 of the 1974 MAFF *Guidance Notes* explains that the Ministry had carried out a survey of land of 250 acres or more in extent 'adversely affected to a major degree by arterial conditions'. Maps showing those areas were sent to WAs accompanying the *Guidance Notes*. Paragraph 12 says by way of explanation: 'The areas are those where inadequacies of arterial drainage including flooding, are such that cropping or stocking *to normally accepted standards* are not possible' (my emphasis). Then (paragraph 13):

To define a problem area or area of benefit *it is necessary to decide in advance the drainage or flood protection standard to be adopted*; . . . The procedure in this respect differs from an urban flood problem, where the choice of design standard is left until consideration of the solutions, . . . design standards should not be adopted on a rule of thumb basis but should be related to soil types and crops. Acceptable standards will thus vary from one area to another. [MAFF, 1974]

No justification is offered for this *obiter dictum*. None in fact could be offered since it is plainly wrong. There is no reason for the imposition of external standards for agricultural drainage and flood protection. There are no considerations of human safety such as may be used to justify the imposition of minimum standards for sea defences and the protection of urban areas. The determination of standards as explained must be an economic one and in that respect agricultural schemes are exactly on a par with urban ones. The difference is that for urban schemes the benefit is damage avoidance so that the link between hydrological conditions and economic consequences appears to be direct, while in situations where the main benefit is from induced investment in higher yielding crops or reseeded grassland the link is anything but direct and needs to be established.

Hydrological standards may be used as a device for indentifying areas where there may be benefits from drainage or flood protection works and which therefore warrant examination. It is clear that MAFF used their standards in this way initially, for the compilation of the maps, but it appears (paragraph 12) that they then carried out preliminary economic appraisals without examining further whether the standards had any justification. Certainly it is intended that Water Authorities should simply apply standards for design purposes. These in turn determine the benefit area: 'The area subject to flooding should be that which . . . corresponds to the frequency standard recommended by the Ministry. . . .' (paragraph 16). Benefit is then calculated for the given design standards, 'Having established as far as possible the area of potential benefit, the annual benefits should be estimated and discounted to given the present value' (paragraph 16).

It is to be expected, given this approach, that the choice of take-up rates will be arbitrary since there is nothing on which to anchor it. The 1978 amendement deals with this in paragraph 8. We quote in full:

8. UPTAKE. Assumptions must be made about the rate at which farmers will take advantage of the drainage and incur any related increases in fixed costs. Experience has shown that it is likely to be fairly slow in the early years, then increase to a maximum and afterwards fall-off. These benefits and costs must be discounted to give their present value. [MAFF, 1978]

It would not be surprising with this guidance if the drainage authorities did not defend the attitude surveys as an improvement on MAFF procedure!

Scheme-specific expedients

Scheme life

The project appraisal period should be determined by the expected life of the structures created. For much private investment it is the economic life rather than the physical life which matters—plant and machinery may become obsolete and uneconomic to operate even though its physical functioning is unimpaired. In the presence of technical progress this can happen equally in the public sector and economic obsolescence is used to determine the appraisal period, e.g. of electricity generating capacity. Another factor determining length of life of equipment is the running-cost function—the cost of maintenance and repair. If this is a rising function with respect to age of equipment, then, in the absence of technical obsolescence, length of life is determined by comparison of annual maintenance cost with annual benefit. When cost equals benefit the equipment is economically dead. These factors determine the length of life of some drainage structures and equipment—pumps, barriers and barrages and also sea banks and river banks subject to scour—and there comes a point when it is necessary to start again. There may be other structures, however, where the maintenance-cost function may not be expected to rise with age, in which case the length of life of the equipment is more or less infinite given a constant real maintenance cost. Railway tunnels and cuttings, canals, are examples of this phenomenon. Whether any drainage structures fall in this category is not clear. A sympathetic interpretation of MAFF guidelines is that all drainage structures are like railway tunnels:

It can almost invariably be said that the maximum life to be allocated to a scheme is that which ensures that the discount curve (qv) has become practically asymptotic, so that the maximum present value can be used. The justification for this is that it is highly unlikely that the works are going to cease to exist at the end of, say, 50 years—even in the case of an earthen embankment, and even in the case of not particularly good maintenance. On the contrary, it seems reasonable to assume that works—being the responsibility of a public authority—will be properly maintained —and will be in almost as good condition at the end of the allocated life as at the beginning. [MAFF, 1974, Appendix 'B', p. 3, paragraph 3, my emphasis]

This would be a very sympathetic interpretation indeed. A fairer one would be that guidelines are misleading if not downright wrong. The choice facing the drainage authority is of a trade-off between length of life and level of maintenance expenditure. Higher expenditure means longer life— hence higher present value of benefits but also higher costs to be offset against them. If the principle is that structures must be properly maintained, then that affects scheme costs as well as project appraisal period. The quoted paragraph is implying but not actually saying that it may be assumed that once the scheme is carried out, the higher hydrological standard will be maintained regardless of cost: the schemes are irreversible; and the Authorities are then invited to add to the appraisal period for as long as doing so increases the return on the project. South West WA, in assuming an appraisal period of infinity for the Seaton Marsh scheme, were sticking to the letter as well as the spirit of the guidelines since the discount curve is asymptotic to infinity.

Assumption that without the scheme farming will cease

Officially it has been argued that '. . . thought needs to be given to the risk of the entire loss of a tract of land owing to failure of neglected defences if an improvement scheme is not carried out' (MAFF, 1974, Appendix 'B'). No explanation is given as to why, in the absence of improvement, maintenance should be neglected. This statement conflicts interestingly with the next paragraph on length of life quoted above, namely, 'it seems reasonable to assume that the works—being the responsibility of a public authority—will be properly maintained'.

The two cases where the assumption that farming will cease is made are interesting. At Halvergate it was argued that the IDB could not afford to replace the pumps, which were in imminent danger of breakdown (Bowers, 1981), without grant aid and that grant aid was only available for improvement (i.e. bigger pumps). They could not afford to replace because the farmers would refuse to pay the drainage rate and instead abandon farming. How abandoning farming avoided liability for drainage rates was not explained. In any case it was not difficult to show that in economic terms the argument was spurious. But the neglect of maintenance arose because it was not economic to replace the pumps (i.e. the decision to replace would fail on CBA: it could none the less be economic to install larger pumps because then the benefit of higher-value enterprises would be obtained). This means that it is no longer economic to maintain drainage on the levels—the cost of doing so exceeds the benefits of agriculture. This is doubtless often the case but normally the drainage authority cross-subsidises the farmers from urban ratepayers. With the IDB concerned it presumably did not have that possibility.

The second case is North Dufield Carrs. The CBA submitted with the application for grant aid assumes, against clear visual evidence to the contrary, that farming has already ceased or that farming is practised but no output obtained. The key to this nonsense was the belief that drainage had deteriorated and that it was not within the powers of IDB to do anything about it.

In neither case can it be said that the assumption made was justified but the invitation to make it, in both cases the only expedient to improve a poor economic case, presumably comes from the guidelines.

Post-scheme flood damage ignored

All schemes that I have examined contain an element of flood risk and none of them attempts to allow for anticipated flood damage in the post-scheme period. As already explained, the principal source of agricultural benefit is the conversion to higher-yielding enterprises—either arable crops or intensive grassland. These enterprises are more prone to flood damage than the enterprises they replace. This fact is central to the case for hydrological improvement: it is the expected losses at existing conditions that inhibits investment. One might have expected, therefore, that the fact that flood risk still exists, even though it no longer inhibits development, would be readily recognised. In fact in section 24.5 concerning appraisals of purely damage-avoidance schemes (usually very small and cheap) this is typically recognised; it is once enterprise change is introduced that the problem is forgotten.

MAFF gives detailed guidelines, with examples, for damage-avoidance problems, but the examples are all for urban schemes and the authorities have presumably assumed that the problem only exists where the scheme purpose is wholly damage avoidance. In fact damage-avoidance benefits to pre-existing enterprises are often ignored also by drainage authorities, though not universally so. MAFF notes offer no specific guidelines on the treatment of damage avoidance for enterprise switching schemes.

Post-scheme cropping patterns

This is an obvious expedient to an analyst whose estimation of benefits is too low for viability. Given a completely unstructured approach to the problem, it can seem perfectly legitimate to adjust cropping patterns provided. In fact forecasting the likely cropping pattern, for a given set of prices (which is what should be done), is difficult, and the MAFF guidelines are of no help. Four points should be made.

First, this is a prime area of true uncertainty where a sensitivity analysis is required, i.e. an investigation of how the benefits are affected by different assumptions of cropping patterns. If the scheme is only viable for some extreme assumptions about cropping patterns then prima facie it should not be proceeded with. Second, some of the high gross margin crops (sugar beet, potatoes and now of course, but not at the period of these schemes, wheat and milk) are quota-controlled and hence cannot be included in a social CBA. Third, as a generalisation of the second point the gains to benefits from juggling with cropping patterns are generally small when correct prices are used (see below) and can even be perverse. This happened on Halvergate where the inclusion of dairying instead of two-year beef on part of the land actually reduced the benefits when they were properly measured.

The fourth point is that there is an interdependence between cropping patterns and requirements for fixed capital. The crops with high gross margins (beet, potatoes, field vegetables) tend to have high fixed capital requirements and furthermore are unlikely to utilise existing spare capacity. To a degree therefore one can increase benefits at the expense of increasing costs.

Treatment of fixed costs

The degree of fixed costs incurred through agricultural improvement will vary with a number of factors, but of central importance is the existing farm structure. Thus the additional capital equipment and labour required by an arable farmer converting a small parcel of pasture into his arable holding may be very small. At the other extreme, the costs of converting a wholly livestock farm to an arable one can be high. Fixed cost requirements are a determinant of take-up rates as well as cropping patterns and the three variables should be examined together and jointly subjected to sensitivity analysis. In practice they are treated separately and rarely examined for sensitivity. The guidelines are again of little value here.

Current yields and cropping

A necessary component of a proper appraisal of agricultural development and the role that drainage works can play in it is an understanding of the existing pattern of agricultural use. There is an inconsistency in postulating a set of profit-maximising farmers waiting to exploit the opportunities afforded by drainage works, if the existing gross margins and cropping patterns assumed are not those which maximise present opportunities. This can happen quite easily if the analyst adjusts margins for pasture downwards and margins of arable upwards to give a high value of benefit per acre. This happened with the Soar scheme. On the Consultant's figures the profitability of livestock rearing was so low that the farmers would have been better off growing spring-sown crops from that land, which technically would have been possible. These same farmers were expected to achieve consistently high arable yields and livestock margins after the scheme was implemented. This inconsistency is avoided by a proper modelling of the farmers' decision-making process as already advocated.

Irrational fears of flooding

The proper modelling of the decision process with the identification of the role of hydrological constraints on the farming pattern avoids giving credence to farmers' views on flood risk. If farmers are abstaining from exploiting their opportunities because of irrational fears of flooding or exaggerated views on its frequency, then a process of education and information is called for. It is certainly not in society's interest to construct flood-protection structures for flood risks which do not exist! It seems extremely unlikely that experienced farmers are under any misapprehension of the risks they face or their significance to them. The 'free rider' effect, however, may lead them to exaggerate their problems if they believe that by doing so they will get relief.

Addition of urban schemes

A part of a drainage scheme is wholly separable from the rest if that part may technically be carried out without implementation of the main scheme, and neither the costs of that part nor the benefits are affected by the main scheme. Parts of schemes may be partly separable in the sense that the objectives may be technically met without implementation of the main scheme, but the levels of costs and benefits are thereby altered. Urban flood-protection components of mainly agricultural schemes are often wholly or partially separable. Thus in the case of the Soar Valley scheme, urban flood protection is provided by the construction of flood banks around urban areas. In some cases (e.g. Ratcliffe-on-Soar) the scheme is partly separable since the main scheme involves lowering river levels. Thus the separate construction of the banks at the same level would afford a slightly lower level of flood protection. Alternatively the same level of protection without the main scheme would involve slightly higher expenditure on higher flood banks. The part of the scheme at Thurcaston Road, Leicester, on the other hand, is wholly separable: it lies up-river of the main scheme and flood problems at Thurcaston Road are not affected by implementation of the rest of the scheme. Separable urban flood schemes are added to agricultural schemes as a means of improving their economic performance.

Yet again this problem arises because of a failure to specify properly the objectives of the flood protection and land drainage schemes that are being considered. WAs and their engineers tend naturally to think in terms of drainage units—reaches of rivers or other definable parts of arterial systems—and to specify projects accordingly, i.e. to look for a programme which deals with all the problems of a given unit. This makes sense in terms of work planning, but none in terms of project appraisal. A given drainage unit can throw up a number of separate drainage problems—flooding of its urban area, low productivity enterprises in the region—and the objectives of drainage works thus differ. A comprehensive scheme embracing separable components is only justified if it costs less than the sum of the separate parts or produces more benefits than the parts. But that can only be determined if the separate objectives are specified, costed and appraised. Only in this way can the schemes be properly assessed and the errors of implicit theorising, e.g. assuming land drainage to be the operative constraint on agricultural improvement, be avoided. The MAFF guidelines take the engineering approach rather than the economic approach to problem identification and thus by implication open the way for window-dressing agricultural schemes by urban accretions.

Write-off of existing structures

The residual value of existing structures is determined by the remaining economic life estimated in the ways previously discussed. In the Yare Barrier, phase 2, the WA decided that all IDB pumps that would need replacing by ones of larger capacity were already at the end of their economic life. On normal accounting practice this would have increased the residual value of written-off equipment rather than reducing it to zero, since some of the pumps would have needed replacing before the optimal time (Bowers, 1978). A similar error was incorporated into the Halvergate Appraisal. MAFF guidelines do not mention the matter.

Notional savings as scheme benefits

Planned expenditure rendered unnecessary by adopted schemes are not resource savings and clearly should not be counted. However, such savings were cited as a benefit in Yare Barrier, phase 2, on the grounds presumably that the Barrier would add less to the WAs expenditure plans than its capital cost. Since the planned expenditure saved was for raising flood banks on agricultural land to levels that could not be justified on economic appraisal, there is a double irony here. This is a classic case of confusion between resource costs and accountancy magnitudes. Whether the confusion was accidental or deliberate is unclear.

Environmental effects

The correct treatment of environmental and other intangible effects is to make an assessment in whatever terms are appropriate to them. This will sometimes involve quantification but not in financial terms. The objective of the exercise is to determine the direction of those effects (positive or negative) and a relative valuation (i.e. serious, trivial). If the sign of intangibles is the same as that of the net present value of tangibles, then intangibles do not affect the decision—if anything they reinforce it. Where the tangible and intangible elements pull in opposite directions then a political decision is required: a subjective weighing of intangibles against the measured economic benefits. For this to be properly done it is necessary both that the appraisal of tangibles be properly conducted and that the intangible 'account' is fully and expertly compiled. We have seen that the treatment of tangibles is unsatisfactory and contains a bias in favour of acceptance of projects. The treatment of intangibles is, if anything, more so, and MAFF guidelines offer little in the way of clarification.

Very few schemes contain any environmental assessment. Phase 2 of the Yare Barrier contains a few pages on the differences between alternative ways of achieving the hydrological objective but no assessment of the consequences of any scheme. An environmental appraisal was produced for the Soar, but only at a late stage, and after the STWA was firmly committed to the scheme. The Soar scheme reveals an interesting expedient. The Authority went through a process of negotiation with NCC about the environmental effects of the scheme, and in consequence introduced some minor design modifications. It then argued that having done this it could henceforth ignore intangibles. This is not so; unless the negotiations eliminate undesirable environmental effects, those remaining should still be brought into the balance in the decision making process.

General defects in guidelines and practice

Here we examine some points more or less general to all schemes, namely the use of sensitivity analysis, assumptions about enterprise yields and the choice of prices for valuing agricultural output.

Sensitivity analysis

Where a degree of uncertainty attaches to the values and variables for CBA, sensitivity analysis is necessary for two purposes: to identify the variables which are critical to the outcome so that research may be concentrated on improving the data at points where it matters; and to indicate the degree of confidence that one has in the economic viability of the project. Sensitivity analysis is not properly used in land-drainage appraisal in either sense. There are cases of great effort being made to obtain precision for variables that have little effect on the outcome with a corresponding lack of care given to those with a critical or strategic role, and often no more than a central projection is used even in areas of great uncertainty. Indeed current practice might be described as being that of finding a set of not obviously absurd values which make the project viable and then acting as though those values were the 'true' ones. MAFF guidelines encourage these practices. The section headed 'Accuracy'

(MAFF, 1978, Supplementary Note, p. 2) makes no mention of sensitivity analysis; instead, after noting that 'a high degree of precision is not to be expected' it urges 'special efforts to produce the best possible estimate' when the project is marginal or where 'other factors such as environmental considerations are likely to enter into the final decision'. This urge for precision is vitiated by the last comment on p. 5 of Appendix 'B' of the 1972 guidelines not amended in 1978, which blatantly urges optimism:

In view of the imprecision of the data and the assumptions that have necessarily to be made *the engineer should carefully judge, at each stage, the upper limit of the various benefits, so that his final figure represents the maximum permissible after allowing for uncertainties.* [my emphasis]

If benefits were replaced by costs in this quotation it would be an acceptable code of practice. The notion of precision is misplaced here in any case. Where uncertainty exists it should be stated. There is a world of difference between the statements: 'the project is viable' and 'the balance of probability is that the project is viable'.

Enterprise yields

There are no printed guidelines on this matter but there is common practice which MAFF *de facto* accepts (and in fact, as I gathered in conversation, approves of.) The practice is that yields for new enterprises resulting from projects should either be those which are technically possible given soil conditions, climatic factors, drainage profiles, etc., or they should be 'best practice' yields as shown, for example, by the high-yield columns in Nix's gross margin tables (Nix, annual). There is a substantial gap between theoretical yields and what is normally attained in practice. Nix's best practice yields are only attained by a minority of farmers and then not consistently. The average yields in Nix, and the average variable input levels that accompany them are intended to be what might be achieved consistently by the average farmer on average. They, or something like them, derived, for example, from the regional Farm Management Surveys, are appropriate for benefit appraisal.

The use of theoretical yields would not matter too much if they were also applied to existing enterprises. They never are; either actual data derived from farm level surveys are used or Nix 'low' or 'average' yields are assumed, usually the former. Hence, we get the phenomenon, already referred to, that a drainage project converts a set of average or below average farmers into some of the industry's leaders. An explicit instruction to assume the average, if not the worst, is needed.